OECD Fiscal Federalism Studies

Making Property Tax Reform Happen in China

A REVIEW OF PROPERTY TAX DESIGN AND REFORM EXPERIENCES IN OECD COUNTRIES

OECD
BETTER POLICIES FOR BETTER LIVES

Please cite this publication as:
OECD (2021), *Making Property Tax Reform Happen in China: A Review of Property Tax Design and Reform Experiences in OECD Countries*, OECD Fiscal Federalism Studies, OECD Publishing, Paris, *https://doi.org/10.1787/bd0fbae3-en*.

ISBN 978-92-64-37037-1 (print)
ISBN 978-92-64-46361-5 (pdf)

OECD Fiscal Federalism Studies
ISSN 2225-403X (print)
ISSN 2225-4056 (online)

Photo credits: Cover © Enkophotography/iStockphoto.com.

Corrigenda to publications may be found on line at: *www.oecd.org/about/publishing/corrigenda.htm*.

Foreword

In OECD and partner countries recurrent taxes on immovable property are among the most important subnational revenue sources and are used to finance key government responsibilities. An efficient and effective design and administration of these growth-friendly taxes are crucial for society to reap their numerous benefits that range from supporting land-use policies to promoting a healthy real estate market. Nonetheless, designing and managing these taxes in an efficient and effective manner is a complex endeavour. Recurrent property taxation is usually an element of a broader discussion on the intergovernmental fiscal framework, land-use policies and property rights, all of which vary widely across countries. As a result, reforms require a careful analysis of a country's particularities, which makes every reform unique and challenging.

Acknowledging the importance and complexities of recurrent property taxation, especially in the context of inclusive growth and intergovernmental relations, the OECD has published numerous studies with empirical evidence and practical policy recommendations aimed at ensuring a more coherent and effective approach to recurrent property taxation reforms. This research draws upon these previous studies and complements them with a range of recent developments on property taxation across OECD and partner countries. This last decade was notably rich in terms of property tax reforms, with more than a dozen reforms being made in the last five years, offering valuable lessons that are here described and analysed.

An important strength of the OECD is its committees. This report was prepared by the Secretariat of the OECD Network on Fiscal Relations across Levels of Government, whose delegates reviewed the draft. The delegates of Working Party No. 2 on Tax Policy Analysis and Tax Statistics of the Committee of Fiscal Affairs also provided comments on the report, including country examples. The report itself was principally drafted by Pietrangelo de Biase, consultant, under the guidance of Sean Dougherty, Senior Advisor and Head of Secretariat to the Network on Fiscal Relations, with Bert Brys of the Centre for Tax Policy and Administration and Andrew Reschovsky, consultant, providing extensive comments on multiple drafts. Colleagues from across the OECD reviewed the report, including Boris Cournède and Margit Molnar (Economics Department), Michelle Harding, Pierce O'Reilly and Sarah Perret (Centre for Tax Policy and Administration), Isabelle Chatry (Centre for Entrepreneurship, SMEs, Regions and Cities) as well as an outside expert, Ehtisham Ahmad (LSE). Responsibility for the report's content remains with the Secretariat and its principal authors.

This report was prepared at the request of the China Development Research Foundation (CDRF), who also provided background information and comments on the report. Therefore, some of the topics explored and recommendations outlined are tailored to the Chinese context. This focus on China is especially relevant now, as China's government has announced that it will start pilot property tax schemes in some regions with the intention of eventually introducing a broad levy on residential properties. Such a tax could be a powerful tool to boost local government revenues while reducing wealth gaps and curbing speculation. Although the report's recommendations are oriented towards China, we believe that most policy lessons in the cases examined and the comparative perspective provided can greatly support member and partner countries aiming at reforming their property tax and intergovernmental fiscal system.

Table of contents

FIGURES

TABLES

Executive summary

This report looks at crucial elements of reforms to growth-friendly recurrent taxes on immovable property. Tax design practices in place in OECD and partner countries are compared and analysed through the lenses of economic theory and empirical analysis. Challenges and practices related to the administration of property taxes are explored as well as their interplay with different tax designs. In addition, the main political and administrative hurdles in approving and implementing property tax reforms are discussed, and the approaches commonly employed to successfully deal with them are examined.

With regard to tax design, a widely adopted and growth friendly tax design involves the use of a value-based property tax with a wide tax base and low tax rate. Typically, member and partner countries tax both land and buildings used for multiple purposes such as residential, industrial and commercial. Wide tax bases allow governments to increase tax revenues while minimising allocative distortions. Tax rates applied by different jurisdictions to these different types of property normally differ but within limits, so taxpayers have little incentives to change the use of land or to move to other jurisdictions solely on tax purposes, minimising distortions and tax avoidance.

The design of property taxes can be set so as to achieve a myriad of policy objectives such as preservation of agricultural land, promotion of business, urban development and reduction in urban sprawl. Usually these objectives are pursued by applying different tax rates across property types/uses/taxable items and by granting tax benefits to specific types of properties. Evidence shows that although these measures can achieve the desired policy objectives, they are better viewed in the context of other policy instruments that usually have a stronger impact on land use such as zoning and transport policies.

The administration of recurrent taxes on immovable property involves the following main activities: fiscal cadastre maintenance, valuation of properties, management of an appeal system, billing, revenue collection and enforcement. A poorly managed property tax system not only shrinks tax revenues but also creates asymmetries in tax obligations that do not reflect design features, treating taxpayers unfairly. Sense of fairness is a driver of tax-revolts, which in many circumstances have undermined property tax reforms and in extreme cases have led to the discontinuation of the levy.

In that light, fiscal cadastres with a higher property coverage increase tax revenues and are crucial to the fairness of the system. They often also have important roles outside the scope of property taxation, such as in urban planning, environment protection, mortgage finances and transportation, housing, recreational and social policies. Therefore, up-front investments to develop fiscal cadastres and keep them updated and accurate are usually worthwhile. In case cadastres are managed by subnational governments (SNGs) that lack capacity, upper levels of government can step in and provide technical and/or financial support.

Property valuation usually is the costlier activity in the administration of recurrent taxes on immovable property and also tends to be the activity that causes more administrative issues. Countries examined commonly use value-based tax bases that require frequent property assessments to properly keep up with the changes in the housing market, since other means of estimating tax bases, such as self-reports and indexation, although useful, can create distortions in the long term if used alone.

Despite this need of frequent property revaluation, value-based tax bases offer unique advantages that more than compensate for these costs. More specifically, they tend to be more progressive, raise more revenues in the long term without resorting to changes in statutory tax rates, have a greater impact on the volatility of house prices, are more growth-friendly, among others. In addition, if there is sales data available, which usually is the case for small properties such as for small offices, retail and most residential properties, properties' values can be assessed by the sales comparison approach. This can be especially relevant since sales comparison can be done in an automated manner through the employment of a computer assisted mass appraisal (CAMA) system, drastically reducing the costs of property reassessments. When SNGs are responsible for these assessments, upper levels of government commonly define guidelines and oversee the process, so properties' values are consistent across jurisdictions.

The billing process is especially important to raise taxpayers' compliance. Countries carefully choose bills' content. Multiple studies have found that a significant increase in tax compliance can be achieved through the disclosure of some type of information such as the compliance rate, a clear explanation of the tax system and a list of public goods that are funded with the tax and sanctions. In addition, allowing payments in multiple instalments also tends to increase compliance as it reduces taxpayers' liquidity issues.

Even in case tax design and administration were satisfactorily planned to meet a reform's goal, a reform can be blocked politically and, thus, failing to have the desired effects. Key factors that can undermine a reform's implementation are their distributional consequences, the impact on the revenue of multiple levels of government, the unpopularity of the tax, transitional costs and timing. In order to deal with these issues, countries by and large bundle recurrent property taxation reforms with the reform of other taxes and/or reforms in fiscal federalism, phase in the reform's impact so that abrupt effects are alleviated, and they put forward reforms in moments that future taxpayers are more willing to support the reform.

There usually are gains in discussing tax reforms taking into account the broader fiscal context. The impact of the reform of a specific tax interacts with the current state of the fiscal system and, hence, discussions of a tax in isolation can be misleading. In addition, seldom can a reform of one tax achieve different policy goals without creating fierce resistance. For instance, recurrent taxes on immovable property tend to be the most growth friendly tax and especially useful to boost subnational autonomy, nevertheless there are other more progressive taxes such as income, wealth and inheritance taxes. As a result, if one of the goals of the reform is to improve the distribution of income, bundling a reform on recurrent property taxation with reforms in income, wealth, inheritance tax or even with cash transfer programmes, can be particularly interesting to achieve multiple policy objectives. For revenue-neutral reforms, the most common case is to bundle a recurrent taxation reform with a reduction in transaction taxes, which are considered to be highly distortive, leading to an overall more growth-friendly tax system.

As recurrent property taxation has a prominent role in funding subnational governments, recurrent property tax reforms are often bundled with inter-governmental fiscal relations reforms to alleviate problems related to the distribution of revenue across and within levels of government. More specifically, reforms of these taxes may exacerbate regional inequalities since richer SNGs are more likely to succeed in the implementation of a well-functioning property tax administration structure and may also benefit more from higher property values. These problems are commonly mitigated by reforming the equalisation system to take into consideration regional differences in revenue-raising capacity and through the use of central or provincial support for introducing the tax. The support can be provided in the form of, among others, capacity development programmes and/or financial incentives that reward efforts to introduce the property tax.

So as to alleviate abrupt effects of the tax reform, countries implement tax reforms gradually. Abrupt changes in tax obligations can lead to undesired changes in resource allocation and public resistance, both of which should be minimised. A more gradual introduction of the tax, starting with low and increasing rates, tied to improvements of visible public services or to income transfer programmes might reduce the resistance to the reform, as payments are linked to benefits received, and provide the necessary time so homeowners and investors have time to adjust to their investment portfolios. Sunset clauses can be used to cease transitional measures at specific dates without further legislative action, increasing the likelihood of the full implementation of the planned reform.

Lastly, regarding timing, economic upswings and booming housing markets tend to create windows of opportunity for putting forward property tax reforms. First, a better fiscal instance as a result of the good economic moment, makes it easier for governments to financially support the introduction of the tax and to compensate losers. Second, evidence points to a small but significant effect of these taxes on reducing housing prices. Hence, tax increases during a slowdown might destabilise the market, whereas tax increases during upswings might act counter-cyclically, stabilising prices. Proper timing can be especially important to raise awareness of the necessity of the tax and, thus, gather public support.

Overview

In contrast to most OECD countries, China does not levy a recurrent tax on residential property. Recurrent property taxes are growth-friendly and versatile, and they are especially valuable for raising revenues at the local level, notably to foster economic development. Despite these benefits, recurrent taxes on immovable property are among the most challenging taxes to administer, primary due to the need to revalue properties frequently. In addition, reforms to recurrent taxes on immovable property are difficult due to the tax's frequent unpopularity as well as its interactions with intergovernmental fiscal frameworks. Nevertheless, many successful recurrent property tax reforms have been implemented by OECD and partner countries in recent decades, especially following the Global Financial Crisis. The aim of this book is to draw on these examples to provide recommendations for the introduction of a recurrent levy on residential properties in China.

China is one of the few countries that does not levy a wide-base recurrent tax on residential properties, despite its rapid urbanisation in recent decades. Chinese municipal governments suffer from a relative scarcity of revenue sources to finance needed spending and they do not have autonomy over any major tax. A main source of revenues for Chinese municipal governments is public land leasing fees (OECD, 2017[1]). Nevertheless, due to the irregular and scarce nature of this source of revenue, it may not be sustainable to rely substantially on this revenue stream (Brys et al., 2013[2]). While the number of urban residents rises, the stock of available land for leasing decreases, shrinking the fiscal capacity of local governments to provide the level of public services that urbanisation demands. A recurrent tax on residential properties could be an alternative source of revenue that has the potential to overcome these difficulties, since it is regular, tends to grow with urbanisation and provides the necessary resources to finance local public services. According to the OECD *Revenue Statistics* and OECD Fiscal Decentralisation database, all OECD countries obtain some portion of their revenues from recurrent taxes on immovable properties, and on average, 88% of this revenue accrues to local governments. This revenue stream represents, on average, 40% of local government total consolidated revenues, usually covering more than all expenditure on housing and community amenities and public order and safety.

Aside from the benefits of increasing government funding, recurrent taxes on immovable property have additional features and purposes that set them apart from other taxes, which could benefit the Chinese tax system in many different ways. More specifically, recurrent taxes on immovable property are a versatile policy instrument that can have a role in the three main functions of the government: attainment of a less unequal distribution of income, maintenance of a stable economy and an efficient allocation of resources. First, due to property taxes' relative inelasticity – taxpayers usually only modestly react to changes in tax policy because their tax base is immovable – they are considered to be relatively efficient and among the taxes that are least detrimental to economic growth, especially when levied on households (OECD, 2021[3]). Second, in the case of residential taxation, there is a close link between taxes paid and public services received, which follows from the benefit principle of taxation in public finance. Third, they are one of the taxes least prone to tax competition, since their burden can be capitalised in house prices. Fourth, they can be used as a policy instrument for property price stabilisation since they tend to reduce the volatility of house prices. Fifth and lastly, it is a relatively transparent tax, potentially improving government accountability, contrasting with land concession revenues, which is a source of revenue that is defined outside the process of establishing a budget.

It is common for property tax reforms to be accompanied by more encompassing reforms of the fiscal system and inter-governmental relations, such as changes on the size and distribution criteria of fiscal equalisation funds. That is because the introduction of a new local tax in the absence of changes in the inter-governmental transfer system is likely to exacerbate existing fiscal disparities. China is among the most decentralised countries in the world from an expenditure perspective and also among the ones with the largest vertical fiscal gaps (i.e. the difference between local spending and local own revenues). At a minimum, the introduction of recurrent taxes on immovable property may narrow the vertical fiscal gap and provide more fiscal autonomy to local jurisdictions.

Despite these benefits, introducing a recurrent property tax system is challenging, given that for a number of reasons recurrent property taxation is among the most unpopular type of taxes. First, the transparency and inelasticity of recurrent property taxes, while they improve accountability and efficiency, make the tax salient and difficult to avoid. Second, the presumptive nature of property taxes makes it prone to unfair value assessments, particularly when revaluations are rare, potentially leading to abrupt and substantially higher obligations. Third, different from most taxes, recurrent property taxes are not levied on income flows, but rather on a stock of a relatively illiquid asset and, thus, can generate liquidity problems for households facing financial difficulties, in particular for asset-rich income-poor households, which are common in rapidly developing economies and regions. Fourth, the redistributive effect of recurrent property taxation hinges on various factors, but overall such taxes are typically less progressive than the personal income tax, inheritance tax and wealth tax. For these reasons, recurrent property reforms may face especially strong public opposition, adding to the typical difficulties of reforming tax systems (e.g. transitional costs, timing, impact on different levels of government, etc.).

Recurrent property taxes are considered among the most challenging taxes to administer, and require a well-functioning property valuation, billing and appeal system. The way that these processes are managed can have a significant impact on administration costs, which can be, as a share of tax revenues, as high as 10% (Almy, 2014[4]) or as low as 1% or less (e.g. in some US states).[1] Moreover, since recurrent property taxes are commonly managed at the local level, multiple jurisdictions may administer these taxes differently and sometimes inconsistently, especially because of asymmetries in local administrative capacity, creating horizontal distortions. China is a large and heterogeneous country and might be prone to this risk.

Although there are major challenges in designing, reforming and managing a recurrent property tax system, it is possible to overcome these in a manner that allows society to reap benefits in terms of a better allocation of resources, more stable house prices and a fairer income distribution. Many successful recurrent property tax reforms were implemented by OECD and partner countries in the last decades, especially after the 2008-09 Global Financial Crisis. This report highlights many of these cases. Some reforms were more comprehensive and disruptive, involving the introduction of new recurrent property tax systems nearly from scratch, whereas others were more incremental, approaching specific features of ownership classification, valuation methods or local government autonomy issues (see Box 0.1 for a sample of the most recent property tax reforms).

Box 0.1. Recent recurrent property tax reforms in OECD countries

In the last five years, recurrent property tax reforms were motivated by very different objectives in OECD countries. Some countries aimed at improving the progressivity of their recurrent property tax system by either giving tax reliefs for low-income households and/or increasing tax rates applied to high-income households. Other countries focused on property revaluation in order to reduce horizontal inequalities, increase fairness and/or tax revenues. In some cases tax rates were increased and/or the tax base was widened so as to boost tax revenues or to curb rapidly increasing housing prices. Temporary exemptions were also given to promote investments.

In **Chile**, a new progressive surcharge applies to taxpayers whose combined real estate fiscal value in Chile exceeds CLP 400 million (regardless of Chilean tax residency). The surcharge rate schedule is as follows: 0.075% for the part of the combined fiscal value of real estate properties that ranges between approximately USD 485 000 and USD 846 000; 0.15% for the part of the combined fiscal value that ranges from approximately USD 846 000 to USD 1 088 000; and 0.275% for the part of the combined fiscal value of real estate above USD 1 088 000. This tax entered into force on 1 April 2020 and is added to the ordinary real estate tax that is payable on a quarterly basis.

Denmark also introduced important changes to housing taxation. From 2021 onwards, housing taxes – including both the property tax and the land tax – will reflect market values, thereby ending the property valuation freeze in place since 2002, which has led to falling effective tax rates for homes experiencing increases in value. This reform will increase cadastral values for many properties. Tax rates will be lowered, however, and homeowners whose overall housing taxes increase with the new system will be compensated through a tax rebate. In an effort to protect homeowners from tax increases while they occupy their home, the payment of tax increases after 2021 will also be deferred until the home is sold.

Finland introduced an increase in recurrent real estate tax rates in 2017 to boost municipalities' revenues. In 2018, for general charges, and in 2019, for residential buildings, the maximum tax rates were raised again.

France's progressive repeal of the dwelling tax for 80% of households is one of the most notable property tax reforms in the last five years. The dwelling tax (*taxe d'habitation*) is due annually by owners or tenants that occupy a dwelling. The repeal has been phased in over three years for a group of households (based on annual income thresholds) with the tax reduction amounting to 30% in 2018, 65% in 2019 and 100% in 2020. For the rest of households, the tax will be gradually removed between 2021 and 2023. The dwelling tax has largely been perceived as unfair because effective tax rates vary widely across municipalities and because the notional rental values upon which the tax is based have not been updated since the 1970s. It should be mentioned that France's reform does not affect the *taxe foncière,* which will continue to be levied on the owners of immovable property.

Greece reduced its property tax (ENFIA) by providing a progressive tax rebate. This rebate ranges from 10% to 30% in a progressive manner – properties valued below EUR 60 000 received a 30% tax rebate while properties exceeding EUR 1 million received a 10% rebate. In addition, in 2018 there was a re-adjustment in real estate taxable values and an increase in the threshold of the supplementary tax – from EUR 200 000 to EUR 250 000. At the same time, the government abolished a property tax cut that was introduced by the previous administration and benefited property owners whose tax liability was below EUR 700.

Germany legislated an overhaul of its property valuation rules to comply with the requirements of the Federal Constitutional Court. In its ruling dated 10 April 2018, the Federal Constitutional Court declared the way in which properties are valued for the purposes of real property tax to be unconstitutional, as the tax is calculated on the basis of property values that are decades old. The values determined in accordance with the new law will be used to calculate charges from 2025 onwards. Overall, the reform is expected to be revenue neutral.

Israel, in order to lower the demand for housing investments and cool the property market, introduced a new tax, which became effective on 1 January 2017. Owners of three or more apartments or houses are now subject to a 1% tax on the value of those properties.

Italy unified its local property taxes, by abolishing the municipal service tax TASI ("*Tributo Servizi Indivisibili*") and merging it with the IMU ("*Imposta Municipale Propria*") local property tax. The sum of TASI and IMU rates will remain the same. Moreover, the IMU deduction from business income taxation has been increased up to 100% as for 2022 (instead of 70%). Italy also introduced an annual property tax on marine platforms for the extraction of hydrocarbons.

In **Korea**, the comprehensive real estate tax, which is a national tax levied on the owners of multiple properties and expensive real estate, was raised as part of an attempt to curb rapidly increasing housing prices.

Lithuania is increasing effective rates of its recurrent property tax by reducing the tax-exempt threshold for non-commercial property from EUR 220 000 to EUR 150 000. It also has increased the minimum tax rates for immovable property used for commercial purposes from 0.3% to 0.5%.

Portugal introduced a new municipal property tax surcharge of 0.7%, 1% and 1.5% on real estates of total taxable values above EUR 600 000, EUR 1 000 000 and EUR 2 000 000, respectively. This surcharge replaces the stamp duty on residential urban properties and on land for construction of a taxable value above EUR 1 million. This reform also introduced a single rate of 0.4% levied on companies' total real estate.

Turkey reformed two elements of its recurrent property tax system. First, it implemented an additional levy on residential houses that are valued above TRY 5 million. The tax rates are progressive (between 0.3% and 1%) depending on the value of the residence. Second, it introduced a five-year exemption from real estate taxation for buildings constructed within the scope of the investment incentive.

Sources: OECD (2016[5]), OECD (2017[6]), OECD (2018[7]), OECD (2019[8]), OECD (2020[9]) and OECD (2021[10]).

This report presents a set of good principles and options for reforming recurrent taxes on immovable property based on the latest experience of property tax reforms around the world that are particularly relevant to the Chinese context. Although these good principles are mostly general, meaning that they can apply to almost any country, the report makes specific points tailored to the Chinese case. The report is divided into four chapters. The first chapter focuses on the role of property taxes in OECD countries; the second chapter discusses good principles for recurrent property tax design; the third discusses good practices on recurrent property taxes administration. Together, the second and third chapters provide the 'end-goal' of a reform, covering topics such as its integration into the tax system, tax rate, scope, valuation of properties and fiscal cadastre management. The fourth and last chapter provides principles to lay out a reform that can successfully overcome the general difficulties in any tax reform, such as transitional costs and communication issues, and the specific difficulties in property tax reforms, such as how to deal with its salience, liquidity constraints, perceived regressivity, inherently arbitrary tax base and lack of sensitivity to economic activity. Box 0.2, below, provides a summary of the main findings.

Box 0.2. Summary of practices

1. Role of recurrent taxes on immovable property

- Recurrent taxes on immovable property often are the most important tax in terms of revenue raising capacity at the local level, although they are only the fourth most important type of tax in terms of overall tax revenue.
- Recurrent taxes on immovable property are the taxes over which subnational governments (SNGs) have most discretion and, thus, have a key role in increasing subnational autonomy and reducing the vertical fiscal gap
- Recurrent property taxes revenues are often enough to supply various public goods commonly assigned to local governments such as housing and community amenities and public order and safety, but usually cannot finance the entirety of local expenditure on education, health or social protection.
- The reliance on recurrent taxes on immovable property is correlated with a country's level of development – not only developed countries tend to rely more on immovable property taxation, but also the more a country develops, the more it tends to increase its reliance on these taxes. Some OECD countries have reformed their property tax system in order to increase the role of recurrent taxes on immovable property while reducing the role of transaction taxes. This can be justified by the fact that a revenue-neutral shift toward a well-designed recurrent tax on immovable property has the potential to minimise economic distortions and increase growth.

2. Tax Design

- The tax base of recurrent taxes on immovable property is typically wide, covering land and improvements, business and residential households, as well as owner-occupied and rented properties. Wide tax bases allow governments to increase tax revenues while minimising allocative distortions.
- The same recurrent property tax usually applies to all types of property and tax bases, and typically tax rates vary little across property types, which minimises distortions and reduces tax avoidance.
- Despite having distortionary effects, property tax reliefs and exemptions are employed to achieve a myriad of policy objectives such as preservation of agricultural land, promotion of business and urban development, increased tax progressivity, reduced salience of the tax, among others.

- The most common measure to increase tax progressivity is to provide tax reliefs to low-income earners. Although progressive rates are employed in some countries, their effect on the progressivity of the tax system depends on the distribution of house ownership.
- Programmes aimed at providing tax benefits to business come in various forms: property tax abatement programmes, firm-specific property taxes, earmarked tax revenues to the development of a specific region and enterprise zones, among others. Despite the use of multiple types of programmes, evidence is unclear about their effect in promoting business.
- Countries often use recurrent property taxation as a tool to reduce housing price volatility. Evidence points to a small but significant effect of these taxes on housing prices. Nevertheless, ultimately, this reduction depends on the incidence of the tax, which is defined by the supply and demand elasticities of housing as well as the frequency of reassessment.
- Owner-occupied housing is commonly taxed at concessionary rates due to lack of imputed rent taxes and capital gains tax exemptions or reliefs. Further concessions are often provided to debt-financed investments in owner-occupied housing through mortgage interest relief. As a result, the tax system often favours housing investments, potentially in a distortionary manner.
- OECD countries often mitigate tax distortions that tend to benefit housing investment in detriment of other investments by levying recurrent taxes on immovable property, capping deductions or providing tax credit when granting tax reliefs for mortgage interest, and capping the value of owner-occupied houses that benefits from exemption from taxation capital gains.
- Designing recurrent property taxes to promote green investments and sustainable land use have become increasingly popular across OECD and partner countries.
- Evidence suggests that property taxes are effective in reducing urban sprawl when designed specifically for that purpose. A more general measure to achieve this objective is the imposition of higher tax levies on land in comparison to buildings (i.e. split-rate taxation). Other measures involve the penalisation of under-used land that was zoned for development and of new developments through fees.

3. Tax Administration

- Administration of a recurrent property tax system can be very costly as a proportion to tax revenues. Nevertheless, many OECD countries employ methods that can significantly reduce these costs, notably computer-assisted mass appraisal systems.
- OECD countries commonly use fiscal cadastres not only as a tool for calculating property tax obligations but also as a tool to support the achievement of other policy goals such as urban, transport and environmental and social policy.
- In decentralised countries, horizontal and vertical co-ordination arrangements are sometimes used to overcome challenges related to the lack of scale that some local governments might have to efficiently administer fiscal cadastres and property valuation systems.
- Capital values are by and large the most used property value basis for recurrent taxes on immovable property in emerging economies, since: 1) there is sufficient sales data; 2) capital values can be used as a basis for other taxes; and 3) they are partially correlated with economic activity.
- The sales comparison approach is the most used method for property valuation across OECD countries. Other methods are particularly employed to appraise properties that lack sales data, such as the cost and the income approach.
- Many OECD economies maintain a frequent revaluation schedule (at least once every six years). Countries that do not maintain a frequent schedule can become prone to distortions that cause horizontal inequities, harming good properties of recurrent taxes on immovable property.
- It is common for upper levels of government to define general guidelines and oversee valuation assessments performed by lower levels of government. This can be justified by the fact that

having some uniformity in the valuation method and basis is important to maintain effective tax rates similar across jurisdictions, reducing horizontal inequities.

- Local governments in most OECD countries can set tax rates within limits set by upper levels of government and cannot define tax bases and/or grant exemptions that are not in the upper level of government law. In that manner local governments have sufficient autonomy to be held accountable for their fiscal policies and, at the same time, cannot create major horizontal distortions across jurisdictions, such as by exporting taxes.
- Most tax administrations grant to taxpayers a right to challenge assessments. Commonly: 1) independent institutions are involved in the judgment of appeals; 2) instructions on how to appeal are available in websites and/or in valuation notices; 3) taxpayer information on how their properties were appraised is provided when requested; and 4) no fee, a small fee or a progressive fee is levied for appeals, allowing low-income taxpayers to appeal.
- OECD countries often try to make tax payments convenient, and allay liquidity challenges as much as possible by allowing tax payments to be in multiple instalments and/or in a joint manner with other payments such as mortgages or utilities. Taxpayer convenience can reduce delinquency.
- Countries carefully choose the text to be sent to taxpayers in bills. Multiple studies have found that a significant increase in tax compliance can be achieved through the disclosure of some type of information such as the compliance rate, a clear explanation of the tax system, the public goods that are funded with the tax and sanctions.
- Internet websites are widely used as a tool to increase transparency. Countries or states usually have websites that centralise information regarding the tax system of local governments. These websites often provide a wide range of information with regards to rates system, valuation, rate setting and the appeal process.

4. Tax Reform

- Payment in instalments, withholding tax at source, allowing payments to be made in conjunction with other payments, tax deferrals for seniors, tax reliefs for low-income households, taxpayer education and consultation, accessible appeal processes, frequent reassessments, phased increases and indexing are among the most promising and widely used approaches to deal with unpopular features of recurrent taxes on immovable property.
- Bundling is an effective strategy that is commonly employed in recurrent property tax reforms as a way to overcome political resistance through losers' compensation and improvements in distributional effects. Often, property tax reforms are bundled with inter-governmental fiscal relations reforms to alleviate problems related to the distribution of revenue across and within levels of government or through the reduction of other taxes to avoid increasing the tax burden.
- Engaging a wide range of stakeholders, obtaining a consensus on a reform's broad long-term goals and focusing the discussions on the systematic rather than individual impact of the reform are all effective communication strategies. In this way, undesired impacts of the reform can be put into a larger/systemic perspective and be communicated in a manner that is more palatable for some actors.
- Transitional measures are typically introduced to alleviate short-term effects of tax hikes. For that purpose, temporary reduction in tax rates, tax credits, tax deferrals or tax reliefs are commonly employed. Nevertheless, reformers need to design and implement these measures in a manner that the full implementation of the reform is secured so the reform can achieve their initial goals.
- Most property tax reforms are made during economic upswings since governments tend to be in a better financial situation to compensate losers and since a potential reduction in housing prices will tend to lead to a stabilisation rather than an attenuation of housing price movements.

References

Almy, R. (2014), "Valuation and Assessment of Immovable Property", *OECD Working Papers on Fiscal Federalism*, No. 19, OECD Publishing, Paris, https://dx.doi.org/10.1787/5jz5pzvr28hk-en. [4]

Brys, B. et al. (2013), "Tax Policy and Tax Reform in the People's Republic of China", *OECD Taxation Working Papers*, No. 18, OECD Publishing, Paris, https://dx.doi.org/10.1787/5k40l4dlmnzw-en. [2]

OECD (2021), *A Review of Local Government Finance in Israel: Reforming the Arnona System*, OECD Multi-level Governance Studies, OECD Publishing, Paris, https://dx.doi.org/10.1787/a5bc4d25-en. [10]

OECD (2021), *Brick by Brick: Building Better Housing Policies*, OECD Publishing, Paris, https://dx.doi.org/10.1787/b453b043-en. [3]

OECD (2020), *Tax Policy Reforms 2020: OECD and Selected Partner Economies*, OECD Publishing, Paris, https://dx.doi.org/10.1787/7af51916-en. [9]

OECD (2019), *Tax Policy Reforms 2019: OECD and Selected Partner Economies*, OECD Publishing, Paris, https://dx.doi.org/10.1787/da56c295-en. [8]

OECD (2018), *Tax Policy Reforms 2018: OECD and Selected Partner Economies*, OECD Publishing, Paris, https://dx.doi.org/10.1787/9789264304468-en. [7]

OECD (2017), *OECD Economic Surveys: China 2017*, OECD Publishing, Paris, https://dx.doi.org/10.1787/eco_surveys-chn-2017-en. [1]

OECD (2017), *Tax Policy Reforms 2017: OECD and Selected Partner Economies*, OECD Publishing, Paris, https://dx.doi.org/10.1787/9789264279919-en. [6]

OECD (2016), *Tax Policy Reforms in the OECD 2016*, OECD Publishing, Paris, https://dx.doi.org/10.1787/9789264260399-en. [5]

Note

[1] For more, see Walters and IAAO Research Committee (2014).

1 The role of recurrent taxes on immovable property

Recurrent taxes on immovable property are not among the largest for governments as a whole in terms of their revenue collection, but because of their immovable tax base, this type of tax is frequently the tax over which local governments can exert the most control. This autonomy is especially valuable as it allows local governments to adjust their revenues intake to fulfil local demands, increasing political accountability. As a result, recurrent taxes on immovable property can raise enough revenues to fund important public services at the local level, such as housing and community amenities, public order and safety as well as a portion of local expenditure on education, health or social protection.

Key messages

1. Recurrent taxes on immovable property represent a significant portion of local governments' revenue, although they are only the fourth most important type of tax in terms of overall tax revenue.
2. Recurrent taxes on immovable property are the taxes over which SNGs have most discretion and, thus, have a key role in increasing subnational autonomy and reducing the vertical fiscal gap.
3. Recurrent property taxes revenues are often enough to supply various public goods commonly assigned to local governments such as housing and community amenities and public order and safety but usually cannot finance the entirety of local expenditure on education, health or social protection.
4. The reliance on recurrent taxes on immovable property is correlated with a country's level of development – not only developed countries tend to rely more on immovable property taxation, but also the more a country develops, the more it tends to increase its reliance on these taxes.
5. The share of local property tax revenues in total local taxation is smaller in China than in the average OECD country, and this gap can be narrowed with a recurrent levy on residential properties.

Property tax revenues and levels of government

Although property taxes are only the fourth most important type of taxes in terms of general government tax revenues, recurrent tax on immovable property represent a significant portion of local governments' revenues

The OECD classifies taxes into six broad categories: 1) taxes on income, profits and capital gains; 2) social security contributions; 3) taxes on payroll and workforce; 4) taxes on property; 5) taxes on goods and services; and 6) other taxes. In terms of tax revenues, taxes on property are the fourth most important category, behind taxes on income, profits and capital gains; taxes on goods and services; and social security contributions. The average share of property tax revenues as a percentage of total taxation in OECD countries is roughly 5.5%, as of 2019, and has not varied much throughout the last three decades (Figure 1.1).

Figure 1.1 Tax revenue as a percentage of total taxation in OECD countries

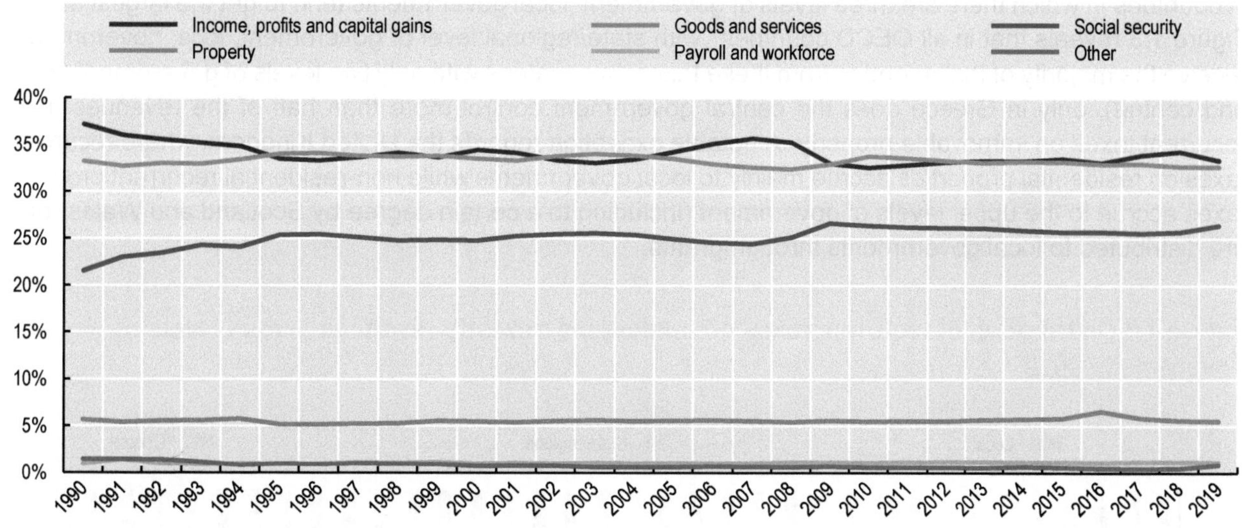

Source: OECD *Revenue Statistics*.

The main subject of this report is recurrent taxes on immovable property, which is a subcategory of taxes on property. For most OECD countries, recurrent taxes on immovable property is the most important category of taxes on property and accounts for, on average, 61% of property tax revenue and 3.2% of total taxation. Figure 1.2, below, depicts tax revenues for each category of property taxes as a percentage of total property tax revenue. In 27 out of 36 OECD countries, recurrent taxes on immovable property are the most important type of property tax in terms of revenue. In countries in which this is not true, a significant levy on net wealth or financial or capital transactions are in place, meaning that in OECD countries recurrent tax on immovable property is by far the most important tax applied to immovable properties.

Brys et al. (2016[1]) suggest that recurrent taxes on immovable property are the least harmful for economic growth, and at the same time, usually do not harm equity. Thus, it is often recommended to boost the share of revenues from these taxes relative to others, more distortive taxes, such as transaction taxes.

Figure 1.2 Tax revenue from categories of property taxes as a percentage of property tax revenue, 2019

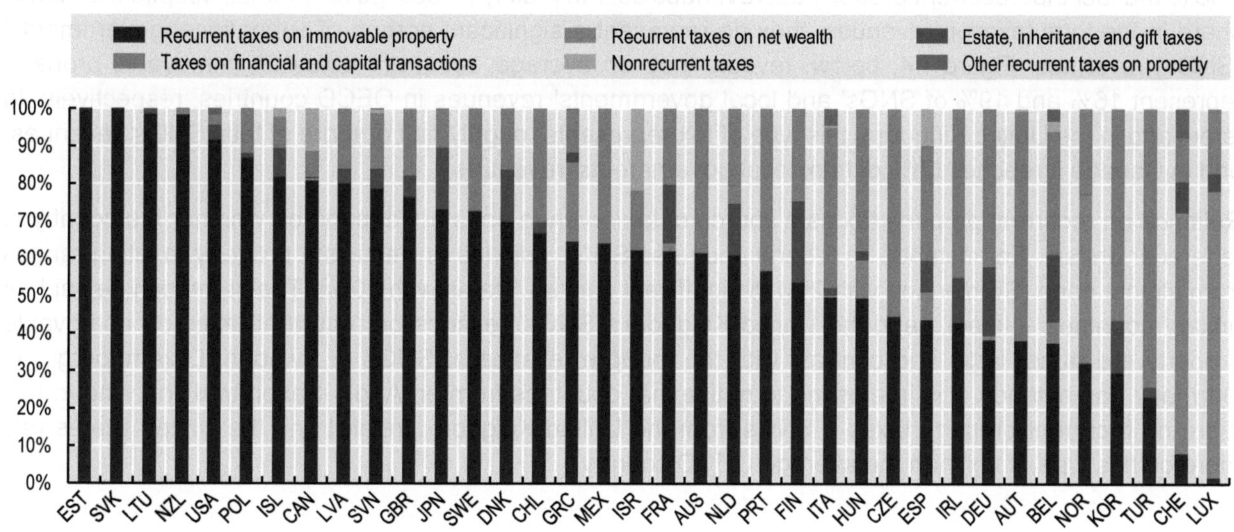

Note: Values as of 2019 or closest year with available data.
Source: OECD *Revenue Statistics*.

Most of the revenues from recurrent taxes on immovable property are assigned to local governments. Even in countries in which there are three levels of government, local governments tend to get the largest share. Figure 1.3 reveals that in all OECD countries[1] with state/regional level of government, local governments receive the majority of the revenues from these taxes. In countries with only two levels of government (local and central), only in Greece does the central government control more than half of the revenues from recurrent taxes on immovable property. A notable exception regards the United Kingdom, where recurrent taxes on residential properties accrue mainly to local governments while non-residential recurrent property taxes accrue to the upper levels of government (including to a certain degree by Scotland and Wales) and are distributed to local governments through grants.

Figure 1.3 Distribution of recurrent taxes on immovable property revenues across levels of government, 2019

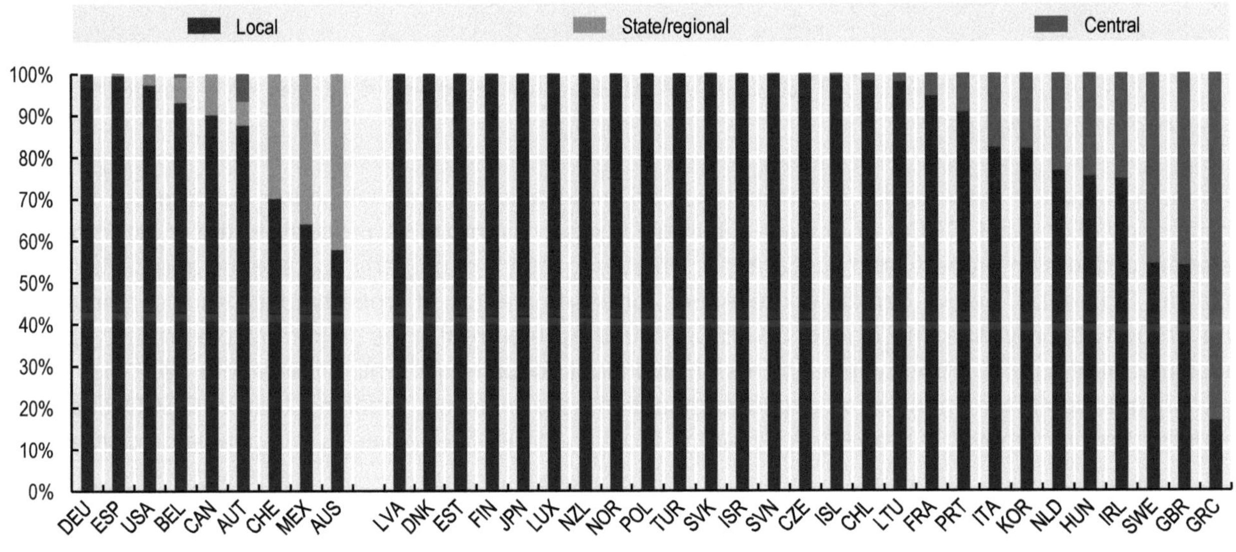

Note: Values as of 2019 or closest year with available data.
Source: OECD *Revenue Statistics* (for recurrent taxes on immovable property) and OECD Fiscal Decentralisation database (for SNGs' revenue)

Due to the fact that recurrent property tax revenues accrue mainly to local governments, despite their small share in the total taxation revenues, they do represent a significant portion of subnational governments' (SNGs) revenues. Figure 1.4, below, reveals that, on average, recurrent taxes on immovable property represent 16% and 19% of SNGs' and local governments' revenues in OECD countries, respectively. In Israel and in the United Kingdom, this type of tax represents roughly half or more of total SNGs' revenues, and in Canada it reaches 58% of total local governments' revenues.

Reliance on recurrent property tax as a source of tax revenue does not depend on whether the country is federal or unitary. For instance, in federal countries SNGs reliance on recurrent property taxation ranges from almost none (Switzerland with 2%) to significant (United States with 20%). The same can be said for unitary countries – Israel's and the United Kingdom's SNGs' reliance on recurrent taxes on immovable property are rather large and contrast with the meagre reliance of SNGs in Sweden, Luxembourg and Germany, for instance. It is interesting to notice that countries from an Anglo-Saxon tradition tend to rely more on recurrent property taxes – SNGs from the United Kingdom, Ireland and the United States rely more on this type of tax than the average OECD country.

Figure 1.4 Recurrent taxes on immovable property as a percentage of local and state government's revenues, 2019

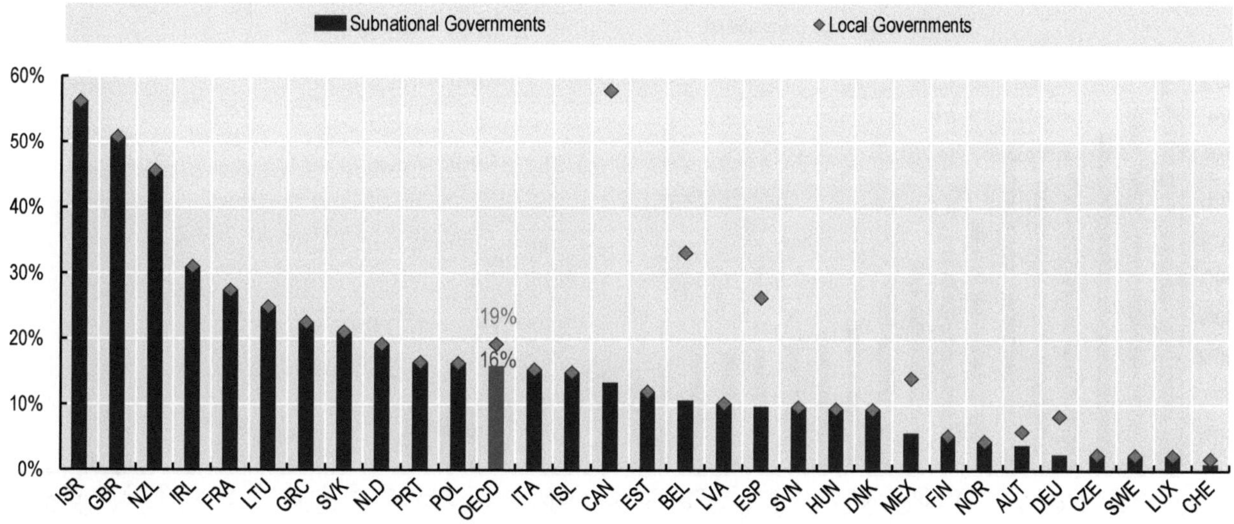

Note: SNGs' revenues are consolidated (defined as total revenue minus the inter-governmental transfer revenue of that government level). Values as of 2019 or closest year with available data.
Source: OECD *Revenue Statistics* (for recurrent tax on immovable property) and OECD Fiscal Decentralisation database (for SNGs' revenue)

Recurrent taxes on immovable properties and subnational autonomy

Recurrent taxes on immovable property are the taxes over which SNGs have most discretion and, therefore, they tend to increase subnational autonomy and reduce the vertical fiscal gap

When considering the importance of recurrent taxes on immovable property as a percentage of subnational tax revenue (instead of total revenues), this type of tax has an even more prominent role. Figure 1.5 shows that recurrent taxes on immovable properties represent roughly 33% and 41% of all subnational and local taxation revenue, respectively. In the case of local governments, they represent more than half of the local tax revenue in 14 countries, and in all OECD countries from an Anglo-Saxon tradition (Australia, the United Kingdom, Ireland, New Zealand, Canada and the United States) their share reaches more than 70% of all local tax revenue.

Figure 1.5 Recurrent tax on immovable property as a percentage of local and state government's taxation, 2019

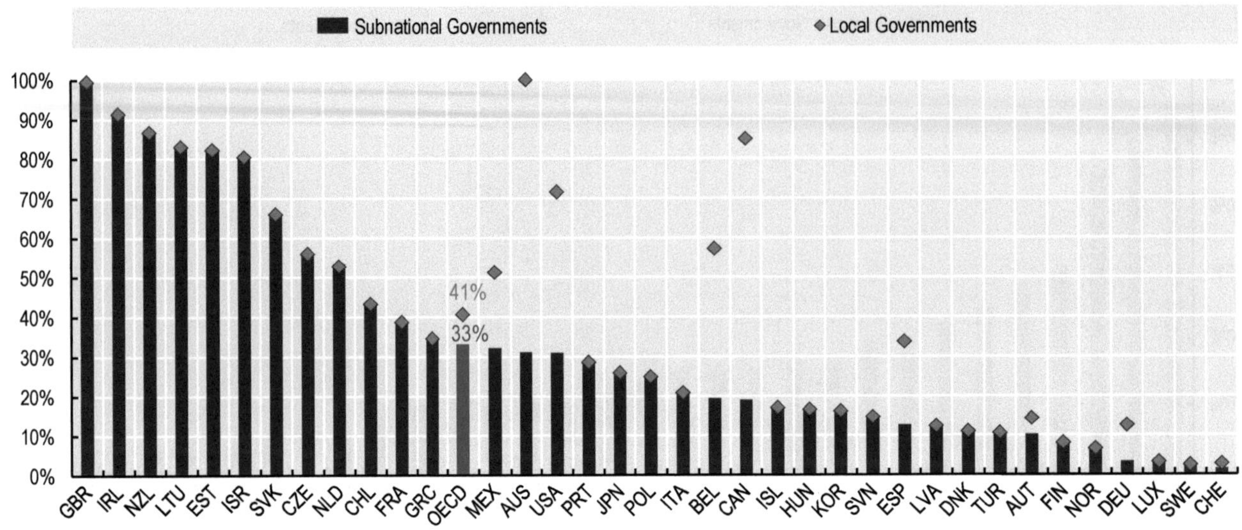

Note: Values as of 2019 or closest year with available data.
Source: OECD *Revenue Statistics*.

Figure 1.6 The subnational tax mix shifts from property to income as decentralisation increases

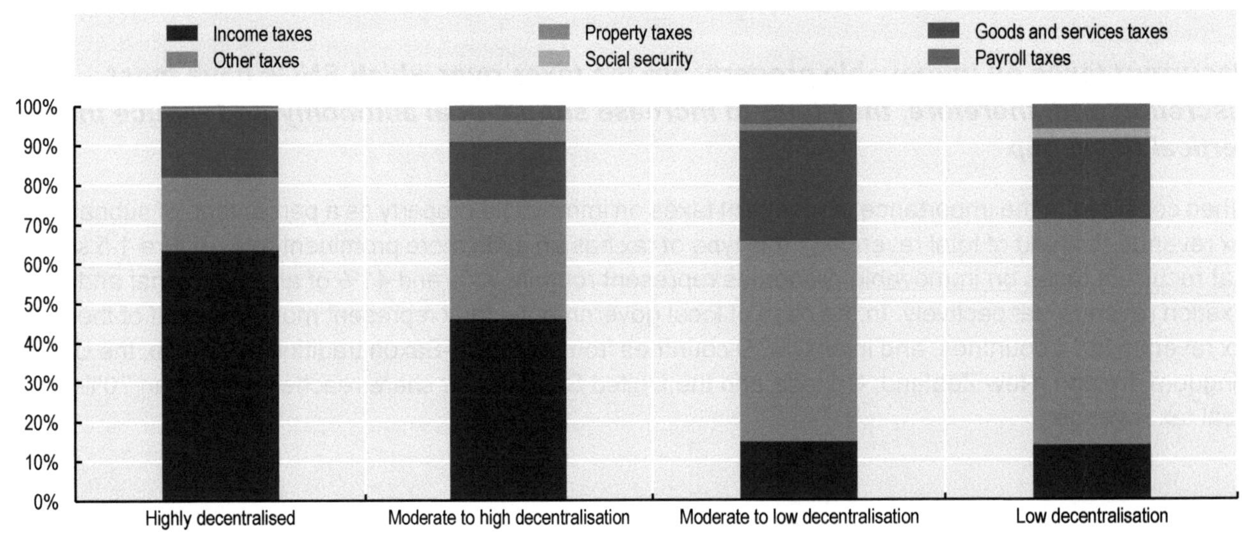

1. Each column represents a quartile of OECD countries in order of decreasing subnational revenues as a share of total government revenue. Revenues from tax-sharing agreements where the SCG does not control the rate are not included. Where data for 2018 was not available at the time of publication, data for 2017 was substituted.
2. Countries were grouped into four categories based on their quartiles with regard to subnational revenue as a percentage of general government's revenue.
Source: Forman, Dougherty and Blöchlinger (2020[2]), based on data from OECD *Global Revenue Statistics*.

The composition of SNGs' tax mix appears strongly related to the extent of decentralisation, as shown in Figure 1.5. In more centralised countries, SNGs rely largely on immovable property taxes. Among the bottom 50% of OECD countries in terms of SNGs' revenues as a percentage of general government revenue, property taxes constitute 48% of SNGs' tax mix, on average. As decentralisation increases, income taxes start to play a greater role. Countries in the top quartile in terms of SNGs' revenue as a percentage of general government revenues have income taxes constituting on average 62% of their SNGs' tax mix. The subnational tax mix has changed relatively little in the last 20 years, with a decline in the share of property taxes and a rise in the share of consumption and income taxes – especially personal income tax. Since around 2010, the property tax share has again been on the rise. Overall, the subnational share of total taxation has hardly increased.

This prominence of recurrent property taxation can be explained to some extent by the fact that SNGs' tax mix is usually less diversified than central governments', since not all taxes are well-suited to be collected at the subnational level. Important aspects to be considered when decentralising the collection of a type of tax are tax mobility and tax competition. Recurrent taxes on immovable properties are both, by definition, levied on immovable assets (low tax mobility) and, as discussed previously, not highly distortive. Thus, they tend to be less prone to regional tax competition when properly designed and as a result, are especially suited to be levied at the subnational level. Nevertheless, when they are levied on business, tax competition can occur in some circumstances since companies might prefer to move to where they pay less taxes.

In addition to these elements, it is worth adding that the lower the administrative capacity of a government the more preferred it usually is to have one tax with large revenue capacity than multiple taxes with small revenue capacity[2] (Mikesell, 2012[3]). That is because there is a fixed cost associated with the administration of each tax and when a type of tax has a small revenue capacity, it might not generate enough revenues to compensate for the additional administrative and compliance burden, not to mention the added complexity to the tax system. In other words: it tends to be easier to administrate one big tax than multiple small taxes and, thus, for governments with limited administrative capacity, one big tax is preferred over multiple small taxes. Therefore, the assignment of multiple minor taxes to subnational governments is not administratively the same as the assignment of a large tax such as the recurrent taxes on immovable property.

Not only are recurrent taxes on immovable property among the most important sources of own-source revenue for local governments, but they also tend to be the one in which SNGs have the most leeway to set their own tax policy (Dougherty, Harding and Reschovsky, 2019[4]). More specifically, SNGs have more discretion over certain aspects of their recurrent property taxation policy such as over decisions to introduce or to abolish a tax, to set tax rates, to define the tax base, or to grant tax allowances/reliefs to households and firms. In that manner, SNGs can use this tax power to tune their fiscal policy to the needs of the local population. Such aspects of recurrent taxes on immovable property cannot be overlooked since much of the economic and political benefit of decentralised public finance comes from the ability of SNGs to make their own decisions.

More precisely, the modern theoretical underpinnings of decentralisation originated with Oates (1972[5]), who posits the decentralisation theorem that, assuming no cost savings from centralisation, aggregate welfare across a set of jurisdictions will be superior when each jurisdiction is allowed to select its own public consumption bundle as opposed to when uniform consumption is provided across all jurisdictions. And enhancing SNG fiscal autonomy allows the bundle of public goods consumed to be selected locally, thus better matching local preferences.

Moreover, increasing subnational own revenues also aligns the incentives of SNGs to reduce moral hazard issues related to fiscal decentralisation. Although the degree of decentralisation varies widely among countries, there is a commonality: spending decentralisation is greater than revenue decentralisation in all countries (Figure 1.7). That is, SNGs own revenues are not sufficient to meet their expenditures. This aspect of fiscal federalism is known as vertical fiscal gap. In order to provide the necessary resources for SNGs, inter-governmental transfers are necessary to fill the gap.

These inter-governmental transfers could also engender a costly misalignment of incentives (Forman, Dougherty and Blöchliger, 2020[2]). More specifically, a "common pool" problem may arise when decentralisation narrows the subnational revenue base and raises the vertical fiscal gap (de Mello, 2000[6]). In this situation, the political costs of raising taxes to transfers to SNGs is borne by the central government but the benefits of the expenditure are enjoyed locally. Rodden (2002[7]) found evidence that SNGs' reliance on inter-governmental transfers is negatively correlated with fiscal performance, particularly when SNGs have easy access to credit. In addition, when SNGs have more autonomy, not only can they be held accountable for their tax policy, but they also have the tax power to raise revenues themselves, not resorting to the "common pool" of higher levels of government taxation. Although in no country do SNGs have the taxing power necessary to finance all of their expenditures, generally, the lower the fiscal gap, the lower the risk of having common pool problems. And to minimise this risk, recurrent taxes on immovable property are among the best tools that there are.

Figure 1.7 Shares of subnational expenditure and revenue in OECD countries, 2020

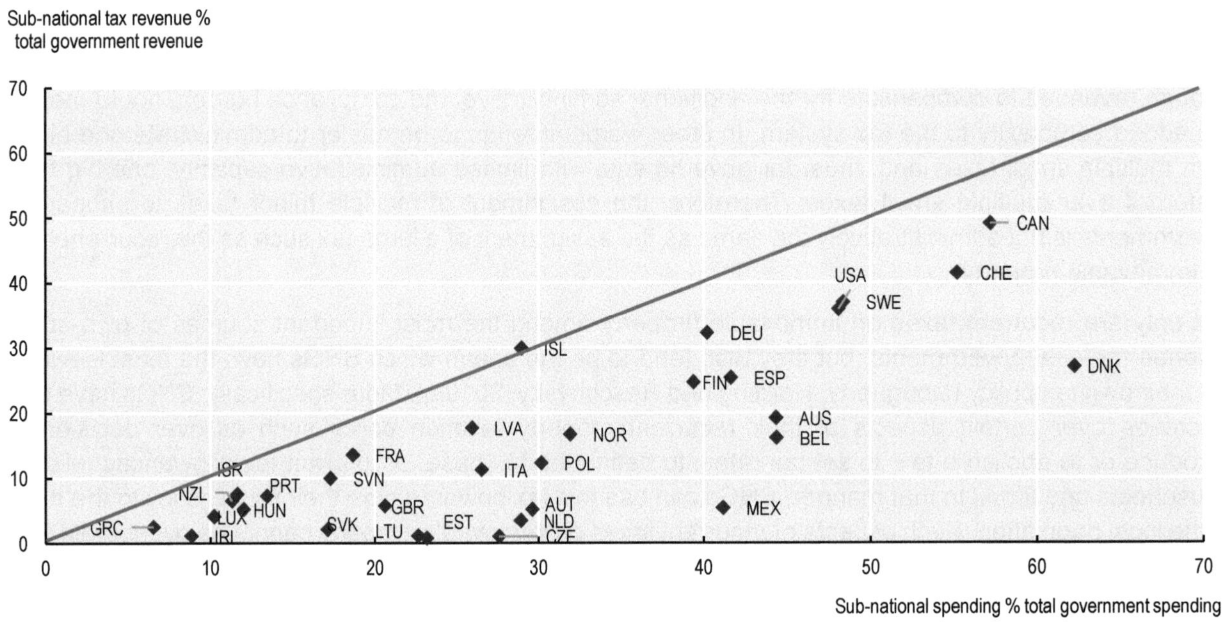

Note: The 45 degrees line shows a situation where revenue decentralisation equals spending decentralisation. The farther away a country is from that line, the larger its vertical fiscal gap.
Source: OECD Fiscal Decentralisation database.

Table 1.1. Local expenditure on selected government functions and property tax revenues, both as a percentage of GDP (as of 2018)

	Social protection	Education	General public services	Recreation, culture and religion	Health	Housing and community amenities	Environ-mental protection	Public order and safety	Local Property Tax
FRA	2.1%	1.3%	2.1%	1.0%	0.1%	0.9%	0.9%	0.4%	2.5%
ISR	0.9%	2.2%	0.6%	0.7%	0.0%	0.3%	0.4%	0.0%	2.0%
JPN	3.9%	2.7%	1.6%	0.4%	1.8%	0.6%	1.0%	1.0%	1.9%
AUS	0.1%	0.0%	0.6%	0.5%	0.0%	0.3%	0.3%	0.1%	1.7%
ISL	2.6%	4.4%	1.5%	2.0%	0.0%	0.4%	0.2%	0.1%	1.7%
GBR	3.2%	2.2%	0.7%	0.2%	0.2%	0.7%	0.4%	0.8%	1.6%
DNK	18.1%	2.8%	1.1%	0.7%	7.9%	0.1%	0.2%	0.1%	1.3%
BEL	1.4%	1.4%	1.3%	0.7%	0.0%	0.2%	0.4%	0.8%	1.2%
POL	2.6%	3.4%	1.2%	1.0%	2.0%	0.5%	0.4%	0.2%	1.1%
ESP	0.6%	0.2%	2.0%	0.6%	0.1%	0.3%	0.6%	0.4%	1.1%
ITA	0.7%	0.8%	2.4%	0.2%	6.6%	0.4%	0.8%	0.2%	1.0%
FIN	5.3%	3.5%	3.9%	0.9%	5.6%	0.2%	0.1%	0.2%	0.8%
LVA	1.1%	3.9%	0.6%	0.9%	0.9%	1.0%	0.2%	0.2%	0.8%
PRT	0.6%	0.7%	1.7%	0.4%	0.3%	0.4%	0.5%	0.1%	0.7%
NLD	3.0%	3.9%	0.9%	0.8%	0.5%	0.3%	1.2%	0.3%	0.7%
KOR	2.8%	3.9%	2.1%	0.6%	0.5%	0.9%	0.7%	0.2%	0.7%
SVN	0.9%	3.0%	0.7%	0.7%	1.0%	0.4%	0.2%	0.1%	0.5%
IRL	0.8%	0.2%	0.1%	0.1%	0.0%	0.3%	0.2%	0.1%	0.4%
DEU	2.7%	1.2%	1.4%	0.4%	0.2%	0.3%	0.3%	0.3%	0.4%
SVK	0.5%	2.6%	0.9%	0.4%	0.2%	0.4%	0.4%	0.1%	0.4%
NOR	4.9%	3.8%	1.3%	1.0%	2.2%	0.8%	0.7%	0.2%	0.4%
HUN	0.7%	0.9%	1.6%	0.7%	0.3%	0.4%	0.2%	0.0%	0.4%
SWE	6.4%	5.3%	2.6%	0.8%	6.5%	0.6%	0.4%	0.2%	0.4%
GRC	0.0%	0.0%	0.0%	0.0%	0.0%	0.0%	0.0%	0.0%	0.3%
LTU	0.8%	2.8%	0.5%	0.5%	1.4%	0.4%	0.3%	0.1%	0.3%
EST	0.7%	3.5%	0.6%	0.8%	1.3%	0.3%	0.3%	0.0%	0.2%
CZE	0.8%	3.1%	1.2%	0.8%	1.4%	0.6%	0.7%	0.2%	0.2%
AUT	1.8%	1.4%	1.2%	0.5%	1.7%	0.1%	0.2%	0.1%	0.2%
CHE	0.0%	0.0%	0.0%	0.0%	0.0%	0.0%	0.0%	0.0%	0.2%
LUX	0.0%	0.0%	0.0%	0.0%	0.0%	0.0%	0.0%	0.0%	0.1%
% of blue cells	**19%**	**19%**	**29%**	**42%**	**45%**	**58%**	**74%**	**84%**	-

Note: Values are painted in blue in case they are both 1) greater than zero and 2) smaller than recurrent taxes on immovable property revenues of the respective country. Last row refers to the percentage of blue cells in the column (i.e. that is, the percentage of countries that can fund the local government expenditure on the respective function using only their local revenues from recurrent taxes on immovable property).
Source: OECD *Revenue Statistics* and OECD *System of National Accounts*.

Public goods financed with revenues from recurrent taxes on immovable property

Recurrent taxes on immovable property revenues are often enough to supply all public goods commonly assigned to local governments such as housing and community amenities and public order and safety, but cannot finance the entirety of local expenditure on education, health or social protection

Local governments in every country provide a wide range of goods and services. A principles-based intuition about which types of services local governments usually provide can be obtained through an analysis of the characteristics of these goods. Some goods supplied by the government have private goods features (i.e. excludable and/or rivalrous) such as sewage, waste collection and some types of recreation like museums. In principle, it makes sense for some of those goods to be at least partially financed by their consumers through government fees, since they can be easily identified, and free-rider behaviour can be partially avoided. Other goods provided by local governments such as those related to public order and safety, recreation and housing benefit local dwellers as a whole (i.e. non-excludable and/or non-rivalrous) and, thus, in principle should be funded with local taxes imposed on residents.

In practice local and regional/state governments are sometimes responsible for the provision of a substantial share of health, education and social protection expenditures. These countries tend to be on the right side of Figure 1.7 (e.g. Canada, Denmark, Switzerland, Sweden and the United States). Usually revenues generated by recurrent taxes on immovable properties are not sufficient to finance these costlier services, but they are, in many OECD countries, enough to cover those services whose benefits are accrued to local communities, mentioned in the previous paragraph (see Table 1.1).

Revenues from recurrent taxes on immovable property as a percentage of GDP ranges from 0.1%, in Luxembourg, to 3.1%, in Canada (Figure 1.8). On average in OECD countries this share is 1.1%.

Figure 1.8 Recurrent taxes on immovable property as a percentage of GDP, 2019

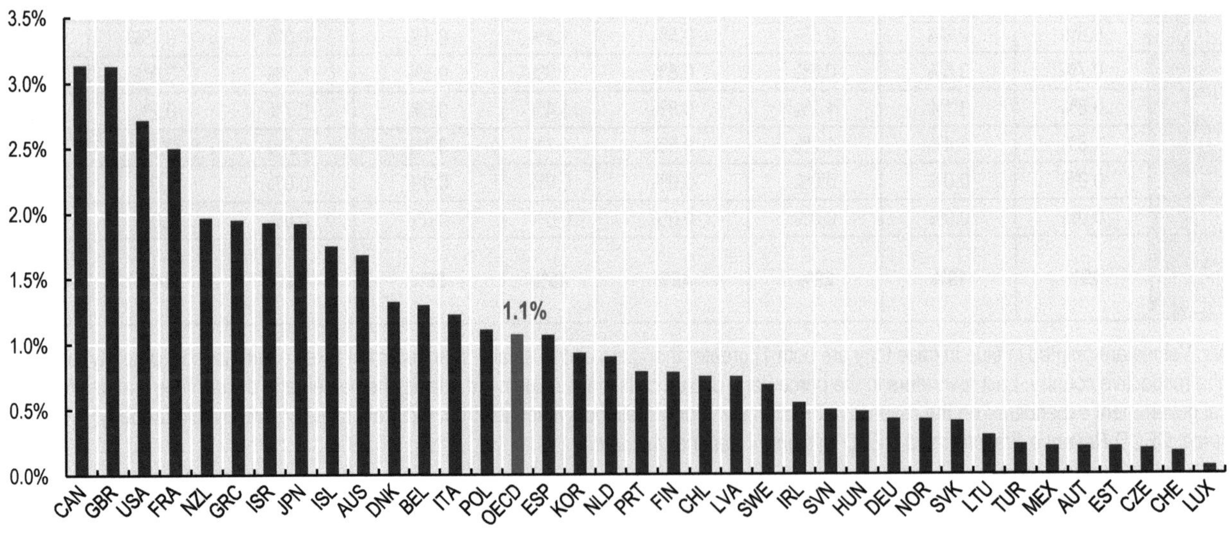

Note: Values as of 2019 or closest year with available data.
Source: OECD *Revenue Statistics*.

In comparison, local government expenditure on social protection, education, health, housing and public order/safety are, respectively, 2.2%, 2.1%, 1.4%, 0.4% and 0.2% of GDP (Figure 1.9). Thus, roughly half of the local revenues from recurrent taxes on immovable property can be used to fund, on average, the entirety of local expenditure on housing and community amenities,[3] and public order and safety. If channelled to fund social protection or education instead, they can fund about half of all local expenditures on these items individually. In the case of health, it could fund roughly 61% of all local health expenditures (see Table 1.1, above, for a country-specific analysis).

Figure 1.9 Recurrent tax on immovable property local revenues and local government expenditure on selected functions as a percentage of GDP, 2018

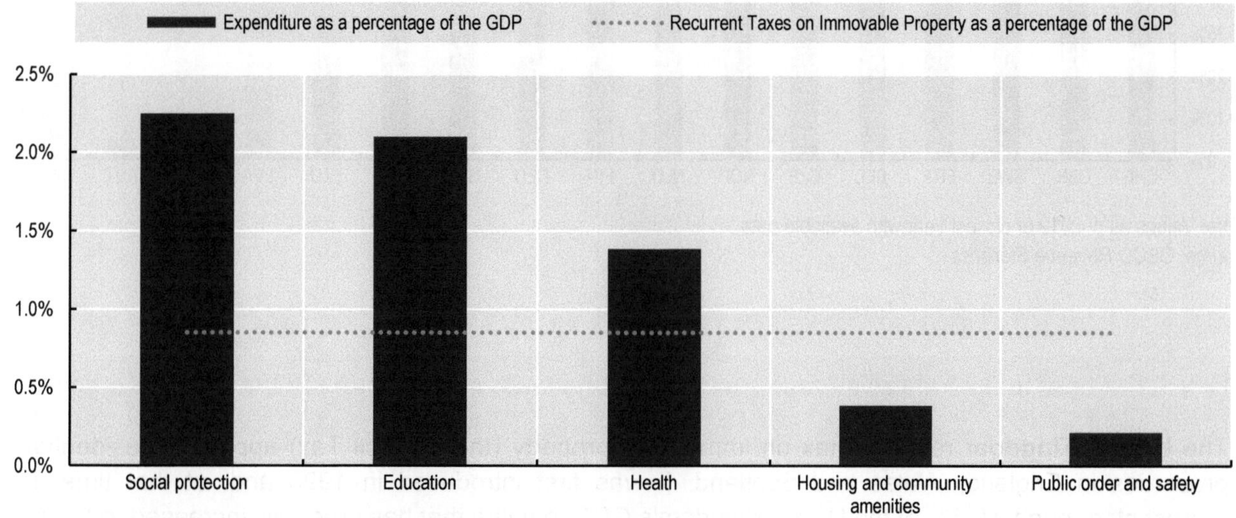

Source: OECD *Revenue Statistics* and OECD System of National Accounts.

All calculations so far considered all revenues collected through the use of recurrent taxes on immovable properties. Nevertheless, these taxes are levied on multiple types of properties. OECD *Revenue Statistics* divides the tax base into two broad tax bases: households[4] and others (mostly business/producers). Figure 1.10 reveals that, on average, 46% of recurrent taxes on immovable properties revenues stem from households whereas the remaining 54% from other types of properties. Therefore, when considering only the levies on households,[5] recurrent taxes on immovable properties generate revenues, as a percentage of GDP, from 0.1% in Mexico[6] to 1.73% in France, averaging roughly 0.38%.[7] Thus, the portion of recurrent taxes on immovable property that is levied on residences is, alone, enough to cover the average local expenditure on housing and community amenities, of 0.37% of GDP. Box 1.1 covers the role of recurrent taxes on immovable property in the United Kingdom.

Figure 1.10 Share of revenues from recurrent tax on immovable property by tax base, 2019

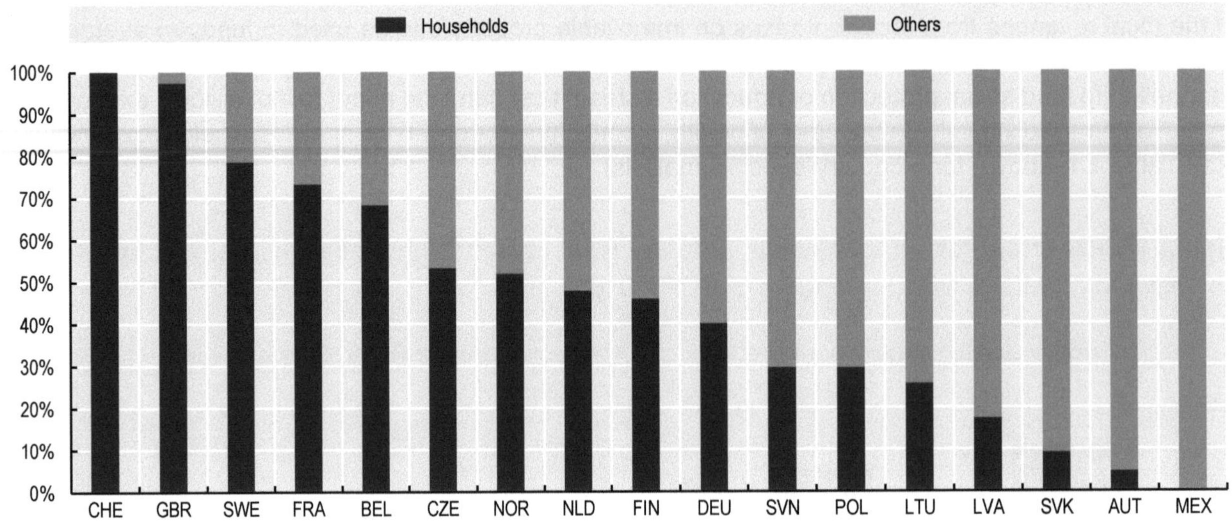

Note: Values as of 2019 or closest year with available data.
Source: OECD *Revenue Statistics*.

Box 1.1. A brief look of the role of recurrent taxes on immovable property in the United Kingdom

The **United Kingdom** recurrent tax on immovable property (the Council Tax) applies to residential properties in England, Wales and Scotland. It was first introduced in 1993 and, at that time, it represented roughly 0.8% of the United Kingdom's GDP, a value that has gradually increased to 1.6%, in 2019. The introduction of the Council Tax significantly changed the source of income of British municipalities. In 1992, the year before the reform, recurrent taxes on immovable property represented only 1.6% of local taxation, against 74% in 1993, the year of the introduction of the new taxes, and from 1994 onwards it has accounted for virtually 100% of total local taxation. It replaced the Community Charge, which was a poll tax in the form of a single flat rate set by local governments on every adult. The Council Taxes, through the use of bands for property values and certain exemptions and discounts, are more progressive than the Poll Tax, and their features haven't changed much since inception.

The business property taxes, in contrast to the levy on households, are managed by the central government, who took over rate-setting in 1990. Since 2009, though, local authorities have been permitted to levy a supplementary local rate (known as a business rate supplement) below an upper limit of 2% of rateable value. Taxes are paid into a central pool and distributed to local governments through inter-governmental transfers largely on a per capita basis. In contrast to the levies on households, the taxes levied on business properties saw their value decrease from 1.7% to 1.4% of GDP and from 5.7% to 4.4% of total taxation from 1993 to 2019.

Together both levies account for approximately 3.1% of the United Kingdom's GDP, about one-third of total local revenues, and represents 9.5% of all taxation in the country, as of 2019. Naturally, their revenues are used to fund important public services at the local level. The levy on households alone is enough to (but not earmarked to) fund roughly all local expenditure on public order and safety (0.8% of GDP), housing and community amenities (0.5% of GDP) and recreation (0.2% of GDP) – all activities that impact the life of local dwellers, potentially being capitalised into house prices. The business property taxes, that are collected by the central government but distributed back to local governments, generate enough revenue to cover all local costs with environment protection (0.4% of GDP) and economic affairs (0.9% of GDP), which refers to general economic and commercial policies, such as those related to the regulation and support of sectors such as agriculture, manufacturing, construction, energy, transport (i.e. construction and maintenance of road transport systems and facilities for all means), communication (i.e. maintenance of communication systems such as postal, telephone, telegraph, wireless and satellite communication systems) and tourism. It is worth highlighting that both sources of revenues are not earmarked to these types of expenditures.

Sources: OECD *Revenue Statistics* and COFOG data; Slack and Bird (2014[8]).

Property taxes and the stage of development

Reliance on recurrent taxes on immovable property is, to some extent, correlated with income levels. Figure 1.11 reveals that, despite the substantial cross-country variation, especially for more advanced OECD countries, there is an overall tendency to rely more on immovable property taxation than in developing ones. Advanced economies that rely the least on immovable property taxation tend to be small or to have a small population such as Luxembourg, Switzerland, Ireland and Norway. Notably more advanced large countries tend to rely the most on these taxes, such as the United States, Canada, France and Japan.

Figure 1.11 GDP per capita against immovable property taxation as a percentage of GDP (as of 2019)

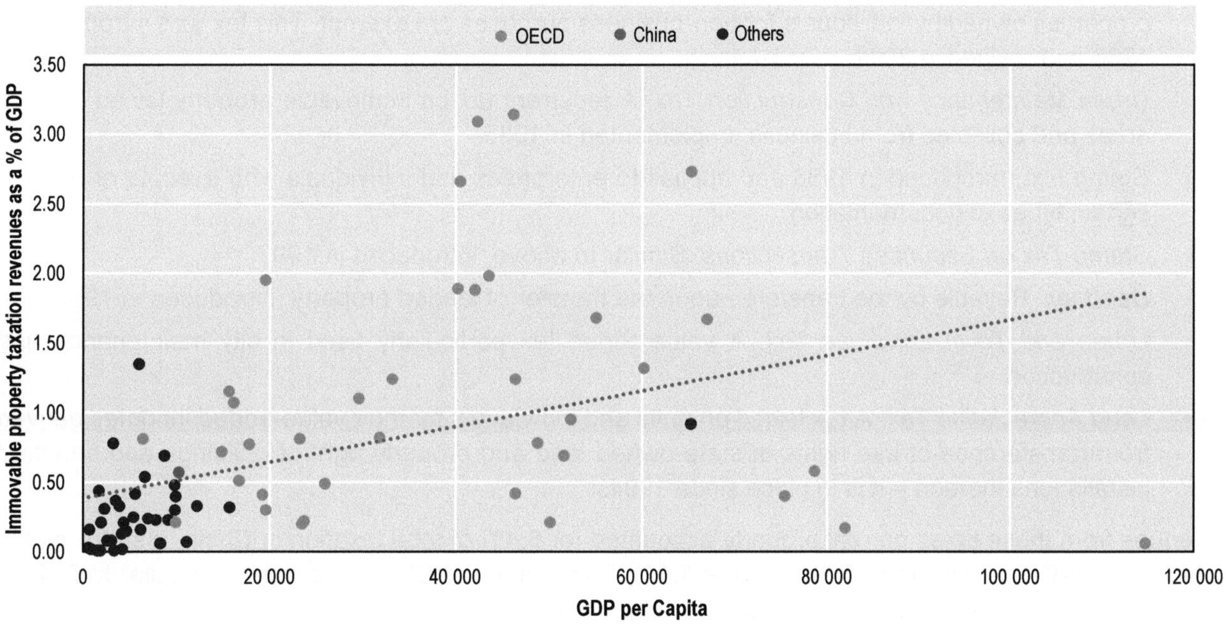

Note: Countries covered: ARG, AUS, AUT, BEL, BGR, BRA, CAN, CHE, CHL, CHN, CIV, CMR, COL, CRI, CZE, DEU, DNK, DOM, ECU, EGY, ESP, EST, FIN, FRA, GBR, GRC, GTM, GUY, HND, HUN, IDN, IRL, ISL, ISR, ITA, JAM, JPN, KAZ, KEN, KOR, LTU, LUX, LVA, MAR, MEX, MLI, MNG, MRT, MUS, NER, NIC, NLD, NOR, NZL, PAN, PER, PHL, POL, PRT, PRY, RWA, SGP, SLV, SVK, SVN, SWE, SWZ, TGO, THA, TUN, TUR, URY, USA, ZAF.
Source: OECD *Revenue Statistics* and World Bank Data.

Clements et al. (2015[9]) explored more rigorously what determines the level of recurrent property taxation and concluded that the country-wise effect of development, urbanisation, openness to trade and legal heritage are positive and significant. In a panel data analysis, they gathered evidence that this effect also occurs over time – that is an improvement in a country's level of development over time tends to be correlated with an increase in the reliance on recurrent taxes on immovable property. In summary, not only developed countries tend to rely more on immovable property taxation, but also as a country develops, it tends to increase its reliance on these taxes.

China's reliance on recurrent taxes on immovable property is close to the average for its income level (see the red dot in Figure 1.11). Nevertheless, this does not mean that China should not reform its property tax system. China has been developing rapidly, which entails that there is room for increasing its reliance on immovable property taxation, following the steps of other large and developed economies. In addition, there are many other reasons for shifting towards recurrent taxes on immovable property, which are treated in detail throughout this report.

The role of property taxes in China's taxation

The share of local property tax revenues in total local taxation is smaller in China than in the average OECD country

Since the late 1980s, China has introduced a myriad of taxes on properties. According to OECD Revenue Statistics, the following property taxes are levied in China[8] (for more details see Annex A):

- *House Property Tax*: Ad valorem levy on the residual value of properties and rental income. House properties owned by individuals for non-business purposes are exempt. This tax was introduced in 1986 and revised in 2011.
- *Urban Maintenance and Construction Tax*: A recurrent tax on immovable property levied on land areas and collected from business, implemented in 1985.
- *Stamp tax*: Introduced in 1988 and applies to enterprises and individuals who execute or receive certain types of documentation.
- *Stamp Tax on Securities Transactions*: Similar to above, introduced in 1992.
- *Deed tax*: Payable by the transferee upon the transfer of landed property, introduced in 1997.
- *Urban and Town Land-use Tax*: A value-added tax particularly used in city maintenance and construction.
- *Land Appreciation Tax*: A tax levied on units and individuals for their value-added incomes derived from transference of use rights of state-owned land and property right of buildings and attached installations thereon – it is in place since 1994.

Revenues from these taxes on real property accounted for 8.4% of total taxation in China, a share that is higher than OECD's average of 5.8% (Figure 1.12). This result put China in a position similar to France and Japan, both countries that rely substantially on property taxes.

Figure 1.12 Property taxes' revenues as a percentage of total taxation by country, 2018

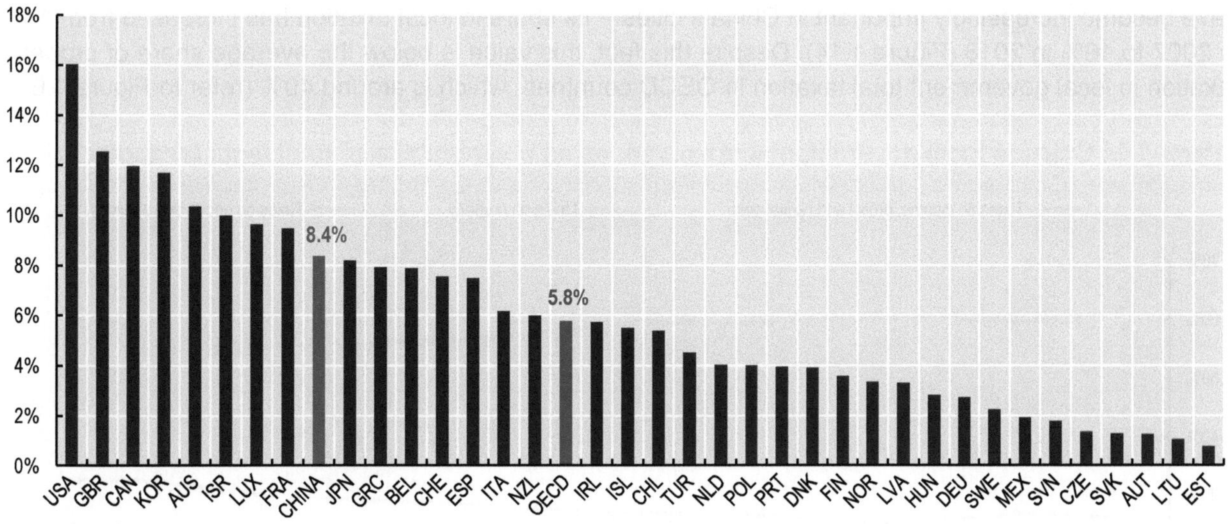

Source: OECD Revenue Statistics.

Nevertheless, it is worth noting that the composition of China's property tax revenues is markedly different than most OECD countries. According to OECD *Revenue Statistics*, in 17 OECD countries with data available on the tax base of recurrent taxes on immovable properties, 16 of them collect some portion of their revenues from households (Figure 1.10, above), while China does not.[9] Revenues collected from these levies on residences range from 0% to 2.1% of GDP in OECD countries, averaging 0.41%. China, on the other hand, collects 43% of its property tax revenues from taxes on financial and capital transactions (Figure 1.13, below), against an average of 25% in OECD countries (Figure 1.10). Transaction taxes are considered highly distortionary, and hence, damaging to economic growth. For this reason, OECD usually recommends countries to reduce these levies in detriment of a greater use of recurrent property taxes (Hagemann, 2018[10]).

Figure 1.13 China's property tax revenues breakdown by specific taxes, 2018

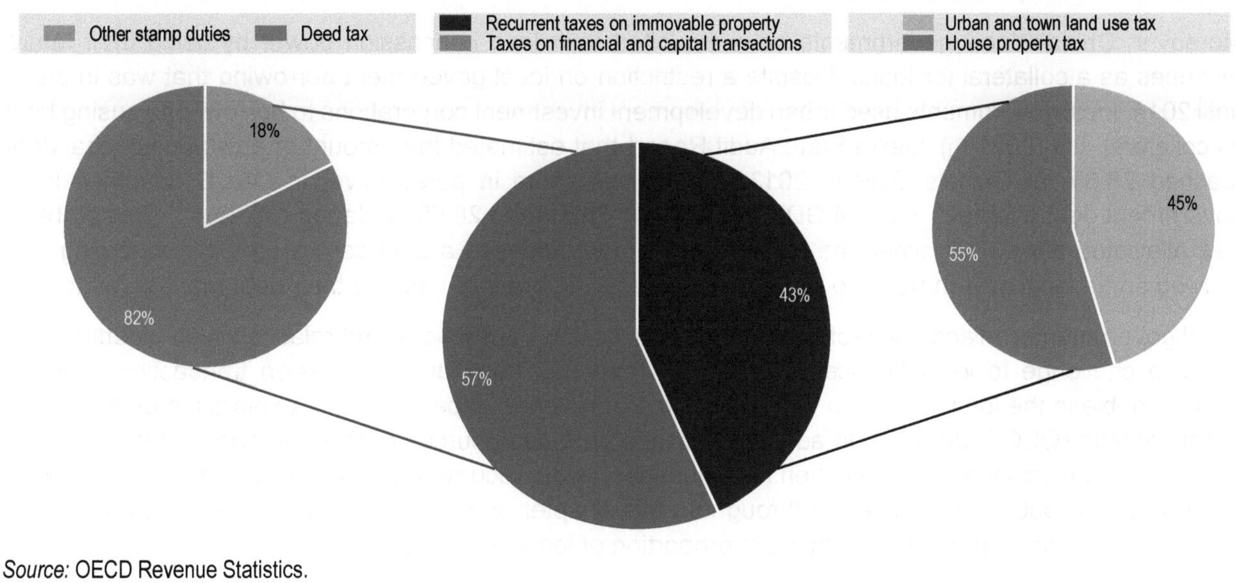

Source: OECD Revenue Statistics.

Apart from the stamp tax on securities transactions and part of the urban maintenance and construction tax, all other Chinese property taxes accrue to local governments. In conjunction, these taxes on properties have become increasingly important in China's cities – its share in local taxation has increased from 13% in 2007 to 16% in 2018 (Figure 1.14). Despite this fact, this value is below the average share of property taxation in local government total taxation in OECD countries, which is around 40% (refer to Figure 1.6).

Figure 1.14 Chinese local government's tax revenues as a percentage of total local taxation, 2018

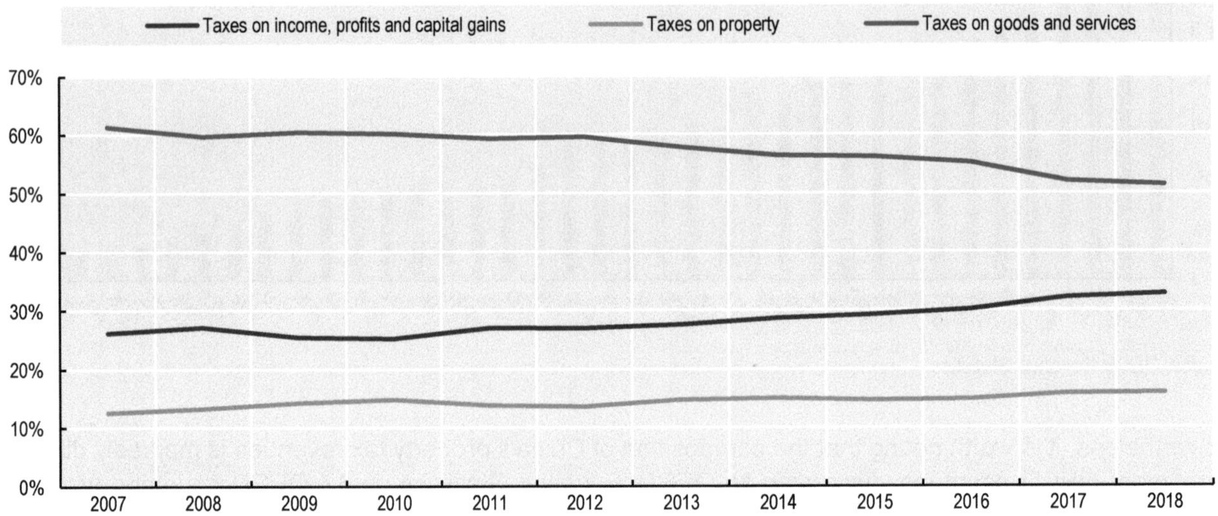

Note: Local governments tax share in general government's taxation is roughly 50%, as of 2018.
Source: OECD Revenue Statistics.

The legal framework currently in place in China gives local governments power to provide land for urban development (Liu, 2021[11]). More specifically, local governments have the power to control and regulate land use, such as by converting rural land into urban land through land expropriation. The expropriated rural land is then sold through market competition to real estate developers that usually offer a higher price for this land than the local government pays to compensate rural villages. As a result, this operation generates revenue for local governments. Liu (2021[11]) shows that land concession revenues are significant – for comparison's sake, they have ranged from 30% to 60% of the locally general budgetary revenues over the past two decades.[10]

Moreover, China's local governments have exploited their land concession power by using their future revenues as a collateral for loans. Despite a restriction on local government borrowing that was in place until 2014, local governments used urban development investment corporations to borrow, often using land as collateral. Liu (2021[11]) cites a State Audit Report that estimated the amount of outstanding local debt reached 28.6% of China's GDP in 2013. To put this value in perspective, in OECD countries local government debt averages 7.2% of GDP and is only higher than 28.6% in Japan (33.2%).[11] This problem was alleviated after 2014, when the central government imposed a debt ceiling on local borrowing and allowed some local governments to issue bonds directly, in order to improve their debt management.

Local governments' reliance on profits from land concession transactions and relatively high indebtedness poses a challenge to local finances. Relying on revenues from land concession transactions can be unsustainable in the long run, given that this source of revenue depends on the exploration of the limited supply of land (OECD, 2017[12]). In addition, reliance on these sources of revenue can incentivise urban sprawl. It is thus important to strengthen local finances, and a recurrent levy on owned residential property is an attractive option. As discussed throughout this chapter, such a levy is widely used across OECD countries and often represents a significant proportion of local revenues.

References

Brys, B. et al. (2016), "Tax Design for Inclusive Economic Growth", *OECD Taxation Working Papers*, No. 26, OECD Publishing, Paris, https://dx.doi.org/10.1787/5jlv74ggk0g7-en. [1]

CDRF (2020), *Background document on China's property taxation*, China Development Research Foundation. [15]

Clements, B. et al. (2015), "Taxing Immovable Property: Revenue Potential and Implementation Challenges", *IMF Working Paper*, Vol. WP/13/129. [9]

de Mello, L. (2000), "Fiscal Decentralization and Intergovernmental Fiscal Relations: A Cross-Country Analysis", *World Development*, Vol. 28/2, pp. 365-380, http://dx.doi.org/10.1016/s0305-750x(99)00123-0. [6]

Dougherty, S., M. Harding and A. Reschovsky (2019), "Twenty years of tax autonomy across levels of government: Measurement and applications", *OECD Working Papers on Fiscal Federalism*, No. 29, OECD Publishing, Paris, https://dx.doi.org/10.1787/ca7ebc02-en. [4]

Eurostat (2019), *Manual on sources and methods for the compilation of COFOG statistics — Classification of the Functions of Government (COFOG) — 2019 edition*, http://dx.doi.org/10.2785/110841. [13]

Forman, K., S. Dougherty and H. Blöchliger (2020), "Synthesising good practices in fiscal federalism: Key recommendations from 15 years of country surveys", *OECD Economic Policy Papers*, No. 28, OECD Publishing, Paris, https://dx.doi.org/10.1787/89cd0319-en. [2]

Hagemann, R. (2018), "Tax Policies for Inclusive Growth: Prescription versus Practice", *OECD Economic Policy Papers*, No. 24, OECD Publishing, Paris, https://dx.doi.org/10.1787/09ba747a-en. [10]

Liu, Z. (2021), "Municipal finance and property taxation in China", in *Local Public Finance and Capacity Building in Asia: Issues and Challenges*, OECD Publishing, Paris, https://dx.doi.org/10.1787/73c69466-en. [11]

Mikesell, J. (2012), "Administration of Local Taxes An International Review of Practices and Issues for Enhancing Fiscal autonomy", in *Primer on Property Tax: Administration and Policy*, John Wiley & Sons, Ltd, pp. 89-124, http://dx.doi.org/10.1002/9781118454343.ch4. [3]

Oates, W. (1972), *Fiscal Federalism*, Edward Elgar Publishing. [5]

OECD (2020), *Global Revenue Statistics Database*, OECD, Paris, https://www.oecd.org/tax/tax-policy/global-revenue-statistics-database.htm. [14]

OECD (2017), *OECD Economic Surveys: China 2017*, OECD Publishing, Paris, https://dx.doi.org/10.1787/eco_surveys-chn-2017-en. [12]

Rodden, J. (2002), *The Dilemma of Fiscal Federalism: Grants and Fiscal Performance around the World*, Midwest Political Science Association, https://doi.org/10.2307/3088407. [7]

Slack, E. and R. Bird (2014), "The Political Economy of Property Tax Reform", *OECD Working Papers on Fiscal Federalism*, No. 18, OECD Publishing, Paris, https://dx.doi.org/10.1787/5jz5pzvzv6r7-en. [8]

Notes

[1] All OECD countries with available data.

[2] Although it is in general better to have small and relevant taxes than having a myriad of taxes with limited revenue raising capacity, it is also important to keep in mind that overreliance on just one or a few types of tax can be risky. That is because any event/policy change that damages these sources of revenue would more vigorously affect a government's revenue.

[3] Housing and community amenities refer to housing development, community development, water supply and street lighting. Housing development regards the development and regulation of housing standards; slum clearance related to provision of housing; acquisition of land needed for construction of dwellings; construction or purchase and remodelling of dwelling units for the general public or for people with special needs. Community development concerns, among others, planning of new communities or of rehabilitated communities and administration of zoning laws and land-use. For more details see Eurostat (2019[13]).

[4] Taxes on dwellings occupied by households, regardless of housing tenure (owner-occupiers, tenants or landlords) are classified under households.

[5] Tax revenues under the code 4110 (recurrent taxes on immovable property applied to households) in OECD *Revenue Statistics* for 2019 (or closest year with data available).

[6] Based on comments from Mexican delegates to OECD Working Groups.

[7] Considering only countries with data available with that level of resolution (the countries in Figure 1.10).

[8] Based on OECD (2020[14]) and CDRF (2020[15]). Urban maintenance and construction tax, and securities stamp transaction tax were assumed to be property taxes, following the methodology from OECD (2020[14]).

[9] According to OECD *Revenue Statistics*, China has no revenues collected under the code 4110 (recurrent taxes on immovable property applied to households).

[10] Note these figures may be overestimated as local governments can typically only make use of about 30% of the funds collected from land transfer fees (CDRF, 2020[15]).

[11] OECD Fiscal Decentralisation database.

2 Designing recurrent taxes on immovable property

The main motivations for introducing recurrent taxes on immovable property are to increase tax system efficiency, boost subnational revenue autonomy, make the real estate market more stable and improve quality of land use. Yet recurrent taxes on immovable property may distort investment allocation decisions and can have positive or negative distributive effects. In order to achieve these multiple advantages while minimising the potential downsides, different tax designs are employed across various OECD countries. Tax rates may vary horizontally (i.e. with property use, property characteristics and/or owner characteristics), vertically (i.e. with property value) and regionally (i.e. across jurisdictions). Most countries provide targeted tax benefits, most of which are aimed at low income homeowners and businesses, with substantial differences in the form of the benefits and on their eligibility. This chapter explores such differences in tax design across OECD countries.

Key messages

1. The wider the tax base of recurrent taxes on immovable property, the more a country can increase tax revenues while minimising allocative distortions.
2. The introduction of recurrent taxes on immovable property can be made in conjunction with the reduction of the levies on property transactions. Such a reform might leave the immovable property prices relatively unaffected and the tax system more growth-friendly and easier to administer.
3. Letting tax rates vary within pre-established bands might improve horizontal equality, mitigating tax avoidance and competition, while providing to local governments sufficient autonomy to tune their fiscal policy to local needs, property type distribution and tax revenue capacity.
4. The use of tax reliefs and exemptions are widely employed in OECD countries. Countries differ significantly with regard to exemptions granted, which reflects the wide range of policy objectives that can be achieved through the use of this instrument. However, these policy objectives can often be achieved more efficiently through other means.
5. Tax reliefs and exemptions are commonly employed to support business. Nevertheless, evidence shows that they have only a limited effect.
6. In countries in which prices of immovable properties vary widely across jurisdictions, progressivity can be improved by giving a tax-free basic allowance that could vary across provinces and cities. An even better effect on the distribution of income can be achieved in a less complex way by providing a tax relief to low-income households or using other tools, such as personal income taxes or even policies unrelated to the tax system such as income transfer programmes.
7. Recurrent taxes on immovable property can be used to reduce house price volatility and to make housing more affordable to low-income households. These desired effects depend on the incidence of the tax, which is defined by the supply and demand elasticities of housing and on the frequency of reassessments – the more reassessments the greater the effect.
8. Granting limited autonomy to local governments over their tax policies and inter-governmental co-ordination in land-use policies can alleviate urban sprawl, leading to a more sustainable and efficient land use in the long run.

Importance of design features

The design features of a tax system determine to a great extent its distributional and allocative impacts

Although taxes are often used to pursue policy objectives, arguably their most important role is to raise revenues to fund government expenditures. Unfortunately, rarely, if ever, can a tax raise revenues without creating economic distortions. Taxes affect relative prices and, as a result, may change behaviour in a way that is harmful to economic activity. Furthermore, taxes levied on households with limited income (i.e. ability to pay) may create economic hardships. Therefore, taxes should be designed so that they can raise sufficient revenues while minimising economic distortions and allocating their burden in a fair and equitable manner.

Each type of tax (e.g. income, product, property, etc.) has its own economic properties. Furthermore, tax design (e.g. definition of tax rates, bases, among other elements) can have large effects on its capacity to raise revenues, on resource allocation and on the income distribution. Moreover, the effects of different taxes are interdependent. Therefore, since tax reforms should ideally consider the impact of the reformed tax in conjunction with other taxes frequently multiple taxes are reformed together.

During the past decades, tax reforms across OECD countries have focused on narrowing the growing income gap[1] while minimising the adverse effects on growth. Consensus has steadily grown on the following ranking of taxes, from least to most harmful to economic growth: recurrent taxes on immovable property, consumption taxes, personal income taxes and corporate income taxes (Hagemann, 2018[1]). However, even for the growth-friendly recurrent taxes on immovable property, their impacts on growth depend on their design features and administrative efficiency. Moreover, recurrent taxes on immovable property are often considered to be more regressive than other important taxes such as income taxes. Nevertheless, while it is indeed true that income taxes tend to be more progressive than recurrent taxes on immovable property, the latter can be designed and administered in a manner that they do not increase income inequality.

This chapter focuses on the design features of recurrent taxes on immovable property so that a government can: 1) raise an adequate level of tax revenues; 2) improve the income distribution; and 3) minimise adverse impacts on resource allocation. First, the chapter delineates general principles of taxation, highlighting specific principles for recurrent taxation on immovable property. Second and third sections discuss tax scope, rates and reliefs. Lastly, the fourth, fifth and sixth section examine potential impacts of a property tax reform on the overall tax system, housing investments, house prices and land use.

General principles of tax design

Ideally taxes should be able to provide a stable and significant source of revenue while minimising allocative distortions in a fair, equitable and transparent manner; nevertheless, seldom can an individual tax achieve all these goals simultaneously

Taxation is often used as a means to support the achievement of fiscal policies' goals, which can be summarised by three functions of government (Musgrave, 1959[2]) – allocative (i.e. efficient use of resources, provision of goods and services), redistribution (i.e. reduction of inequalities) and stabilisation (i.e. full employment and price stability). These functions of government, along with other principles/criteria, are often used by economists to design/evaluate tax systems, such as capacity to generate revenues and transparency. The list below summarises some of these principles – based on Slack (2012[3]):

1. *Capacity to generate revenues*: Net (of administrative and compliance costs) tax revenues should be sufficient to fund government spending.
2. *Allocation of resources*: This refers to the effects of taxes on the behaviour of individuals and/or businesses. Some taxes are designed to change behaviour (e.g. sin taxes are designed to reduce, for instance, tobacco consumption), but, in most cases, behavioural changes may influence resource allocation in an undesirable manner. For recurrent taxes on immovable property, shifts in behaviour may involve decisions about where to open/locate a business, where to live and about how much to invest in land and buildings, including deciding whether buying or renting a house.
3. *Equity*: Taxes are commonly analysed through the lenses of the benefit principle and of taxpayers' ability to pay. The benefit principle refers to the idea that public services should preferably be funded by those who benefit from their supply. Although the application of the principle is straight-forward, beneficiaries of public services are not always easily identifiable (e.g. for streetlight, public infrastructure, national security, among others), and in these cases, the tax burden should ideally be borne proportionally to taxpayers' ability to pay. For recurrent taxes on immovable property, the ability to pay is often estimated through taxpayers' property value, income and, sometimes, personal characteristics such as age, phase of life, number of dependents, among others. Both

vertical equity (i.e. the higher the income the higher the tax burden) and horizontal equity (i.e. taxpayers with similar conditions should have similar tax burden) are desirable.

4. *Stability*: Taxes should provide a stable source of revenue to fund the relatively stable government expenditures. This principle is linked to the concept of buoyancy, which is related to the relation between tax revenues and economic activity. In general, a small buoyancy means that the source of revenue tends to be more stable under economic fluctuations, which is desirable for its predictability. Nevertheless, in the long-term a source of revenue that is not directly linked to economic activity might create imbalances between government revenues and the necessary funds to supply public service. In the case of recurrent taxes on immovable property, the tax base tends to be relatively less buoyant than for other taxes.
5. *Transparency*: Tax obligations should be transparent. That is, taxpayers should be able to understand how charges were calculated and for what purposes these funds are being used.

It is often the case that a tax reform cannot follow all these principles simultaneously. Some decisions regarding tax design might involve a gain in one of the principles, such as equity, at the cost of damaging another principle, such as allocative efficiency. As a result, although it is possible to lay out a set of good practices based on these principles, in some cases there is no best option that satisfies everyone – trade-offs exist. Hence, tax design is a political choice that depends on country-specific factors and conditions such as culture, the tax system in place, the state of the economy, the income distribution, among others.

Scope of taxes

Wide tax bases tend to increase revenue-raising capacity while minimising allocative distortions

The scope of property taxes refers to the types of property that are taxed. It is a crucial element of any tax system that has implications on all the principles mentioned in the previous section. By and large, for multiple reasons economists recommend policy makers to set tax bases as wide as possible and tax rates as low as possible (Cornia, 2012[4]). First, a wider tax base has a larger revenue generation capacity as more properties are taxed. Second, a narrow tax base can encourage tax avoidance, since potential taxpayers may shift their type of property to avoid taxes. Third, since many public services benefit all the population, in case all citizens contribute financially for their provision, the tax system can become fairer and more equitable, following the benefit principle. Fourth, a wide tax base is more diversified than a narrow one, entailing that the former is less vulnerable to sector-specific shocks. Fifth, the revenue-raising capacity of a wide tax base allows tax rates to be lower, which reduces the income effect on taxpayers (i.e. the change in demand for a good or service caused by a change in a consumer's purchasing power resulting from a change in income) and, as a result, minimises possible changes of behaviour, reducing popular resistance and increasing compliance.

Therefore, a narrow tax base may facilitate free-rider behaviour (i.e. enjoying the benefits of services provided with tax revenues without bearing its costs) and requires a higher tax rate to collect the same amount of revenue, which can affect the decisions of the group that is being taxed, creating stronger resistance to the tax reform, as well as room for tax avoidance and delinquency. In the case of the property tax, a wide tax base means that all types and forms of land use (e.g. improved and unimproved land for multiple uses such as residential, businesses, agricultural, industrial, land dedicated to special infrastructure purposes, etc.) are taxed and that exemptions are kept to a minimum.

Covering the tax scope in the legislation in a precise manner can help maintain the salient recurrent taxes on immovable property applied to a wide tax base (Plimmer, 2012[5]). Tax bases that are covered in a legislation that cannot be easily changed may resist better recurring political pressures to benefit select groups of taxpayers. In addition, the clearer the definition of the tax scope, the less room there is for changes as a result of judicial interpretation or administrative regulation.

Most OECD countries have a single integrated property tax that applies to different types of property, but there are also cases in which different levies are applied to different types of property

The scope of the recurrent property tax can be assessed along two lines: 1) the purpose of use (i.e. residential and business property; rented or owner-occupied); and 2) the taxed items (i.e. land and improvements). All OECD and partner countries analysed[2] (Figure 2.1, left plot) levy taxes on both types of properties (residential and business), and in all countries but Lithuania both owner-occupied and rented houses are taxed[3] (in Lithuania only owner-occupied properties are taxed). Most countries have a single integrated property tax that applies to these two types of property – notable exceptions are Australia, Belgium, Ireland and the United Kingdom. Australia has two types of recurrent taxes on immovable property – the Council rate, which applies to owner-occupied and rented residential properties and business properties, and a land tax, which applies only to residential rented and business properties. Similarly, Ireland has two levies – the Local Property Tax (LPT), which applies to owner-occupied and rented residential or business properties, and the Non Principal Private Residence (NPPR), which only applies to residential rented and business properties. Belgium also has two separate types of recurrent taxes on immovable property, being the "Ménages" tax applied to residential property (owner-occupied and rented) and the "Societés" applied only to business. The United Kingdom also levies a separate levy to residential properties (owned-occupied and rented) and a different one to business.

Figure 2.1 Scope of immovable property taxes across OECD countries

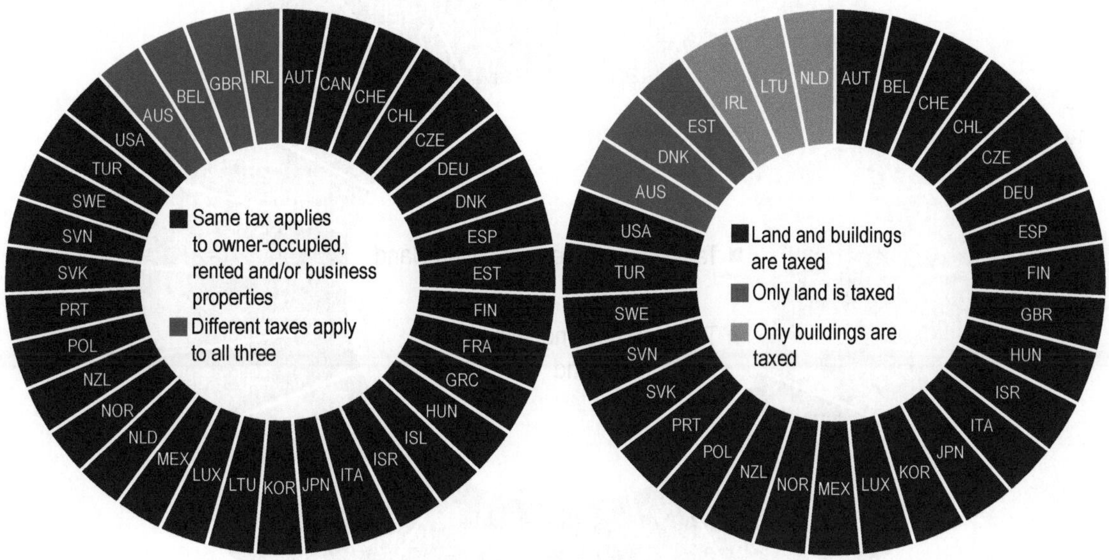

Source: Responses from OECD Survey on Recurrent Taxes on Immovable Property.

Regarding the taxed items (land and improvements), in most countries (26 out of 31) both land and buildings are taxed (Figure 2.1, right plot). Only three OECD countries feature a pure land tax, which can help to promote densification (a discussion on the benefits of taxation on land can be found on Box 2.6). These are found in the state of New South Wales in Australia, Denmark and Estonia. On the other hand, property taxes in Ireland, Lithuania and Netherlands comprise improvements only.

Concerning improvements, each country considers a different set of taxable items. For instance, in the United Kingdom certain items of plant and machinery can also be included in the assessment. In Australia assessments include basic site improvements such as sewerage, but not the value of buildings or other capital improvements. In the Irish LTP, the assessment considers shed, outhouse, garage, yard and other building structures.

Some OECD countries do not tax agricultural lands in order to protect them from urbanisation

Agricultural land is one type of property that is excluded from the tax base in some countries (Figure 2.2). Precisely, 8 out of 29 countries do not include agricultural land in their tax base. Farmlands are usually favoured in order to protect them from conversion to urban use. Such protection can also be granted in other forms. As Maurer and Paugam (2000[6]) pointed out, another way to protect farmland is through favouring them in property value assessments – that is, rather than assessing agricultural land at their market value, their values can be assessed considering their value in current use. In that manner, it is likely that agricultural land will have a smaller cadastral value in comparison to other types of land, which reduces their tax obligations in comparison to urban land. Countries such as Canada (in some jurisdictions) and New Zealand employ this strategy (Maurer and Paugam, 2000[6]).

Figure 2.2 Agricultural land treatment in OECD countries for recurrent property taxes

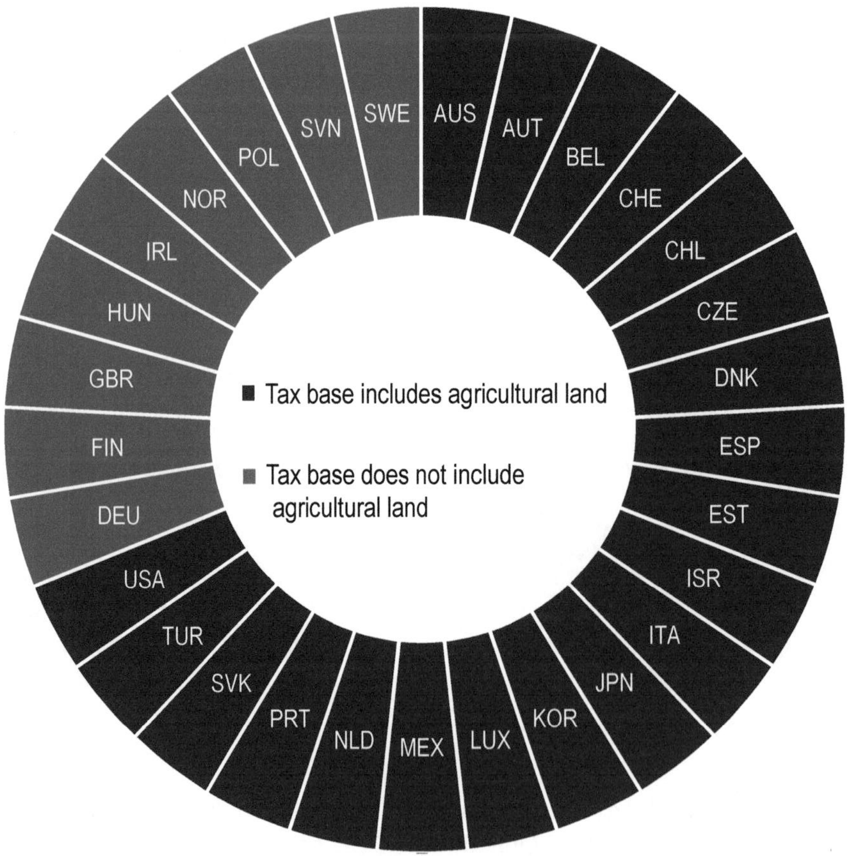

Source: Responses from OECD Survey on Recurrent Taxes on Immovable Property.

It is worth noting that a favourable property tax treatment is often not sufficient to protect farmland from urbanisation due to the fact that effective tax rates that are applied to land are typically small. More precisely, differences in tax obligations between urban and agricultural land are commonly not large enough to compensate for the much higher prices that the land could have in case it was converted to urban land (Maurer and Paugam, 2000[6]). Furthermore, favourable treatment of rural land can increase speculation at the urban fringe, potentially leading to an increase in urban land prices (Slack, 2012[3]). As a result, granting favourable tax treatment to agricultural land might not be the most efficient way to protect farmland – land-use planning and transport policies tend to have a greater influence on land-use decisions (Brandt, 2014[7]).

Property tax bases in China

China levies urban land-use taxes that are not applied to residential households.[4] These taxes are levied on land areas. Properties exempt include, among others, land for directly productive use of agriculture, forestry, animal husbandry, fishery industries, municipal roads, squares, greenbelts and energy, transportation and water conservancy facilities. The most unusual type of property that China exempts is personal residence. In addition, China also levies a tax on the residual value of properties or rental income (house property tax). Again, house properties owned by individuals for non-business purposes are exempt.

As a result, the Chinese system has two recurrent levies on properties with some degree of overlap with regard to taxed items and a significant amount of exemptions in terms of number of properties – the urban home ownership rate in China reaches 96%. A levy on personal residence buildings can, thus, widen substantially its property taxes' tax base and reduce, proportionally, tax rates in a manner that the tax burden on other types of property are reduced. This can potentially make the Chinese system more growth-friendly through a reduction in allocative distortions.

Tax rate and reliefs

Tax rates may vary horizontally (i.e. with property use, property characteristics and/or owner characteristics) and vertically (i.e. with property value)

Tax rate setting is directly linked to the definition of tax bases. Since tax revenues are the result of the interaction between tax rates and tax bases, the decision regarding the level of tax rate necessary to raise a certain amount of tax revenue greatly depends on the tax bases that the rates are applied to. In the case of recurrent taxes on immovable property, tax rates may vary horizontally (i.e. with property use, property characteristics and/or owner characteristics), vertically (i.e. with property value) or even regionally/locally.

Despite these numerous possibilities of setups, a case for uniformity of tax rates across different types of property can be made. First, uniformity increases transparency, reduces complexity of the tax system and minimises distortions on land-use decisions. A second consideration regards tax avoidance – when tax rates differ widely across tax bases, taxpayers may avoid taxation by concealing the true nature of their property. On the other hand, non-uniform tax rates can be used to foster some types of development or decisions; for instance, it is common to encourage homeownership with tax exemptions and reduced rates on owner-occupied houses, as homeownership can reduce wealth inequality (Kaas, Kocharkov and Preugschat, 2015[8]).

In OECD countries tax rates are usually allowed to vary by jurisdiction with property characteristics within pre-established bands

Figure 2.3 depicts property tax rate structures across OECD and partner countries. It shows four classifications: 1) Multiple structures, which regards the situation in which within the same country there are different structures depending on the jurisdiction and, thus, one single classification does not represent the structure of the country; 2) Based on type of property or owner; 3) Compound, which is the case in which different levels of government levy their own recurrent property taxes that are compounded into the final levy; and 4) Uniform, which concerns the structure in which tax rates do not vary with the property use, characteristics, owner or jurisdiction.

No OECD or partner country has a uniform tax structure[5] and only the Netherlands reported to have a compound structure, which means that the majority of OECD and partner countries have either a multiple structure or a structure in which the tax rate varies with the type of the property or owner. In the latter case, limiting the range from which tax rates vary can reduce tax competition across jurisdiction (for business property taxation) and reduce the incentives for tax avoidance. For this reason, it is common practice across OECD and partner countries to limit the range within which tax rates can vary both across jurisdictions and with regard to property type and owner.

Figure 2.3 Property tax rate structures in OECD and partner countries

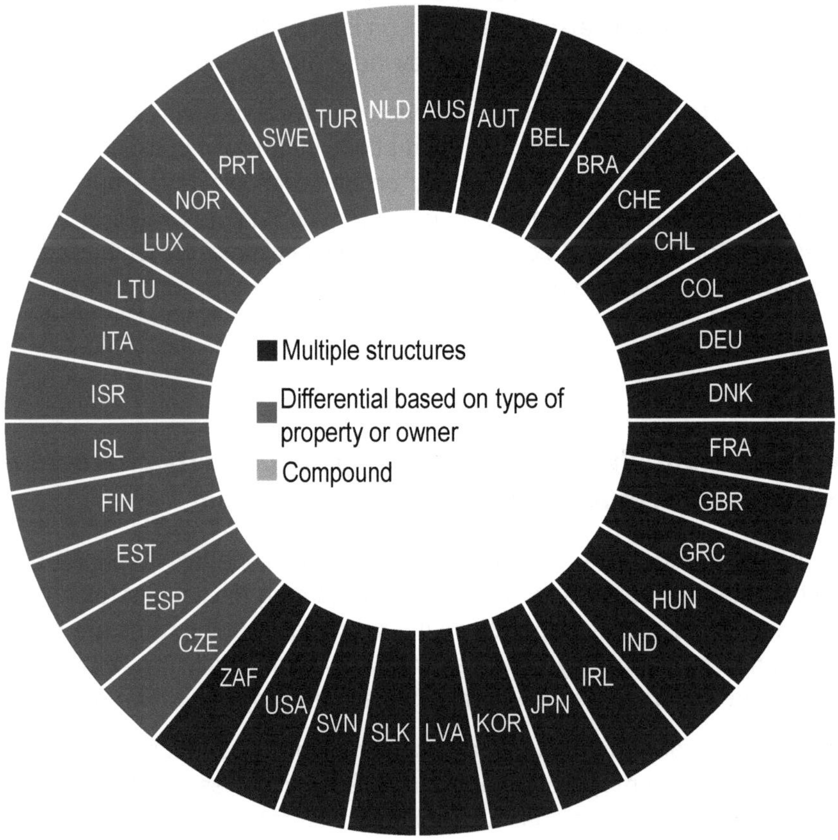

Source: Adapted from Almy (2013[9]).

For instance, in Chile, tax rates vary with property use – tax rate is 1.0% for agricultural properties, vary between 0.98% to 1.143% for non-agricultural residential properties and is 1.2% for non-agricultural and non-residential properties. In Finland business and residential properties are taxed differently – general property taxes (land and commercial buildings) are allowed to vary from 0.93% to 2.00% while residential building taxes are allowed to range from 0.41% to 1.00% (separate tax rates can be used for leisure homes, undeveloped residential land and power plants). In Turkey, tax rates vary with the characteristics of the location of the property – tax rates vary from 0.1% to 0.3% and are doubled for properties within the borders of metropolitan municipalities and contiguous areas. In Spain, not only are different rates applied to urban properties (from 0.4% to 1.10%) and rural properties (from 0.3% to 0.9%) but these rates can also increase up to 1.3% depending on certain circumstances (for instance, when a municipality provides certain services, or when it is the capital of a province or region). Furthermore, Spain's local governments may establish a surcharge of up to 0.5% to the vacant urban properties or different rates depending on the use of the property. Annex B has a summary of the tax rates applied across OECD countries.

Tax rates can be made progressive, nevertheless effects on income distribution from recurrent taxes on immovable property depend greatly on home ownership patterns

In some countries tax rates grow with asset values, which are correlated with taxpayers' ability to pay.[6] Nevertheless, there is a significant distinction that needs to be made between property values and income. Property values are, indeed, correlated with the owner's/tenant's income but this correlation is not perfect. Thus, it is possible for tax rates that are progressive in terms of property values to be, in some cases, actually regressive in terms of income. More notably, although imposing progressive tax rates tend to increase the equity of the property tax system due to the correlation between income and assessed values, it may aggravate the liquidity problem of asset rich income poor households.

The effect of recurrent taxes on immovable property on the distribution of income depends greatly on home ownership patterns in a country. For instance, in Ireland, a shift in the tax mix towards residential property taxes[7] may have had an adverse effect on the income distribution because of Ireland's high rates of home ownership throughout the income distribution (O'Connor et al., 2015[10]). By contrast, in a country where home ownership is highly concentrated at the top of the income distribution, an increase in recurrent taxes on immovable property will have less negative distributional effects on low and middle-income households. Nevertheless, in practice middle-income families tend to hold a high proportion of their wealth in immovable property (i.e. the family home) whereas top earners may hold a significant proportion of their wealth in more liquid forms that are not subject to property taxes (Brys et al., 2016[11]).

Another problem with the introduction of progressive tax rates for property tax is that introducing tax progressivity for a specific type of asset (i.e. property in this case), as opposed to overall wealth, can be distortion-prone, and thus, sub-optimal. Properties are just one type of asset and in case progressive rates are only applied to property taxes, then the resulting progressivity of the overall tax system will depend greatly on the differences of the composition of taxpayers' asset portfolio across income brackets. This can be worrisome, since property ownership is usually more evenly distributed than ownership of other types of assets, and thus, the introduction of progressive rates might not have the desired effect. In addition, in case only one type of asset is taxed at progressive rates, investors might decide to change their investments depending on the value of the asset to be invested in, leading to distortions (see section on "Housing investments" for a detailed analysis and solutions for these distortions).

Despite these considerations it should be noted that the pro-growth nature of recurrent tax reforms can alleviate potential regressive distributional effects. For instance, Vermeulen (2018[12]) analysed the potential impact of a shift towards recurrent taxes on immovable property on the distribution of disposable income in the Netherlands. The analysis concluded that this shift would yield a moderately positive impact on employment that minimised adverse distributional effects. In other words, after taking into account an increase in employment generated by the pro-growth features of these taxes, the impact on the distribution of disposable income would be minimal – it would only exceed 4% of the disposable income in less than 5% of the households in the lower-income group.

Some OECD and partner countries increase the progressivity of their recurrent taxes on immovable property by increasing tax rates with property values and by imposing a lump-sum exemption

Thirteen OECD countries reported to have a progressive feature in their tax rate structure (Figure 2.4). No country reported to increase tax obligations with owner's/tenant's income, eight countries reported to raise tax rates only with property values, only Estonia applies a fixed lump-sum exemption alone and four countries employ both methods. The tax rate structure differs widely across these countries. For instance, Mexico City (the largest and most representative city in Mexico) applies a myriad of tax rates that ranges from 0.017% to 0.23% (approximate numbers) of the cadastral values. Ireland only applies a higher rate for properties valued over EUR 1 million. For Australia's land tax, a marginal rate of 1.6% applies above a tax-free threshold of AUD 412 000, and 2% on landholdings that exceed AUD 2 519 000. In Sweden, the tax rates rise with the value of the property, however, there are relatively low limits for how much property owners have to pay. In the United Kingdom, only businesses are subjected to progressive property tax rates. In these cases, there are only two possible rates, and the applicable rate is selected based on the size of the property.

Figure 2.4 Property tax rate structures with progressive features

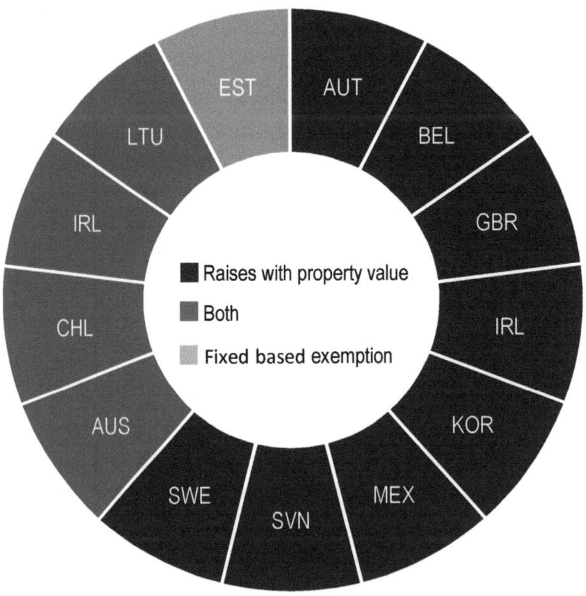

Source: Responses from OECD Survey on Recurrent Taxes on Immovable Property.

Effective tax rates can differ across country depending on valuation rules, tax bases and taxable values

A comparison of statutory values of tax rates across countries may be misleading for at least three reasons. First, many governments set the taxable value of a property below assessed (or cadastral) property values (see Box 2.1 for more details). Second, valuation methods may change the relation between the property value as recorded and the real market value of properties. Therefore, countries differ with regard to the percentage of market value that is being captured through the valuation process. Third, the taxable items differ across countries – land, buildings or land and buildings can be taxed, which may drastically change the tax burden. In order to have a better idea of the actual tax burden, a different indicator can be used, such as the percentage of tax revenue as a percentage of GDP or the ratio between the tax revenues and the number of properties.

Nevertheless, the tax rate structure, here referring to the relative changes in tax rate within a country, can be compared across countries to grasp the relative tax burdens of properties – that is, the differences of tax burden for different types of property and property values. The idea is to analyse which country over or under tax which types of properties or property owners. Still, caution is advised since valuation methods may vary depending on property types within the same country, which can distort even relative comparisons. For instance, it is common for countries to use a market-based valuation method for residential properties and a cost approach[8] for properties for which there is no active market, such as industrial properties, transport infrastructures (e.g. train stations) and large buildings (e.g. football stadiums). In these cases, the valuation method may create relative distortions, hindering a fair comparison of tax rates across property types.

Box 2.1. Taxable property value as a fraction of assessed values across OECD countries

In some countries it is practice to set all taxable property value below assessed property values (i.e. taxable values are a fraction of assessed values). In other countries the taxable values of certain types of property (e.g. owner-occupied property) are set below assessed values. In the OECD Survey on Recurrent Taxes on Immovable Property, eight countries reported to follow these practices.

Some countries use this instrument with the purpose of alleviating tax hikes that may occur due to property revaluations (e.g. Denmark, Spain, Sweden), others as a way to reduce the tax burden over some portion of properties (e.g. Chile, Italy, Japan, the United Kingdom).

In **Chile**, for urban properties (residential and non-residential), both land and buildings are taxed. Land is valued using 60% of the market value, while buildings are valued through the cost approach. In Chile's case the combination of these two methods leads to, on average, a taxation of only 63%/79% of the market value of residential/non-residential properties. The difference between these averages is a result of non-residential properties having more building value than residential properties, as assessed by the cost method.

In **Denmark**, the government has imposed a limit on how much the taxable land value is allowed to increase each year. The taxable land value is the minimum of the assessed land value or the taxable land value of the previous year increased by a factor capped at 7%.

In **Finland**, the target rates are 75% for buildings and for lands. In practice, the land values often lag behind due to limits to increases in values.

In **Italy**, the 50% of exemption is applied for partially destroyed or unfit for use properties.

In **Japan**, the assessed value of some types of residential land is multiplied by a special measure rate (one third for small residential land, and two-thirds for other residential land).

In **Spain**, cadastral values (assessed value) coincide with the taxable property value. However, when the real estate is subject to reassessment, a decreasing reduction coefficient is applied over a period of 9 years (0.9 in the first-year linear decreasing to 0.1 in the ninth). This reduction aims to soften the increase in the tax burden resulting from value reassessments.

In **Sweden**, two years prior to the taxation assessment, only 75% of the market value of the property is taxed.

In the **United Kingdom**, there is one very small exception where the taxable value for stud farms is discounted by a flat amount.

Sources: Responses from OECD Survey on Recurrent Taxes on Immovable Property.

Tax benefits are an important tool to improve the progressivity of the property tax system, reduce the liquidity problem of asset-rich income-poor households, promote non-profit activities and incentivise building construction/renewal

Tax obligations are also often reduced by tax benefits granted under certain criteria that the property or the property owner fulfils. Some benefits are temporary or phased in to alleviate transitional issues. Others are permanent and aim at achieving various policy goals. When permanent, these benefits are often targeted at taxpayers who do not have sufficient ability or liquidity to pay or to encourage economic, environmental or social activities that the government wants to promote.

Tax benefits, thus, can make recurrent taxes on immovable property more progressive and help the achievement of policy goals. Nevertheless, these benefits come at the cost of either a loss of tax revenues or a compensation for this loss of revenues that must be paid by other taxpayers in the form of higher tax obligations. In addition, there are also costs in the form of distortions of land-use decisions. Due to these costs, tax benefits may be politically and/or socially contentious and must, in order to be considered fair in the eyes of the taxpayers, reflect the cultural and societal views of the respective society (Plimmer, 2012[5]).

Issues with tax reliefs and exemptions arise when they are provided to specific individuals or companies that have the ability to pay the tax in full. When such concessions are done mainly for political reasons, the tax system can become inefficient and unfair. Since it is important for the compliance of taxpayers that the tax system is considered both efficient and fair, the arbitrary provision of tax benefits to certain groups might create popular resistance against tax reforms, undermining potential improvements in the tax system (see Box 2.2 for more on tax incentive for business). This is easier said than done, especially in the case when local governments can give tax reliefs and exemptions as they tend to be more vulnerable to local political pressures.

Before exploring the main practices adopted across OECD countries, it is worth highlighting the main types of tax reliefs as well as their properties. The following discussion is based on Langley and Youngman (2021[13]). Tax reliefs differ markedly with regard to, at least, four aspects: 1) how they reduce the tax liability (i.e. exemptions/deductions reduce the taxable value of a property whereas abatements/credits reduce the tax obligation); 2) which taxpayers they apply to; 3) the level of government that is paying the costs of the relief programme; and 4) the timing of the payment. There is no best tax relief programme since there are many trade-offs involved in their design. Some properties and examples of tax reliefs granted by US states are described below:

- Flat-value exemptions/credits tend to make the property tax distribution more progressive, given that these reliefs represent a larger share of the tax obligations applied to low-income property values.
- Percentage exemptions/credits are better employed to shift the tax burden away from the group that is receiving the benefit. That is because they do not substantially affect the distribution of property taxes among taxpayers that are in the same group. Thus, for instance, a revenue-neutral tax rate reduction for pensioners would shift the burden away from pensioners to other taxpayers and will only improve the progressivity of the tax in case pensioners (i.e. the group receiving the benefit in this case) have lower incomes than the average taxpayer.
- Lump-sum credits is the only tax benefit that can provide relief to taxpayers without changing the marginal tax rate of its beneficiary (i.e. if the tax rate increases, the benefit will remain constant). That is because: 1) reliefs that reduce a percentage of taxable value/tax obligation are also applied to tax hikes, reducing the marginal tax rate for beneficiaries; and 2) exemptions reduce the taxable amount to which the tax increase is applied.
- Income-based tax credits refer to reliefs in which the tax obligation is reduced by either a fixed amount or a percentage depending on the income of the taxpayer. Income-based programmes are

usually more cost-effective given that they are more targeted towards low-income taxpayers, but their administrative and compliance burdens tend to be higher, since information on income is necessary.

- Deferrals regard a tax relief that does not reduce tax obligations but rather delay tax payments to some future period, usually when the property is sold or the owner dies. In case interest rates applied to the deferred values are in line with market values, there are not real costs to either the taxpayer or to the tax administration. In other words, the tax obligation is not changed but, at the same time, the beneficiary can have a temporary full reduction in their tax obligations. Usually only some types of taxpayers are eligible for deferrals, such as low-income seniors. Nevertheless, since seniors often want to leave their property to their heirs without many tax obligations attached, participation rates tend to be very low.

With respect to the level of government that is responsible for funding the tax relief, when funding is provided by upper levels of government, disparity in revenue capacity across local governments is less of a concern. In other words, programmes that are funded by upper levels of government are typically applied to all localities for which this level of government is responsible. Thus, even taxpayers from poorer local governments that would not have the necessary funds to establish such a programme can benefit from it.

Lastly, regarding taxpayer eligibility, the higher the coverage of the programme, the higher the costs. Nevertheless, limiting eligibility can be problematic and lead to distortions in case limitations were introduced only for the sake of reducing costs. For instance, in case the objective of the programme is to grant relief to low-income households, this goal can be better achieved in case all low-income households are eligible, regardless of, for instance, the age of the homeowner or the ownership status of the property (these two requirements are commonly found in OECD countries). In addition, other commonly found requirements are income ceilings, net worth limits, maximum property value and residency requirements.

Box 2.2. Property tax incentives for business in the United States

Tax incentives

Each one of the 50 US states employ at least one type of property tax incentive for business. There are many different types of incentives provided such as property tax abatement programmes, firm specific property tax incentives, tax increment financing, enterprise zones and the combination of property tax exemptions with industrial development bonds. Some states employ multiple programmes. This box explores these programmes in more detail.

Property tax abatement programmes allow partial or full reduction in property tax liability for certain types of properties. There are a myriad of property tax abatements in the United States. Tax abatements may vary depending on the types of eligible properties. In the United States the most common types of properties that benefit from tax abatements are industrial (51 programmes) and commercial (44) properties, but there is a wide variety of other types. Regarding the type of tax that is abated, there also is a significant variation, being the most common in the United States the following: real property taxes (70 programmes), personal property taxes (46) and taxes on improvements (24). The form of abatement can also vary, and in US states, among the most common there are exemptions (50 programmes), tax credits (12) and freezes (8). They can also be geographically targeted. Concerning the duration of abatements, 10 years is the most common in US states, but they are frequently renewable. Lastly, nearly half of these programmes have no limiting provisions; about one third of the programmes can be terminated in case companies do not meet policy targets (e.g. regarding job creation targets); about one fifth include “clawbacks” that attempt to require these companies to pay back some portion of the abatement; and 7% have a pre-established end date.

Firm-specific property tax incentives regard partial or full reductions in property tax liability for some specific companies. They are offered on a case-by-case basis and commonly to companies considering relocation. There is little systematic data on these incentives. Nevertheless, it is worth noting that there is a significant concern regarding these benefits – once a firm-specific incentive is given to one firm, similar companies will lobby for their own tax incentive package. Granting similar incentives to many companies can greatly reduce tax revenues.

With **tax increment financing (TIF),** growth in property taxes or other revenues in a specific territorial area is earmarked to support economic development in that area. These funds are commonly used to improve infrastructure. It is worth noting that TIF is not a tax reduction programme, but an earmarking one. As a result, it aims at promoting business through an improvement in the conditions of the area not through a tax reduction. More advanced schemes allow the issuance of bonds backed by future revenue growth, which can make these programmes self-financing. Usually there is an end date for TIF in which afterwards tax revenues will accrue normally to governments.

Enterprise zones are a more all-encompassing type of tax benefit. The objective is to promote business development in a region facing economic problems (i.e. unemployment, poverty and low-income) through the provision of special tax treatment and other benefits. In 2010 there were 48 enterprise zone programmes in 42 US states plus the District of Columbia. Most programmes (31 out of 48) include some type of property tax benefit such as a reduction or exemption. Another goal is to increase employment opportunities for residents in the zone.

Impact

Despite this widespread use of property tax incentives for business in the United States, evidence suggests that they have only a limited impact on general economic growth (Kenyon, Langley and Paquin, 2012[14]). That is because property taxes are only a small portion of all costs for most firms and, thus, they are commonly outweighed by other factors that are relevant for business placement such as labour market, proximity to suppliers and consumers, as well as transportation costs. There is also evidence that these benefits can have a significant impact on economic growth for individual jurisdictions. Nevertheless, these benefits cease to exist when neighbouring jurisdictions adopt similar measures, reducing their relative property tax advantage and leading to an overall reduction in property tax revenues.

Principles

Despite their downsides, there are ways that these tax incentives can be designed to maximise their potential benefits. First, criteria for granting incentives can increase investment quality (i.e. restricting incentives to projects that meet certain standards). Second, incentives can be limited to mobile facilities that export goods or services out of the region – in that way the room for tax exporting[1] can be minimised. Third, place limits on the number or total dollar value of incentives in order to curb a continued growth in tax benefits over time. Fourth, enforce an open process for deciding on incentives. Fifth, encourage co-operation with other localities to avoid potentially harmful tax competition.

1. Tax exporting refers to the practice of one jurisdiction imposing tax burdens on residents/businesses of another.
Sources: Kenyon, Langley and Paquin (2012[14]).

Figure 2.5 shows which types of property/owner tax reliefs are provided in OECD countries (Box 2.3 explores the specific case of US States and Annex C provides in detail the reliefs provided by OECD countries). Tax reliefs are more commonly applied to low-income owners and certain businesses, such as new businesses or businesses from a specific sector. In some countries reliefs apply to all properties that a taxpayer owns (Chile, Estonia and Lithuania), while in others these benefits are restricted to one property, such as the main residence (Belgium, Portugal and the United States). For the United Kingdom some reliefs apply to all properties while others just to one property. Under-used properties (e.g. if the number of people living in a house is below a critical number) also enjoy tax benefits in some countries (Belgium, Chile, Korea and the Slovak Republic), as well as certain types of spending on property (e.g. investments).

Figure 2.5 Recurrent taxes on immovable property in OECD countries: Tax reliefs

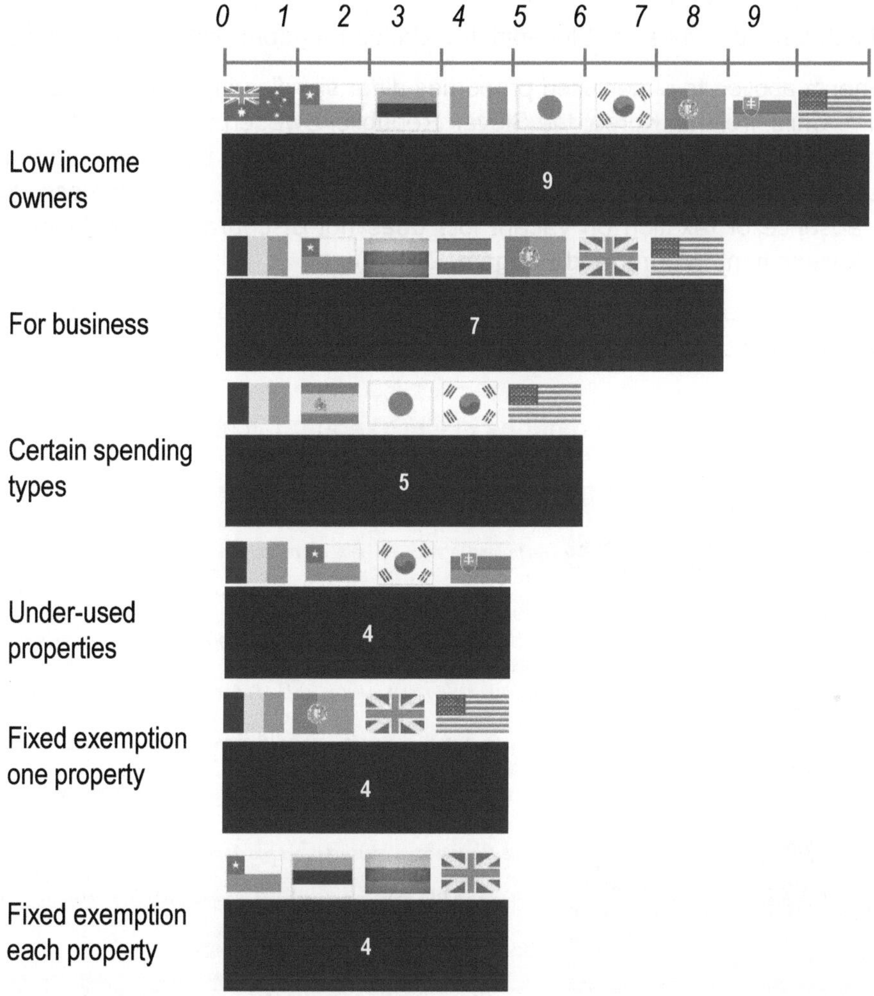

Note: For more details regarding the US system see Boxes 2.2 and 2.3
Source: Responses from OECD Survey on Recurrent Taxes on Immovable Property.

It is interesting to note that some countries (Estonia, Italy, Japan, Portugal, the Slovak Republic and the United States) did not report having a progressive tax rate structure but these countries provide benefits to low-income households in the form of tax reliefs. These reliefs can improve the income distribution without the need to introduce progressive tax rates, and are likely to broaden political support for a property tax reform. However, the overall consistency of such allowances with other parts of the tax and transfer system must be carefully checked.

Apart from low-income households, pensioners also often benefit from tax reliefs (in Australia, Chile, Estonia, the Slovak Republic and some US states) as they tend to compose the group of asset-rich but cash-poor taxpayers. Newly constructed buildings are also subjected to tax reliefs in many OECD countries with the purpose of promoting the construction sector while improving the quality of the buildings or to promote the supply of new homes (Australia, Belgium, Norway,[9] Slovenia and some US states). In Spain, local authorities are allowed to establish tax deductions for installed systems that use thermal or electrical energy from the sun. Properties that are put to some specific use are also commonly exempt, such as properties used by charities, churches, government, non-profit and international organisations (Berne-Switzerland, Finland, Ireland, Lithuania, Slovenia, the United Kingdom and some US states).

Special tax treatments applied to under-used properties differ significantly across OECD countries. Seven countries (Belgium, Chile, Ireland, Korea, the Slovak Republic, Sweden and the United Kingdom) provide benefits or exemptions to these types of properties. These benefits can be given on the grounds that the tax burden should be a charge on the actual use of urban services. Nevertheless, from a land-use perspective, the absence of taxation on vacant lots does not discourage speculation nor encourages advancement of development (Maurer and Paugam, 2000[6]).

To summarise, Figure 2.6, below, provides a list of tax reliefs that are granted the most by OECD countries and gives one example of a country that provides the respective relief.

Figure 2.6 Common tax reliefs and exemptions in OECD countries along with country examples

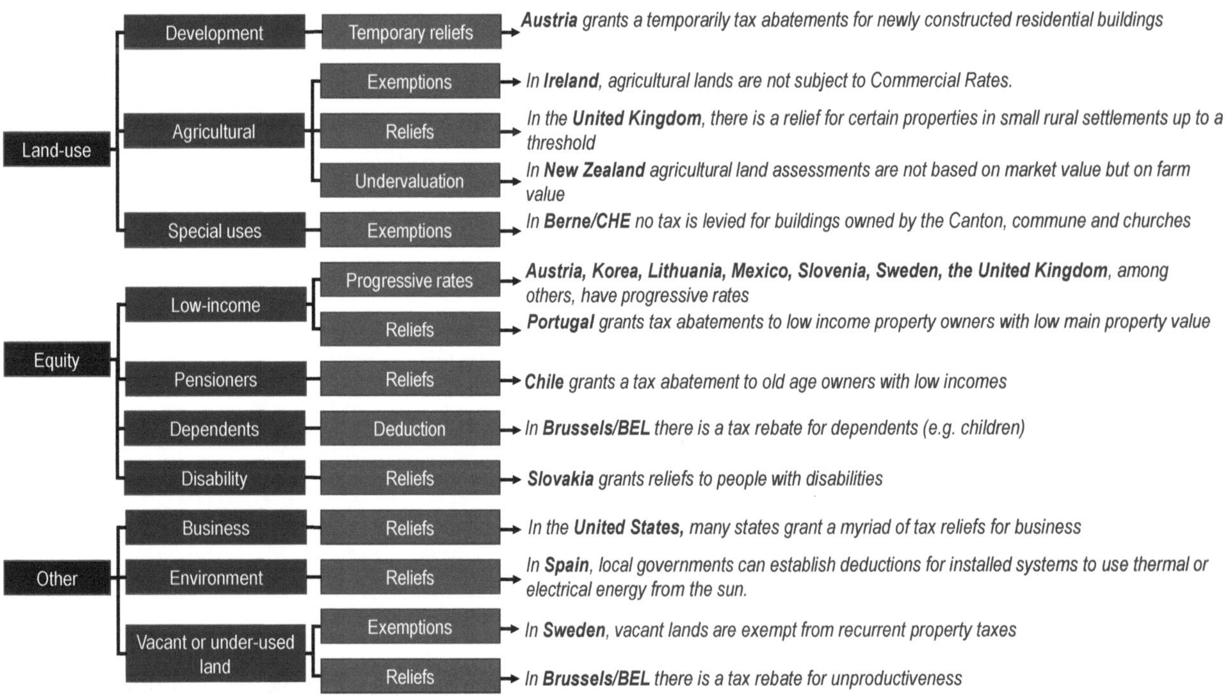

Note: For New Zealand the information comes from Maurer and Paugam (2000[6]).
Source: Responses from OECD Survey on Recurrent Taxes on Immovable Property.

Box 2.3. Recurrent property tax exemptions in US states

Types of Programmes

As in multiple countries, many exemptions granted by US states aim at reducing the public opposition towards recurrent taxes on immovable property. All but three states have at least one of the two programmes: homestead exemptions and property tax credits. Homestead exemptions reduce the amount of property value subject to taxation while property tax credits directly reduce the tax obligation. Both can be reduced either by a fixed dollar amount or by a percentage of the value.

Despite these commonalities among states, the design of these exemption programmes varies markedly across them. As of 2012, 59% of state programmes provided flat dollar exemptions while 19% provided percentage exemptions and roughly 20% employed property tax credits or other benefits based on a more complicated formula.

States vs. Local Funding

The costs of these programmes are, in some cases, funded by the state and, in others, by the local governments. As of 2012, most commonly (57% of the cases) local governments bear these costs while in 28% of the cases the state fully covers local revenue losses. In the remaining 15% of the cases, the cost is shared between states and local governments. Usually, costlier and broad-based programmes are funded by states whereas cheaper and more specific programmes are funded by local governments.

Programme costs

In proportion to total property tax revenues, the costs of these tax benefits are normally small but vary widely across states. In 14 of the 45 states with these programmes, total savings are less than 0.5% of property tax revenues while in 27 states, the savings are less than 2.5%. In 9 states the costs are equal to or exceed 10% of total property tax revenues.

Eligibility

It is also worth highlighting that most states employ more than one property tax exemption or credit programme. These programmes usually differ in terms of eligible taxpayers. The most common groups are homeowners, seniors, veterans, or the disabled.

Homeowner's programmes in 26 states are for nearly all homeowners, but usually limited to owner-occupied primary residences. In an "average state" the median homeowner receives a 12.5% cut compared to 25% in the top quarter of states that offer more generous programmes. Seniors' property tax relief programmes are present in 18 states. These programmes tend to grant larger benefits in comparison to the benefits granted to homeowners. The median benefit is a tax cut of nearly 30% in the typical state. More than half of these programmes provide a median tax cut of at least 25%, while only a sixth of them provide a median tax savings of less than 10%. In the typical state, roughly 20% of homeowners are eligible for these senior targeted programmes. It is worth noting that eligibility rates vary significantly across states depending on whether there is an income ceiling. In the seven states that provide property tax relief to seniors regardless of income, 25–30% of homeowners are typically eligible. But in seven states with low-income cut-offs (USD 10 000 to 30 000), only 5–10% of homeowners qualify.

Regarding veterans, only 10 states provide property tax exemptions or credits for all veterans, even those without disabilities. The average tax cut is just 3.2%. Tax reliefs usually differ when veterans have service-connected disabilities are considered (15% of veterans qualify in the typical state). Currently, 31 states provide property tax exemptions or credits specifically to veterans with service-connected disabilities. It is worth noting that only 0.6% of homeowners are eligible for these programmes in the median state and, thus, their impacts tend to be small.

In 23 states there are programmes covering disabled homeowners. The criteria used to determine the eligibility of taxpayers vary across states. In the median state, 2.3% of homeowners are eligible for these types of programmes, and they receive a median property tax cut of 21%.

Sources: Langley (2015[15]).

Under certain circumstances, there might be other policy tools that can achieve the same desired goals that tax reliefs programmes aim at achieving but, potentially, in a more cost-effective manner. Tax reliefs tend to increase the complexity of the tax system and can create distortions. As explored throughout this section, most tax relief programmes target low-income earners. In the realm of intergovernmental relations, equalisation grants are widely employed to offset differences in revenue-raising capacity or public service cost across jurisdictions and, as a result, can at times be an effective tool to reduce income inequality within a country – see Dougherty and Forman (2021[16]). In the realm of social programmes, there are a myriad of anti-poverty and housing policies that can be used to improve the situation of low-income earners. As it will be discussed further in the last chapter of this report, bundling a reform of recurrent taxes on immovable property with other policies outside the realm of taxation can be a good strategy to offset undesired effects of property taxation and, in this context, can also be an alternative to the use of tax reliefs.

In that light, addressing distributive problems using income-transfer programmes can be even more transparent, since it is unlikely that many taxpayers will notice a clear link between their income bracket and the tax benefit that they receive. In addition, the outcomes of tax relief programmes depend greatly on many elements, such as the distribution of homeownership in a country and tax evasions rates. For that reason, Kitchen (2012[17]) argues that "uncertainty over regressivity of the property tax and the tendency to provide relief that varies directly with property values argues strongly in favour of eliminating property tax credits and using other components of the state, region or provincial government's income-transfer system to improve inequities in the overall distribution of income."

Exemptions in the Chinese property tax system

It is worth noting that many of the properties that are exempt in OECD countries are also exempt from China's land tax – such as land used by state organs, religious temples, parks, among others (CDRF, 2020[18]). In addition, exemptions can be based on criteria that vary across jurisdictions. That is, in the case of China, in which the price of immovable property varies widely across jurisdictions, progressivity can be achieved in a fair manner by giving a tax-free basic allowance that could vary across provinces and cities (Brys et al., 2013[19]). A similar outcome can be achieved in a less complex way by providing a tax reduction to low-income occupiers. Such tax benefits based on income are already in place in China's property tax system – taxpayers who are facing financial difficulties may enjoy a reduction or exemption from China's house property tax for a determined period.

Impact on the overall tax system

A revenue-neutral shift from transaction taxes towards a well-designed recurrent tax on immovable property has the potential to increase economic growth while improving the income distribution

When carrying out tax reforms, policy makers balance efficiency and pro-growth objectives of tax reforms with distributional objectives, while also taking into account the impact on revenues, tax avoidance and evasion opportunities, as well as the costs of compliance, administration and enforcement. Such objectives rarely can be achieved in isolation – that is, when reforming a specific form of taxation, the actual impact of the reform might deviate from the expected impact in case the interplay between taxes and benefits are not considered. In particular, recurrent taxes on immovable property are a form of capital/property taxation and user fees (depending on the incidence considered) and, thus, their impact can be better assessed in conjunction with other taxes such as capital taxes and user fees. Income taxes are also particularly relevant to properly assess the distributive impact of a certain types of design for recurrent taxes on immovable property. This section analyses how recurrent taxes on immovable property can be reformed in a harmonised and consistent manner with the tax system already in place (see the Greek and Italian case in Box 2.4).

First, recurrent property taxes are considered among the least damaging to economic growth, even when compared to other property taxes such as inheritance taxes, net wealth taxes and transaction tax (Hagemann, 2018[1]). Property transaction taxes, especially, are generally considered to have distortionary effects. For instance, imposing taxes on a house transaction will, for example, discourage the owner from moving to an area with better labour market opportunities. As a result, revenue-neutral shifts from transaction taxes towards immovable property taxation tend to have positive allocative impacts by minimising the influence of the tax system on transaction decisions.

Second, as discussed previously, the impact of recurrent property taxes on the distribution of income greatly depends on the design of the tax and on the distribution of homeownership in a country. When considering revenue-neutral shifts towards recurrent taxes on immovable property, the progressivity of the taxes that are being discontinued/reduced are of great importance to determine the overall effect of the reform on the progressivity of the tax system.

Although the distributive impact of recurrent taxes on immovable property can be increased through an adequate tax rate and relief structure, as discussed previously, it still is the case that, in principle, some other types of taxes are better equipped to improve tax system's progressivity. In the case of property taxes, it is unclear whether transaction taxes are either regressive or progressive[10] but net wealth taxes and inheritance taxes tend to be more progressive than recurrent taxes on immovable property (Cournède, Fournier and Hoeller, 2018[20]). That is because in general wealth is much more unequally distributed than home ownership and even income, entailing that the distributive effects for both net wealth and inheritance taxes are larger than for immovable property taxes and income taxes.

Therefore, in summary, reforms aimed at increasing the share of recurrent taxes on immovable property tend to improve the allocation of resources while the impact on income distribution is heavily dependent on the distribution of homeownership in a country, on the tax design and, in case of revenue-neutral reforms, the tax that is being shifted from. When a country's tax design involves a mildly progressive tax rate structure and/or a sound tax relief policy that benefits asset rich income poor households, the progressivity of recurrent taxes on immovable property tends to improve. Thus, in principle, a reform that simultaneously reduces transaction taxes while increasing recurrent taxes on immovable property might not only improve economic output but also possibly make the income distribution more equal. For this reason, it has been relatively common for OECD and partner countries to shift from transaction taxes to recurrent taxes on immovable property.

Recurrent taxes on immovable property are not the best tool to reduce income inequality

Joumard et al. (2012[21]) analysed the income redistribution effects via taxes and cash transfers and they concluded that the latter reduce income dispersion more than the former in most OECD countries. In other words, cash transfers tend to be more effective in improving the progressivity of fiscal policy than tax reforms. More specifically, family, housing, disability and unemployment benefits are especially important to improve income distribution. Regarding taxes, income tax tends to be the most progressive tax, but its overall effect on the distribution of income depends on its design and, thus, varies by country.

As a result, usually taxes are not the best fiscal policy tool to reduce income inequality, nor are recurrent taxes on immovable property the best type of tax in this respect. Nevertheless, a shift towards recurrent property taxation can improve both efficiency and equity, especially in more globalised economies (Dougherty and Akgun, 2018[22]). The main motivations for the introduction of recurrent taxes on immovable property are: 1) increasing tax system efficiency; 2) increasing subnational revenue autonomy; 3) making the real estate market more stable; and 4) improving the quality of land use. In case improving the progressivity of the tax system is the main goal of the reform, a shift towards other taxes is often a better option – notably income taxes, inheritance taxes and wealth taxes.[11] In addition, a revenue-raising recurrent property tax reform could have a more substantial effect on income equality if revenues collected are used to fund progressive policies such as cash transfers to low-income households and the design of the tax does not exacerbate income inequality.

China's tax system and the introduction of recurrent taxes on immovable property

As noted above, the impact of recurrent property taxes on the distribution of income greatly depends on the distribution of housing assets in a country. According to McGregor (2021[23]), approximately 70% of China's household wealth is held in real estate. In addition, the urban homeownership rate in China is roughly 98%, among the highest in the world (CDRF, 2020[18]). In this situation, recurrent taxes on immovable property can be an effective tool in reducing wealth inequalities (OECD, 2019[24]).

In addition, as suggested by Ahmad (2021[25]), the cost of the provision of public services can be explicitly linked to the revenues raised by the new recurrent levy on residential property. In that scenario, even if the new tax may not be progressive, the overall fiscal system could become more progressive if the revenues raised were spent on programmes/services that have an income-equalising effect. As discussed in the last chapter, this strategy could also increase the public support for tax reform.

With regard to the other property taxes, among the main Chinese local taxes there are the house property tax (3.51% of local tax revenue as of 2018),[12] the urban land-use tax (3.36%) and the land value added tax (6.8%). Hence, the absence of a major tax managed at the local level might lead to a low efficiency of the tax administration and collection activities, as well as to an increase in compliance costs for taxpayers. Moreover, China also levies a deed tax that accounts for roughly 7.4% of total taxation at the local level.[13] As a result, in case the introduction of recurrent taxes on residential property is combined with the discontinuation or reduction of other property taxes, especially the deed tax, the Chinese tax system could become more growth-friendly and simpler to administer. Such a reform might leave the housing price level relatively unaffected, as these measures have opposite price effects (Brys et al., 2013[19]). Another interesting option is to introduce recurrent taxes on immovable property along with a reform on inheritance taxes. As OECD (2019[26]) recommended, the introduction of these taxes together could lead to a reduction in wealth inequalities.

Box 2.4. Italian and Greek property tax reforms that reduced the number of tax levied

In **Italy**, the property tax on primary residences (ICI) was abolished in 2006 but reintroduced in 2013 under a new single municipal tax (IMU), which incorporates three taxes:

1. the IMU ("*Imposta Municipal Propria*"), which is a real estate tax paid by owners of secondary residences only. The taxable base is determined in connection with the value of the property according to the cadastre. The regular tax rate is 0.76% of the taxable base, but municipalities may increase or reduce the rate, with a maximum of 0.3%.
2. the TASI or "tax for indivisible services" is a supplementary real estate tax, which is supposed to meet the expenses for the delivery of lighting, street cleaning, green areas and services that are provided equitably by municipalities to all citizens;
3. and the TARI (waste tax), which must cover the costs of the service of collection and treatment of waste.

Both the IMU and the TASI were repealed on primary residences (except luxury homes) in 2014 and 2015. From 2020 onwards, in order to simplify the fiscal system, the government unified its local property taxes by abolishing the municipal service tax TASI and merging it with the IMU local property tax (both taxes are described below). The sum of TASI and IMU rates remain the same. Despite a reform of cadastral values is still pending to fully exploit the potential of the property tax, municipalities can intervene to re-evaluate cadastral rents of under-valuated areas or properties. In 2019, the recurrent property tax accounted for 1.2% of GDP, in line with the OECD average.

In **Greece**, a new property tax (Unified Property Tax, ENFIA) was established in 2014 to replace two previous property taxes, the real estate-based wealth tax (FAP) and the property tax that is collected through the Electric company utility bill. The new tax applies to individuals and legal entities owners of land and buildings. The ENFIA comprises a "main tax" and a "supplementary tax". The main tax applies for buildings, plots, fields and so on. The main tax is calculated on the basis of "objective values" based on several criteria such as the location of the property, its size, use, age, the floor on which the property is located, etc. The supplementary tax (so called sumptuary tax) is imposed on very expensive property. The tax rate ranges from 0.1 to 1% of the assessed value. In 2018, the government reassessed the "objective values", resulting in a decrease of paid taxes for 23% of property owners (23%), a stability for 62% and an increase for the remaining 15% of taxpayers.

Sources: OECD (2020[27]) and OECD (2021[28]).

Housing investments

The impact of property taxes on housing investments can be non-neutral and distortive

The non-neutrality of the taxation of housing assets has the potential to distort investment allocation decisions (Millar-Powell et al., 2022[29]). In this light, the effects of recurrent taxes on immovable property can be better understood when analysed in the broad context of taxation on housing investments. Multiple other tax levies and reliefs affect housing investments, and their effects are felt in different investment phases. Transaction taxes can be levied when the asset is acquired; income taxes, recurrent taxes on immovable property and net wealth taxes can be levied during the holding period; and capital gains taxes can be levied upon disposal of the asset. Mortgage interest relief, which can apply during the holding period, is one example of the range of deductions, credits and exemptions that apply to housing investments (Figure 2.7). Box 2.5 delves into the details of these taxes and reliefs in OECD countries.

Figure 2.7 Taxes levied over the life of housing investments

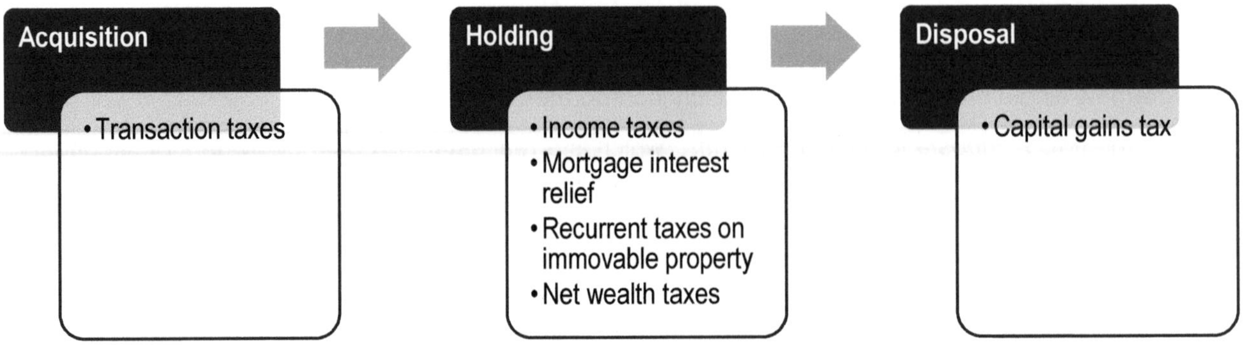

Source: Based on Millar-Powell et al. (2022[29]).

Box 2.5. Taxes levied over the life of housing investments in OECD countries

Taxes on acquisition of housing assets

- **Transaction taxes are levied on owner-occupied and rented housing in 30 out of the 40 countries analysed.** They are generally applied at flat rates, but occasionally can depend on the value of the asset (for example, in Canada). Transaction taxes are typically levied on the purchase of an existing housing asset, and not on the sale of the asset. New residential housing may be exempt from transaction taxes, but some countries levy Value Added Taxes (VAT) when a new property is sold for the first time. The buyer may be liable for remitting the transaction tax or the VAT, but the economic incidence of the tax will depend on many factors and may lie on the buyer, the seller or they may share the burden.

Taxes on holding of housing assets

- **Taxation of rental income is more common than taxation of imputed rent**. Different tax treatment of income typically applies to owner-occupied and rented housing. The return generated by owner-occupied housing in the form of imputed rent is typically tax exempt. Only four countries (Denmark, Greece, the Netherlands and Switzerland) tax imputed rental income, though this is generally at low rates and only when at least partially debt-financed in the case of the Netherlands. In contrast, 34 out of 40 countries tax actual rental income, while two (Belgium and the Netherlands) apply a tax on deemed rather than actual rental income. Rental income is typically taxed at progressive rates. However, four countries tax rental income at flat rates (Denmark, Iceland, Italy and Slovenia). In some cases, tax rates on rental income are applied at concessionary levels, or on a reduced base (e.g. Latvia, Spain, Iceland and Italy). There are also income-based exemptions applied to the taxation of rental income in Korea and the Slovak Republic.
- **Mortgage interest relief is widely available in the countries analysed.** Twenty-one out of the 40 countries provide tax relief (via either a deduction or a tax credit) for mortgage interest on owner-occupied property. In 17 countries, this tax relief takes the form of a tax deduction for mortgage interest. The total value of the deduction is capped in two countries (Estonia and Luxembourg), while two countries restrict eligibility for mortgage interest relief to taxpayers who earn below an income threshold (Chile) or to taxpayers whose housing asset falls below a value threshold (Korea). Four countries provide a tax credit for mortgage interest, which is capped in Belgium, Italy and Spain but not in Japan. 27 out of the 40 countries also provide mortgage interest relief for rented property. The majority of these 27 countries provide an uncapped tax

deduction for mortgage interest on rented property, though interest is not deductible in Chile if taxpayer income exceeds a threshold and tax relief is capped in Estonia. Some regions in Belgium provide a capped tax credit for mortgage principal repayments (but not for interest payments) for loans contracted before 2015.

- **No country provides an allowance for housing equity.** In the area of corporate finance, different tax treatment may apply to firms that finance investments with debt and firms that finance with equity. In order to mitigate this differential treatment and reduce the incentive for firms to use debt finance, some countries provide an Allowance for Corporate Equity (ACE). Individual taxpayers may face similar incentives to employ debt finance; however, no country attempts to address any resulting incentives in a similar way (e.g. an allowance for housing equity).
- **The few countries that impose a net wealth tax have special treatment for owner-occupied housing.** In all six countries with net wealth taxes, owner-occupied and rented property are included in the tax base (Argentina, Colombia, France, Norway, Spain and Switzerland). However, all six countries have a considerable minimum wealth threshold before a positive rate or rates apply and several provide special treatment for residential property. A 30% rate reduction applies for owner-occupied housing in France and Spain applies a specific exemption threshold to the main residence of up to EUR 300 000, which is in addition to the EUR 700 000 general net wealth tax exemption threshold. Only 25% of the owner-occupied property value is subject to the tax in Norway, which rises to 90% in the case of rented property (secondary homes). The basic general allowance in the wealth tax is NOK 1 500 000 (EUR 150 000) per taxpayer.

Taxes on disposal of housing assets

- **Concessionary rates are often applied to capital gains on owner-occupied property.** Countries tax capital gains at a mix of progressive and flat rates and capital gains are typically taxed on a realisation rather than an accrual basis. Beyond these two commonalities, however, the tax treatment of owner-occupied and rented housing differs substantially. Of the 40 countries analysed, only 14 countries tax capital gains on owner-occupied housing. These taxes are often imposed at concessionary or zero rates and in many cases are subject to a minimum holding period test. At least some capital gains for rented housing are taxed in 34 out of the 40 countries. However, concessionary (or zero) rates are often applicable for rented housing and, as is the case for owner-occupied housing, these concessionary rates are generally subject to a minimum holding period test.

Sources: Millar-Powell et al. (2022[29]).

Debt-financed investments on owner-occupied properties are commonly taxed at lower effective rates relative to investments on other assets due to the lack of imputed rent taxes, capital gain taxes and mortgage interest reliefs

Not only is it challenging to analyse the joint effect of these tax levies/reliefs on housing investments, but these effects are also asymmetrical across investment's, taxpayer's and property's characteristics. Three of the most important determining factors in the tax system that can affect the tax treatment of housing investments are related to: 1) whether the property is owner-occupied or rented; 2) whether the property is debt-financed or equity-financed; and 3) taxpayer's income and wealth (Millar-Powell et al., 2022 [29]). In principle, unless it is a policy objective to provide benefits[14] to some type of investments, properties or taxpayers, these differences are non-desired consequences of the design of the tax system and, thus, should be minimised. In general, owner-occupied and debt financed properties are favoured in terms of marginal effective tax rates in comparison to rented and equity financed properties. The effect of taxpayers' income and wealth and the length of the investment is not clear cut – it depends heavily on the characteristics of the tax system. According to Millar-Powell et al. (2022[29]), regarding:

- *Debt-financed and equity-financed properties*: Mortgage interest relief is considered the cause of the differences in tax treatment between them. Tax relief for mortgage interest can significantly reduce the tax burden on housing, as it allows taxpayers to reduce their taxable income by the partial or full value of the interest they have paid on their mortgage. In the case of owner-occupied housing, which receives a tax subsidy on average, the reduction in tax liability provided by mortgage interest relief tends to outweigh the combined effect of all other taxes levied on a housing investment.
- *Owner-occupied and rented properties*: There are two main drivers for the tax benefits that owner-occupied properties enjoy. First, with respect to income taxes, rental income is commonly taxed while imputed rents are often not. Second, while many countries provide tax exemptions for capital gains on owner-occupied housing, capital gains on rented housing are typically subject to taxation.
- *Taxpayer's income and wealth levels*: There are many potential drivers that may affect their tax treatment. First, tax deductions that allow taxpayers to reduce their taxable income at their marginal personal income tax rate may provide a greater benefit to high-income earners, who are often taxed at higher marginal rates. In this light, mortgage interest deduction provides a greater benefit to taxpayers with higher income because many countries provide a deduction at the taxpayer's marginal rate, which is higher for high-income taxpayers in progressive tax systems, and because most countries do not cap the mortgage interest relief. Second, taxation of the main residence raises complex distributional questions since higher-income households hold more wealth in main residences than lower-income ones, but main residences of lower-income households tend to make up a larger share of their assets. In any case, the very poorest of households tend to not own a home and in this situation concessionary taxation of owner-occupied property relative to other forms of assets could provide a greater tax benefit to those in the middle and top of the income distribution compared to those at the very bottom. When tax benefits are extended to second homes, high-income taxpayers tend to benefit the most since they more commonly have multiple properties.

It is worth noting that due to the amount of exclusive benefits that debt-financed investments on owner-occupied receives, investment decisions can be distorted in a manner that favour this type of investment. First, the income generated by owner-occupied properties are often exempt of taxation while the income generated by other assets are not. Second, capital gains of owner-occupied properties are commonly not taxed. Third, interest paid to finance these investments are often subjected to tax relief, either as a tax credit or a deduction against labour and/or other income. While, from a neutrality perspective, this tax relief is difficult to justify, this position reflects the fact that a large number of countries place considerable importance on the policy objective of supporting home ownership[15] (OECD, 2018[30]).

Distortions can be alleviated by levying recurrent taxes on immovable property, capping deductions or providing tax credit when granting tax reliefs for mortgage interest, and capping the value of owner-occupied houses that benefits from exemption from taxation capital gains

In order to make the tax system more neutral with regard to investments, OECD (2018[30]) recommends a number of measures. First, the recurrent taxes on immovable property can be used to increase the tax burden on investments in residential housing. Another option related to a shift towards other types of tax involves increasing transaction taxes but since these are highly distortive, a growth-friendlier solution is to increase further recurrent taxes on immovable property.[16] Second, following the practice found in a number of countries (explored in Box 2.5) a cap on relief for mortgage interest can be imposed in order to reduce the magnitude of the tax benefit in a manner that it is not distortive enough to change investment decisions. Third, tax reliefs for mortgage interest can be provided in the form of tax credits rather than deductions, so there is no regressive impact of deductions against income taxed at progressive rates. Fourth, a limit on the value of owner-occupied housing that benefits from an exemption from taxation on capital gains can be imposed so as to mitigate the adverse distributional effects of this incentive when providing equality to all taxpayers.

It is worth highlighting that this special treatment given to low-income households with regard to mortgage interest reliefs can be especially relevant since these households may have substantial housing debts as a percentage of their income. These good practices are taken by some countries (see Box 2.5). Three countries cap the value of the mortgage interest deduction and a further two countries restrict eligibility for the deduction based on taxpayer income or the value of the housing. Three countries instead apply a capped tax credit, which provides the same value to all taxpayers where the credits are wastable.

China incentives to home ownership

In the Chinese case,[17] the income from securities investment (i.e. levied on the interest and dividends from securities investment) are taxed but no taxes are levied on capital gains from housing investments. There is no comprehensive levy of recurrent taxes on residential property, while mortgage interests are deductible when calculating taxable comprehensive income. Rental income is only taxed in one province (Hebei Province) and imputed rental income is not taxed. China does levy taxes on properties, but most are either minor or they exempt large categories, such as residential houses owned by individuals (i.e. house property tax, urban land-use tax) or personal transactions (i.e. land value added tax). China also collects lease administrative fees and house leasing taxes.

As a result, the Chinese tax system seems to support home ownership, which might contribute to the urban homeownership rate of 96%[18] and to the relatively high house vacancy rate in the country. These values are very high in comparison to OECD countries. In OECD countries, the average ownership rate is roughly 43% and, considering houses paying mortgage, this number grows to 65% (OECD Affordable Housing database, as of 2018). In this light, the introduction of recurrent taxes on residential property can shift the tax system towards neutrality with regard to investments in different types of assets.

One important remark regarding the Chinese tax system is that the proportion of homeowners in China that are subjected to an individual income tax is substantially smaller than in the average OECD country. According to OECD (2019[26]), roughly 82% of China's taxpayers do not pay personal income taxes. As a result, the impact of the interplay between income and property taxation is not as significant as in OECD countries. Nevertheless, in the future, personal income taxation might become more prominent in China, which could aggravate the distortions here mentioned. In that scenario, in anticipation of this possible tendency, it might be interesting to consider these elements in designing a recurrent property tax system.

House prices and land use

Apart from the attainment of fiscal policy goals, recurrent taxes on immovable property can also be used as a tool to influence house prices and land use. Regarding the former, many countries intentionally reform recurrent property taxes aiming at alleviating undesired movements in house prices. Regarding the latter, taxes provide strong incentives for particular forms of spatial developments and, as a result, can be used to, for instance, reduce the amount of vacant land or to increase the supply of an economic activity that greatly depends on land availability (OECD, 2017[31]). It is worth noting that in order to attain these policy goals, housing, land use and fiscal policies should be implemented in a harmonised manner. This harmonisation might involve multiple levels of government and, in this scenario, inter-governmental co-ordination is crucial.

Recurrent property taxes can be used to make housing more affordable and to reduce the volatility of housing prices, nevertheless these effects depend on the frequency in which properties' value are reassessed and on the supply and demand elasticity of housing

First, property taxes can be used to make land and properties more affordable to low-income households. Although mortgage financing can also be used for that purpose, it has some limitations given that a certain level of disposable income is necessary to get a mortgage and, in some cases, low-income households do not have such levels of income. In that situation, a property tax levy can be used to reduce house prices. The mechanism driving this reduction is the capitalisation of the tax obligations into the expected future cash flows generated by a property. Although it is true that a low-income household will probably have to pay the respective property tax obligations as well, tax payments are distributed throughout the whole lifespan of a property and, thus, they are not paid in full when purchasing. As a result, the imposition of a property tax levy can especially help households with limited liquidity to obtain a mortgage since the reduction in house prices might capitalise the tax obligations in perpetuity while the household will only pay the property taxes in the period in which they own the property, which leads to a net effect that favours their purchase (Smolka and De Cesare, 2012[32]).

Despite this potentially desirable net effect, the actual effect depends on supply and demand elasticities of properties, which ultimately depends on the structure of the housing market. In case housing is undersupplied, owners may shift the property tax burden onto their tenants, which does not affect their expected future cash flows and, thus, their property's prices. Conversely, in case housing is oversupplied, owners won't be able to shift the property tax burden and, thus, house prices are expected to decrease. In practice, the tax burden is commonly shared between owners and tenants and their incidence greatly depends on the local context, potentially being asymmetric across a jurisdiction. It is worth noting that a high tax incidence on tenants may have negative equity implications,[19] particularly in areas (such as big cities) where rents represent a significant share of individuals' spending (Brys et al., 2016[11]). These effects can be particularly harmful if policy makers try to use recurrent taxes on immovable property as a "wealth" tax – instead of reducing wealth inequality, the tax can increase inequality, as the tax burden could get passed on to renters of these properties.

Second, taxes on immovable property can be used as a policy instrument for asset price stabilisation. House price volatility is negatively associated with property tax revenues as a share of GDP and, hence, higher property taxation tends to stabilise house price fluctuations. An empirical analysis from Blöchliger et al. (2015[33]) revealed that doubling the property tax-to-GDP share – e.g. by lifting it from 0.5% towards the current OECD average of 1% – would dampen house price volatility by between 1% and 4% and reduces house price growth. That is because, everything being equal, the effect of the capitalisation mechanism is larger the higher the tax obligation. More specifically, since, in most cases, tax obligations are based on properties' capital values, when property prices are increasing, property tax obligations will grow as well, alleviating the magnitude of the upswing. As a result, higher property taxation may also reduce the amplitude of house price fluctuations around the long-term trend and thereby help avoiding property boom-and-bust cycles and, in turn, can dampen GDP fluctuations, given the various channels between house price developments and GDP (Blöchliger et al., 2015[33]).

Nevertheless, it is worth noting that this effect only occurs in case the taxable value of properties increases in line with the market prices. In case property values are not re-valued frequently, which is the case in some OECD countries,[20] property tax obligations will remain constant over an upswing and, thus, would not alleviate the boost in house prices (OECD, 2017[31]). In other words, infrequent updates are going to affect house prices with a delay, which may occur only after the upswing movement. In case prices are updated through indexing, properties are going to have their values updated by the same index and, thus, the effect on house princes will disregard local-specific price movements. This situation can create unwanted and potentially harmful asymmetries. For instance, an index that reflects a mild increase on the average property price could, 1) in a region in which prices are increasing substantially, not be sufficient to alleviate the "asset bubble"; and 2) in a region in which prices are decreasing, further reduce house prices. In the first case the indexation led to an insufficient effect on house prices and in the second it generated a pro-cyclical undesirable effect on prices. This reveals one of the potential troublesome effects of not re-valuating properties frequently.

Recurrent taxes on immovable property can and are employed around the globe to reduce urban sprawl and to promote sustainable use of land and buildings

Recurrent taxes on immovable property impact land use in various ways. It can incentivise or alleviate urban sprawl (i.e. an expansion of urban development characterised by low density, segregated land use and limited infrastructure provision in more sparsely developed areas), affect the composition of new developments (mostly residential versus commercial) and be used to foster sustainable and eco-friendly use of land.

Urban sprawl is a major concern across the globe. The pace in which open land is being converted to residential and commercial zones through low-density settlements can be harmful. Open space has well-being and environmental benefits, among many others. In addition, dispersed land usually brings more transport and energy costs, while potentially excluding groups from having access to some public services such as sanitation and transport infrastructure.

Different tax solutions can be employed to minimise urban sprawl. In theory, one way to achieve this goal is by taxing land at higher rates than improvements since properties with a higher building to land ratio are going to enjoy a tax benefit (see Box 2.6). Nevertheless, in practice, although this tax design does increase building development, its impact on urban sprawl and density is not clear (Blöchliger et al., 2015[33]). A second way is by making new residents internalise the cost of new development by imposing impact or development fees. A third way is to tax more heavily underdeveloped land (i.e. land that is zoned for development but remains undeveloped or not developed to the densities it is zoned for). In that manner, new properties are going to be developed in the land that was reserved for it, potentially reducing urban sprawl. The application of such penalties to undeveloped land are found in Chile and Slovak Republic, while Slovenia and Portugal are either attempting or recently attempted to do so (OECD, 2017[31]).

Nonetheless, it is worth noting that property taxes are only one among many government tools that are employed to promote sustainable and efficient land-use. Pure land-use policies or restrictions, such as land planning (e.g. zoning), land expropriation, expiration of planning and/or building permissions and even transport policies can have a much stronger effects on land-use than property taxes, which are typically low; property taxes are too broad to target specific land plots or foster specific land-use patterns and, thus, in the context of land use, are better employed when aiming at broad land-use goals and as a complement to other land-use policies (Blöchliger, 2015[34]).

Box 2.6. Split-rate taxation with higher rates on land and pure land taxes

A pure land tax or a split-rate taxation with higher rate on land as compared to improvements can reduce urban sprawl given that it favours dense developments. More specifically, the effective tax rate on a property that has a high proportion of capital to land will tend to be less than for a similar property with a lower ratio. As a result, landowners will enjoy a tax benefit in case they make denser buildings. Denser buildings tend to reduce urban sprawl since more people can live in the same area, without needing to spread out.

A pure land tax maximises this benefit since it favours the densest constructions. Nevertheless, Brandt (2014[7]), pointed out that land values are only a fraction of property values, so in order to keep tax revenues constant, land tax rates would have to be raised substantially. In addition, due to political reasons, resistance to proper valuation of land and collection of land taxes can be fierce and effective (Ahmad and Stern, 1989[35]). As a result, land-only property taxes are seldom employed. One exception in the OECD is Estonia, which features such a pure land tax.

The use of split-rate taxation with higher rate on land as compared to improvements also has its difficulties: lands and improvements must be assessed separately, complicating the valuation process. Finland and some US states feature a split-rate taxation scheme. For instance, in Finland the rate applied to land ranges from 0.93% to 1.90% while for buildings it ranges from 0.41% to 0.90%. Some countries, like Poland and Japan do not necessarily have a different levy on land and buildings (i.e. the rates in Japan are set by the municipalities within a predefined range and, thus, some local governments can implement by selecting a higher rate for land) but they assess buildings and lands separately.

Assessing land and buildings separately

In **Austria**, agricultural land is evaluated through a lump-sum method (i.e. net present value of the expected income) in contrast to assessed value for other properties.

In **Finland** lands are valued using the sales comparison approach while buildings the cost approach (i.e. reconstruction cost).

In **Japan**, all assets are assessed by their fair market value. Similarly to Finland, fair market value of land is assessed through a sale/price comparison approach and the fair market value of buildings is assessed by the cost method.

In **Hungary**, local governments have two options for setting the taxable base: 1) area, divided in constructed area and land parcel; and 2) half of the market value of the building and land evaluated together.

In **Poland**, the tax base for land is the area, whereas for buildings is the usable area. Structures used for economic activity are assessed based on their acquisition value.

Impact of split-rate taxation in the US state of Pennsylvania

In Pennsylvania, local governments levy various split-rate taxes on land and improvements, which offers an interesting case for analysing the effect of this tax policy. Banzhaf and Lavery (2010[36]) found that within Pennsylvania, split-rate taxes increased the ratio of capital to land, mostly through additional dense residential development. As a result, jurisdictions with split-rate taxes experience less urban sprawl. In the same vein, Hanson (2021[37]) found that a move to split-rate taxation is associated with growth in the number of business establishments in a municipality. Yang (2018[38]), using municipality-level panel data, concluded that split-rate taxation leads to an increase in land value per acre. As a result, municipalities from Pennsylvania offer evidence of the potential impact of split-rate taxation in the development of properties, which reduces urban sprawl.

Land-use regulations, property market and split-rate taxation

As argued throughout this section, when fostering certain types of developments, recurrent taxes on immovable property are better employed when used as a complementary tool to other land-use policies. If there is no more room for developments in a certain region because of, for instance, land-use policies, the use of property tax as a tool to affect land-use decisions could be inefficient. In this situation, the entire tax burden would be translated into higher property prices rather than affecting land-use decisions. Thus, although pure land taxes and split-rate taxation can be used to foster dense developments, their success depends on their interaction with other land-use policies and with the current stage of development of the targeted region. For newly developing areas, with few restrictions, such taxes may have more effect on land use and, therefore, leading to more dense development.

Sources: Responses from OECD Survey on Recurrent Taxes on Immovable Property.

Designing recurrent property taxes for promoting green investments and sustainable land use have become increasingly popular

Policies aimed at reducing urban sprawl tend to benefit the environment in numerous ways. Urban sprawl not only reduces the amount of natural lands, but it also increases air pollution and increase energy demand. The latter is particularly damaging to the environment when energy sources are not environmentally friendly. Nevertheless, this is not the only way in which property taxes are employed to promote sustainable use of land and development.

Designing property taxes in order to promote green investment have become increasingly popular. Brazil, Czech Republic, Italy, Spain and the United States are examples of countries that promote renewable energy installations, renewable energy use and efficient sources of energy through property tax design (see Box 2.7 on the case of the Municipality of Salvador, in Brazil). Usually these governments grant tax relief for buildings that meet certain energy efficiency standards and/or exemptions to value increases that are due to energy efficiency investment.

Box 2.7. Brazilian recurrent property tax rebate to incentivise environmentally friendly buildings

Brazil has a very decentralised recurrent property tax system in which virtually all aspects of tax design are defined at the subnational level. Some Brazilian SNGs are designing their recurrent taxes on urban immovable property (IPTU – *Imposto Predial e Territorial Urbano*) in a way to foster "green" development.

The municipality of Salvador is a former Brazilian capital and currently the capital of the Brazilian state of Bahia. It is the fourth largest Brazilian city with a population of roughly 2.6 Million people. The Salvador municipal government has recently provided property tax reliefs to encourage the development of sustainable buildings. Salvador "IPTU Verde" (Green recurrent taxes on urban immovable property) rates properties differently based on their ability to reduce CO_2 emissions through the use of sustainable technologies. This assessment is done through a checklist that has 70 items concerning, for instance, environmental certifications, waste management process, use of natural lighting, the source of energy that the property uses (i.e. wind and solar energy provide benefits), the technology of the lifts, ventilation infrastructure, water reuse, among others. Depending on the score of a property it can be eligible for a discount on the property tax of 5%, 7% or 10%. Salvador also provides to owners of land located in environmental protection areas who opt not to build or exploit the land economically an 80% discount on their property tax. The local government expects to promote a market of green technologies in Salvador.

Sources: Prefeitura Municipal de Salvador (2020[39]); and C40 Cities (2020[40]) (accessed in September 2020).

It is worth noting that these benefits come at the cost of a reduction in tax revenues and potential creation of horizontal inequalities. As a result, the efficiency and effectiveness of these property tax benefits have to be weighed against these costs (Brandt, 2014[7]). A few studies reviewed by Brandt (2014[7]) revealed that the evidence regarding the effectiveness of tax incentives and government subsidies to promote energy efficiency investment is mixed. Some studies found no relevant impact on sustainable development investments while others found a significant positive and others a negative impact due to free-riding effects. Therefore, it seems to be too early to draw conclusions about the long-term effects of these green-friendly tax designs; this type of design is an innovation that is likely to mature in the future and possibly accelerate the transition towards the use of green buildings and technologies.

Local governments have an incentive to steer land to its highest tax use, so limits on local autonomy might be appropriate

The composition of new developments can be affected to some extent by the design of recurrent taxes on immovable property. When effective tax rates differ based on the use of the property (e.g. industrial, commercial, residential), the relative profitability of investments can change, leading to an undersupply or oversupply of some property types. Blöchliger et al. (2017[41]) summarise a handful of studies in which these effects were examined in specific country's/region's situations.

When local governments benefit from sales taxes, they may prefer to favour retail buildings to the detriment of others – this has happened to some extent in, for instance, California and Florida. In Israel, the imposition of different tax rates for different property types has led local governments to oversupply industrial and commercial zones in order to maximise tax revenues (see Box 2.8). In the United Kingdom, since taxes levied on commercial real estate are collected by the central government and taxes levied on residential properties are levied by local governments, local governments can maximise their tax revenues by using land-use policies to favour residential zones.

Box 2.8. The distortive effect of differentiated recurrent property tax rates in Israel

Land use and recurrent property tax revenues are often intertwined. Tax revenues that are collected in a jurisdiction depend on the use of its properties and, simultaneously, the use of properties depend on, to some extent, the effective tax rates that they are subjected to. As a result of that, governments may have an incentive to employ land-use policy tools, such as zoning, and design their recurrent property tax system in a manner to maximise tax revenues instead of fostering a suitable use of land. This can lead to an oversupply of some types of properties that generate more tax revenues to the detriment of others.

Effective tax rates can differ depending on, among others, the statutory tax rate, tax reliefs, taxable value of a property and property value that is actually captured by the valuation method employed. It is worth noting that due to the fact that multiple variables affect effective tax rates, sometimes the differentiation is not even intended. One case in which it is intended, though, eventually happens when local governments have substantial autonomy over these elements that affect the effective tax rate and, simultaneously, recurrent property tax revenues accrue to them. Since they fully enjoy the benefits of a higher tax revenue, and the benefits from a good land-use policy is, to some extent, exported, they can have an incentive to employ land-use policies and design their tax system to maximise tax revenues.

Israeli property tax system is an example of a system that gives incentives for local governments to prefer one type of development (business/commercial) in detriment to another (residential). Local governments are free to choose tax rates for different types of properties within bands set by the central government. These rates can vary widely. For instance, the commercial property can be up to 10 times higher than for residential units. In addition, multiple tax reliefs and exemptions apply to residential properties. Residential developments are, thus, typically associated with a net loss in local government revenues while commercial and industrial developments are associated with a net gain in revenues. In other words, the cost for service provision to new residents exceeds the revenue from residential property taxes and fees, while the tax revenues from new industrial and commercial properties exceeds the cost for service provision to them.

It is worth noting that oversupplying business/commercial properties can backfire even in terms of tax revenues in the long run. The lack of residential development, which is greatly needed in order to accommodate population growth, can lead to a shortage of workers in local communities that followed this short-term tax revenues boosting policy, leading to industries and commerce to settle elsewhere.

Sources: Blöchliger et al. (2017[41]).

All these examples reveal perverse incentives for SNGs that can use their autonomy to maximise tax revenue in detriment of promoting a good use of land. In addition to the problem related to the "fiscalisation" of land policy, when jurisdictions can vary substantially their land-use and property tax policy, heterogeneity is expected in these policies within a country/region. This heterogeneity can allow households to circumvent restrictive local fiscal and regulatory policies by moving elsewhere, thereby causing erratic sprawl in a different jurisdiction (Blöchliger, 2015[34]). This behaviour can be, though, minimised if policies are enforced in a co-ordinated manner.

Recurrent taxes on immovable property and urban sprawl in the Chinese context

Recurrent taxes on residential property in China could help to alleviate urban sprawl. The use period of residential property is 70 years, higher than leases put to other uses. Furthermore, when these lands are used to build residential properties owned by individuals, they pay no recurrent property taxes. At the same time, land used for business purposes can pay both a land-use and a house property tax. As a result, there is a tax incentive for building commercial properties. In addition, Chinese local governments are an interesting case of the "fiscalisation" of land-use policies. Some Chinese local governments have overdeveloped land for urbanisation due to, among other reasons, the leasehold fees they obtain, leading to urban sprawl (Liu, 2021[42]).

In this light, an adoption of recurrent property taxes that apply to residential properties owned by individuals can not only reduce the tax incentive given to housing investments but also strengthen local finances in a manner that they are less dependent on leasehold fees. This can discourage urban sprawl from both the local government and investors' side. Nevertheless, despite the revenue gains from property taxes, this levy alone may not completely discourage local governments from oversupplying zones for development. That is because profits from land expropriation and development can still be significant. In light of this, the involvement of upper levels of government in land-use policies in a co-ordinated manner with local governments can help mitigating urban sprawl further.

References

Ahmad, E. (2021), "Multilevel financing of sustainable infrastructure in China — policy options for inclusive, resilient and green growth", *Journal of Infrastructure, Policy and Development*, Vol. 5/1, pp. 1-24, http://dx.doi.org/10.24294/jipd.v5i1.1251. [25]

Ahmad, E. and N. Stern (1989), *Taxation for Developing Countries*, Elsevier Science Publishers. [35]

Almy, R. (2013), "A Global Compendium and Meta-Analysis of Property Tax Systems", *Lincoln Institute of Land Policy Working Paper*, https://www.lincolninst.edu/sites/default/files/pubfiles/almy_wp14ra1-v2.pdf. [9]

Banzhaf, H. and N. Lavery (2010), "Can the land tax help curb urban sprawl? Evidence from growth patterns in Pennsylvania", *Journal of Urban Economics*, Vol. 67/2, pp. 169-179, http://dx.doi.org/10.1016/j.jue.2009.08.005. [36]

Blöchliger, H. (2015), "Reforming the Tax on Immovable Property: Taking Care of the Unloved", *OECD Economics Department Working Papers*, No. 1205, OECD Publishing, Paris, https://dx.doi.org/10.1787/5js30tw0n7kg-en. [34]

Blöchliger, H. et al. (2015), "The stabilisation properties of immovable property taxation: Evidence from OECD countries", *OECD Economics Department Working Papers*, No. 1237, OECD Publishing, Paris, https://dx.doi.org/10.1787/5js0cqq93djg-en. [33]

Blöchliger, H. et al. (2017), "Local taxation, land use regulation, and land use: A survey of the evidence", *OECD Economics Department Working Papers*, No. 1375, OECD Publishing, Paris, https://dx.doi.org/10.1787/52da7c6a-en. [41]

Brandt, N. (2014), "Greening the Property Tax", *OECD Working Papers on Fiscal Federalism*, No. 17, OECD Publishing, Paris, https://dx.doi.org/10.1787/5jz5pzw9mwzn-en. [7]

Brys, B. et al. (2013), "Tax Policy and Tax Reform in the People's Republic of China", *OECD Taxation Working Papers*, No. 18, OECD Publishing, Paris, https://dx.doi.org/10.1787/5k40l4dlmnzw-en. [19]

Brys, B. et al. (2016), "Tax Design for Inclusive Economic Growth", *OECD Taxation Working Papers*, No. 26, OECD Publishing, Paris, https://dx.doi.org/10.1787/5jlv74ggk0g7-en. [11]

C40 Cities (2020), *Cities 100 Salvador Tax rebate incentivizes building green*, https://www.c40.org/case_studies/cities100-salvador-tax-rebate-incentivizes-building-green. [40]

CDRF (2020), *Background document on China's property taxation*, China Development Research Foundation. [18]

Cornia, G. (2012), *Tax Criteria: The Design and Policy Advantages of a Property Tax*, http://dx.doi.org/10.1002/9781118454343.ch9. [4]

Cournède, B., J. Fournier and P. Hoeller (2018), "Public finance structure and inclusive growth", *OECD Economic Policy Papers*, No. 25, OECD Publishing, Paris, https://dx.doi.org/10.1787/e99683b5-en. [20]

Dougherty, S. and O. Akgun (2018), "Globalisation, decentralisation and inclusive growth", in *Fiscal Decentralisation and Inclusive Growth*, OECD Publishing, Paris, https://dx.doi.org/10.1787/9789264302488-5-en. [22]

Dougherty, S. and K. Forman (2021), "Evaluating fiscal equalisation: Finding the right balance", *OECD Working Papers on Fiscal Federalism*, No. 36, OECD Publishing, Paris, https://dx.doi.org/10.1787/253da2b8-en. [16]

Hagemann, R. (2018), "Tax Policies for Inclusive Growth: Prescription versus Practice", *OECD Economic Policy Papers*, No. 24, OECD Publishing, Paris, https://dx.doi.org/10.1787/09ba747a-en. [1]

Hanson, A. (2021), "Split-Rate Taxation and Business Establishment Location: Evidence from the Pennsylvania Experience Working Paper WP21AH1", No. WP21AH1, Lincoln Institute of Land Policy, https://www.lincolninst.edu/sites/default/files/pubfiles/hanson_wp21ah1.pdf. [37]

Journard, I., M. Pisu and D. Bloch (2012), "Less Income Inequality and More Growth – Are They Compatible? Part 3. Income Redistribution via Taxes and Transfers Across OECD Countries", *OECD Economics Department Working Papers*, No. 926, OECD Publishing, Paris, https://dx.doi.org/10.1787/5k9h296b1zjf-en. [21]

Kaas, L., G. Kocharkov and E. Preugschat (2015), "Wealth Inequality and Homeownership in Europe", *CESifo Working Paper Series*, No. 5498, CESifo. [8]

Kenyon, D., A. Langley and B. Paquin (2012), *Rethinking Property Tax Incentives for Business*, Lincoln Institute of Land Policy, https://www.lincolninst.edu/sites/default/files/pubfiles/rethinking-property-tax-incentives-for-business-full_0.pdf. [14]

Kitchen, H. (2012), "Property Tax: A Situation Analysis and Overview", in *A Primer on Property Tax*, Blackwell Publishing Ltd, Oxford, http://dx.doi.org/10.1002/9781118454343.ch1. [17]

Langley, A. (2015), "How Do States Spell Relief?", *Land Lines, Lincoln Institute of Land Policy.* [15]

Langley, A. and J. Youngman (2021), "Property Tax Relief for Homeowners", *Policy Focus Reports, Lincoln Institute of Land Policy.* [13]

Liu, Z. (2021), "Municipal finance and property taxation in China", in *Local Public Finance and Capacity Building in Asia: Issues and Challenges*, OECD Publishing, Paris, https://dx.doi.org/10.1787/73c69466-en. [42]

Maurer, R. and A. Paugam (2000), "Reform Toward Ad Valorem Property Tax in Transition Economies: Fiscal and Land Use Benefits", *Background Series*, No. 25393, The World Bank, https://documents1.worldbank.org/curated/en/544251468762625226/pdf/253930Urbanbackground13.pdf. [6]

McGregor, G. (2021), *Evergrande and property speculation force Beijing to consider an idea that's radical in China: Taxing real estate*, https://fortune.com/2021/10/26/china-property-tax-real-estate-tax-evergrande-crisis-speculation/. [23]

Millar-Powell, B. et al. (2022), "Measuring Effective Taxation of Housing: Building the foundations for policy reform", *OECD Taxation Working Papers*, No. 56, OECD Publishing, Paris, https://dx.doi.org/10.1787/0a7e36f2-en. [29]

Musgrave, R. (1959), *The Theory of Public Finance: A Study in Public Economy*, McGraw-Hill. [2]

O'Connor, B. et al. (2015), "Searching for the inclusive growth tax grail: The distributional impact of growth enhancing tax reform in Ireland", *OECD Economics Department Working Papers*, No. 1270, OECD Publishing, Paris, https://dx.doi.org/10.1787/5jrqc6vk3n30-en. [10]

OECD (2021), *A Review of Local Government Finance in Israel: Reforming the Arnona System*, OECD Multi-level Governance Studies, OECD Publishing, Paris, https://dx.doi.org/10.1787/a5bc4d25-en. [28]

OECD (2020), *Tax Policy Reforms 2020: OECD and Selected Partner Economies*, OECD Publishing, Paris, https://dx.doi.org/10.1787/7af51916-en. [27]

OECD (2019), *OECD Economic Surveys: China 2019*, OECD Publishing, Paris, https://dx.doi.org/10.1787/eco_surveys-chn-2019-en. [26]

OECD (2019), *Tax Policy Reforms 2019: OECD and Selected Partner Economies*, OECD Publishing, Paris, https://dx.doi.org/10.1787/da56c295-en. [24]

OECD (2018), *Taxation of Household Savings*, OECD Tax Policy Studies, No. 25, OECD Publishing, Paris, https://dx.doi.org/10.1787/9789264289536-en. [30]

OECD (2018), *The Role and Design of Net Wealth Taxes in the OECD*, OECD Tax Policy Studies, No. 26, OECD Publishing, Paris, https://dx.doi.org/10.1787/9789264290303-en. [43]

OECD (2017), *Land-use Planning Systems in the OECD: Country Fact Sheets*, OECD Regional Development Studies, OECD Publishing, Paris, https://dx.doi.org/10.1787/9789264268579-en. [31]

Plimmer, F. (2012), *Legal Issues in Property Tax Administration*, Chichester: John Wiley & Sons, http://dx.doi.org/10.1002/9781118454343.ch8. [5]

Prefeitura Municipal de Salvador (2020), *Ações sustentáveis*, http://iptuverde.salvador.ba.gov.br/. [39]

Slack, E. (2012), *The Politics of the Property Tax*, Chichester: John Wiley & Sons, http://dx.doi.org/10.1002/9781118454343.ch3. [3]

Smolka, M. and C. De Cesare (2012), "Property Tax Collection and Enforcement", in *A Primer on Property Tax: Administration and policy*, John Wiley & Sons. [32]

Vermeulen, W. (2018), "Decentralised funding and inequality in education", in *Fiscal Decentralisation and Inclusive Growth*, OECD Publishing, Paris, https://dx.doi.org/10.1787/9789264302488-7-en. [12]

Yang, Z. (2018), "Differential effects of land value taxation", *Journal of Housing Economics*, Vol. 39, pp. 33-39. [38]

Notes

[1] Income gap refers to the gap in income between the top income earners and the bottom income earners (e.g. top 20% richest and 20% poorest).

[2] The OECD Network on Fiscal Relations across Levels of Government in collaboration with the Centre for Tax Policy and Administration (CTP) periodically survey OECD and partner countries on property tax policies. The questionnaire aims at collecting information on taxes on immovable property as recorded under category 4100 in the OECD *Revenue Statistics*. The last questionnaire, held in 2014 and updated with new information as of 2021, was divided into four sections regarding: 1) the scope of the tax on immovable property; 2) assessment and updates of immovable property values; 3) abatements that reduce the property tax base and tax liabilities; and 4) immovable property tax rates.

[3] It is worth noting though that in some countries the scope of their recurrent taxes on immovable property rests with subnational governments and, thus, there may be different tax bases within the same country.

[4] Information on the Chinese tax system and ownership rate was gathered from CDRF (2020[18]).

[5] According to Almy (2013[9]), a uniform rate structure is found in some African (e.g. Cape Verde, Gabon, Sao Tome & Prince) and Asian countries (e.g. Cambodia, Jordan, Mongolia, Thailand, Yemen).

[6] Progressivity is often discussed in terms of income. However, policy goals can align more closely with progressivity by wealth or lifetime income. In the latter case, the value of assets owned, including immovable property, is highly correlated with wealth. Wealth taxes, though, are superior to immovable property taxation in case progressivity with regards to wealth is one of the main goals of the reform.

[7] It is worth noting that the impact of this shift on the distribution of income also depends on the tax that a country is shifting from.

[8] These approaches are defined in Chapter 3.

[9] Norway's local governments decide whether or not to have such a tax relief.

[10] Brys et al. (2016[11]) concluded that the distributional effects of immovable property transaction taxes are unclear and more empirical analysis is needed. Given that homeownership tends to be lower for lower income people and property transaction taxes increase with the value of the property, transaction taxes can be considered progressive. Nevertheless, the value of the immovable property as a percentage of lifetime income is not necessarily increasing in income across the entire income distribution, possibly pointing to an inverse U-shaped relation. Moreover, property transaction taxes are borne more heavily by those that need to move more often for their employment, and these may well be poorer workers with less job security.

[11] For a detailed examination of the role and design of wealth taxes, see OECD (2018[43]).

[12] CDRF (2020[18]).

[13] Data from OECD Revenue Statistics, as of 2018.

[14] For instance, governments often aim at reducing income inequalities by increasing the tax burden on high-income and wealthy taxpayers. In this case, it is desirable to have an asymmetrical tax treatment across taxpayers with different levels of income and wealth.

[15] There are various reasons why governments may wish to support home ownership. For example, home ownership may be seen as a way to encourage long-term savings similar to tax relief for private pensions.

[16] It is worth noting that there may be a case to retain transaction taxes where there are concerns about asset bubbles (2018[43]).

[17] Based on CDRF (2020[18]).

[18] It is worth noting that one of the main causes of this high home ownership rate in China was the privatisation of formerly state-owned housing that happened in the late nineties. Nonetheless, the fact that home ownership is exempt from recurrent taxes may also help keep this rate that high.

[19] This same mechanism may apply to tax benefits – targeted exemptions and tax reliefs can also be capitalised into property prices or rents and, thus, shifting the beneficiary of tax benefits and undermining a tax benefit that aimed at improving income equality (Brys et al., 2016[11]).

[20] This topic will be covered in detail in the next chapter.

3 Property tax administration

Recurrent taxes on immovable property are among the costliest taxes to administer. That is because their administration involves several activities: fiscal cadastre maintenance, valuation of properties, management of an appeal system, billing, revenue collection and enforcement. A dysfunctional tax administration can lead to asymmetries in tax obligations that can undermine the goals of the tax design while creating horizontal inequality that make charges unfair. As most of the benefits from recurrent taxes on immovable property can only be reaped with value-based tax bases, it is especially challenging to keep a fiscal cadastre with a good coverage and updated property values. Computer assisted mass appraisal (CAMA) systems can be especially relevant for such purposes. Lastly, the billing and appeal process are particularly relevant for raising taxpayers' compliance, with the bills' content and frequency being relevant for raising tax revenues and alleviating taxpayers' liquidity problems.

Key messages

1. A good tax administration is necessary for recurrent taxes on immovable property to have the desired impact on the economy in terms of allocative efficiency, equity and revenue capacity. When cadastres are incomplete, valuations are outdated, or taxpayer compliance is low, taxpayers in similar situations will be taxed differently, damaging the fairness of the tax system.
2. Co-ordination across levels of government and/or agencies responsible for performing the main activities related to property tax administration (i.e. cadastre management, property valuation and billing) is crucial, regardless of the delineation of activities.
3. In decentralised cadastre management systems, horizontal and vertical co-ordination can be used to overcome challenges related to the lack of scale that some local governments might have to administer efficiently their property tax system.
4. Fiscal cadastres can also be used as a tool to support the achievement of other policy goals such as urban, transport, environmental and social policy. In that regard, the registration of informal settlements can improve the property tax system by generating more tax revenues and reducing horizontal inequities, and as a means to increase the access of the poor to public services.
5. Upper levels of government can help lower levels to have some uniformity in the valuation method and basis. In that way, they can maintain similar effective tax rates across jurisdictions and reduce horizontal inequities due to differences in property valuation policies.
6. Implementation of computer assisted mass appraisal (CAMA) system can drastically reduce the costs of property reassessments. Nevertheless, the effectiveness of these systems depends on sales and property data, scale and specialised human resources.
7. A transparent tax system combined with a convenient payment procedure and a fair appeal system can significantly improve compliance. This can be achieved by enabling the taxpayer to pay through multiple methods and by communicating in advance all steps involved in the tax collection and appeal process.

The prominent role of the property tax administration

Balancing administrative costs and operational effectiveness is a major challenge in administering recurrent taxes on immovable property

In OECD countries, costs related to the administration of recurrent taxes on immovable property vary widely and can be, as a share of property tax revenues, as high as 10% (Almy, 2014[1]) or as low as 1% or less (e.g. in some US states).[1] That is because these costs can be drastically reduced when more advanced methods are used such as Computer-Assisted mass Appraisal (CAMA). Despite this high share of costs in tax revenues, it is still challenging to reduce it further without affecting the operational effectiveness of the property tax system, which could defeat the purpose of having this levy in the first place. Differently than for most other taxes, recurrent taxes on immovable property are levied on notional property values, which requires expertise on the part of the assessors and a sound appeal system so taxpayers can contest the estimations. Thus, in summary, the collection of these taxes requires labour-intensive steps, as follows: 1) fiscal cadastre maintenance; 2) valuation of properties; 3) billing, revenue collection and enforcement; and 4) appeal.

As a result of this costly administration, officials might be tempted to reduce the costs of the property tax system through the postponement of revaluations (the most expensive task in the tax administration)[2] and by neglecting the necessary training that the staff requires to perform satisfactorily the necessary operational activities. In the short term, a reduction in costs might increase the net property tax revenues, but in the long run this effect will be reversed and, in addition, vertical and horizontal imbalances in the valuation and collection processes may arise. The latter is particularly damaging for a property tax administration since, in many cases, policy makers might face popular resistance to re-invest in a dysfunctional property tax system, further harming the perceived fairness of the system, in a vicious cycle that, in some cases, can contribute to the total discontinuation of the levy on immovable property (see Box 3.1 on the French case). Thus, balancing administrative costs and operational effectiveness is a major challenge of managing a property tax system.

The following conceptual model shows the administration role in revenue collection for this type of tax (Kelly, 2012[2]):

Eq 3.1 $\text{Tax Revenue} = (\text{Tax Base x Tax Rate}) \text{ x } (\text{Coverage Ratio x Valuation Ratio x Collection Ratio})$

1. The coverage ratio can be defined as a measure of the amount of taxable property that is registered within the government, compared to the total amount available (both registered and unregistered). As such, one of the key steps in a recurrent property tax reform is to identify the properties being taxed, in essence, preparing a cadastre.
2. The valuation ratio compares properties' value as appraised by the government with its real market value.
3. The collection ratio is the ratio of the tax revenue collected versus the total tax billed for a fiscal year. In order to guarantee a high collection ratio, both positive and negative incentives can be used.

The tax base and rate are defined in the tax design process while the coverage, valuation and collection ratios depend on the tax administration. As a result, much of the tax revenue that is collected from taxes on immovable property is a result of administrative efforts rather than policy choices.[3] The effects of all these ratios on the tax revenue are multiplicative and, thus, no ratio can be low for the system to be effective.

Some of these ratios are easier to increase than others. The priority in establishing a tax system with more coverage and higher liability for taxpayers is necessary before the valuation ratio becomes the focus, especially due to the difficulty and expense of determining an accurate market value of all taxable properties. Thus, in many cases, although the valuation ratio still holds its importance, focusing on the other administrative ratios will theoretically increase the tax revenue more significantly at the early stages of the introduction of the property tax.

In addition to revenue collection, other potential aims of the property tax system, such as those related to land use and equity, are unattainable in case the tax administration is inefficient (Kelly, 2012[2]). For instance, if fiscal cadastres do not cover some types of property (e.g. this happen, for instance, in the case of informal settlements),[4] if property valuation assessments are biased (i.e. they estimates values that are systematic higher for some types of property in comparison to others), the distributional and allocative effects of the property tax system are going to be different than the intended. Hence, it is absolutely crucial for a property tax system to be properly administered, otherwise the design features of the tax are going to be drastically hampered.

The second chapter of this report focused on the design features of recurrent taxes on immovable property. This third chapter focuses on the administration of recurrent tax on immovable property. The next three sections focus on the main steps described above: fiscal cadastre management, property valuation and administrative measures for collection of tax revenues. The last section of this chapter focuses on the delineation of responsibilities related to property tax administration across levels of governments.

Box 3.1. Lack of update of property and cadastral values in OECD countries and the discontinuation of the French residence tax

Administrative issues are common in property tax administration. Out of date property values have been identified as lowering SNG property tax revenues and generating distortions across a range of surveys including Austria, Belgium, Estonia, Finland, France, Germany, Greece, Indonesia, Mexico, Portugal and Sweden (Hagemann, 2018[3]; OECD, 2015[4]). In particular, the Austrian survey noted that "up-to-date valuation of real estate is a precondition for strengthening revenue-raising powers of municipalities on the basis of real estate taxes" (OECD, 2005[5]). In some cases, out of date values have been linked to infrequent updating of property registries. In Mexico, the lack of regular valuation kept taxed property values well below market value with data showing cadastral values 55% below market values in about half of the 32 states. In the Belgian case, a similar problem of infrequent valuations was observed. One solution discussed was devolving responsibility for updating the cadastre to the regions by creating regional cadastres. This would resolve the mismatch between the federal responsibility for updating valuations and the increases in regional revenues that would arise from the updates.

Partially due to the lack of update of property values, which is a pure administrative task, the French residence tax (*taxe d'habitation*) will be discontinued. As a result, governments will lose 3.4% of France's GDP in tax revenues. It is worth noting that other recurrent taxes levied on properties will continue to be applied in France such the land tax, the property tax on building, and the business real estate tax.

One of the reasons for the discontinuation of the *taxe d'habitation* regards the fact that it is considered and perceived as unfair. There are two sources of unfairness: horizontal and vertical. Horizontal unfairness is caused by the fact that 1) effective tax rates vary across municipalities for comparable properties; and 2) cadastral values have not been updated in four decades. Vertical unfairness is caused by the tax structure that taxes more, as a proportion of taxpayer income, low-income households. The repeal has been phased in over three years for a group of households (based on annual income thresholds) with the tax reduction amounting to 30% in 2018, 65% in 2019 and 100% in 2020. For the rest of households, the tax will be gradually removed between 2021 and 2023 for the remaining 20% of French.

Sources: Forman, Dougherty and Blöchliger (2020[6]), OECD (2020[7]) and OECD (2021[8]).

Fiscal cadastre

Fiscal cadastres usually have at a minimum all the information necessary to calculate tax obligations such as land use, taxpayers' characteristics, properties' features and geographical records

Fiscal cadastre is a term that usually refers to the repository in which the information about properties and taxpayers are stored for the purpose of managing a property tax system. This cadastre is distinct from the cadastre of property rights (the legal or juridical cadastre), which contains information about the persons who possess the right to property. Such distinction is usually justified on the ground that landlords should not believe that one of the costs of a title registration is the property taxation, which could, as a result, generate an incentive for them to avoid registration. Nevertheless, having both the fiscal and the legal cadastre merged in a multipurpose cadastre brings benefits – more notably a better data consistency and co-ordination across cadastres. Managing such multipurpose cadastres has become easier due to the computerisation of cadastral maps and records. Therefore, although historically different agencies were responsible for fiscal and legal cadastres, the number of countries with single multipurpose cadastres is growing – examples include Iceland, Northern Ireland and New Zealand (Almy, 2014[1]).

According to Enemark (2004[9]), these multipurpose cadastres have four main functions: land tenure (securing and transferring rights in land); land value (valuation and taxation of land and properties); land use (planning and control of the use of land and natural resources); and land development (utilities, infrastructure, construction planning, permits and implementation). It is worth noting that having a complete and multipurpose cadastre yield benefits beyond the collection of revenues through the tax system – fiscal cadastre can be a useful source of information for other policies and activities related to, for instance, urban planning, environment protection, transportation, housing and community amenities, recreation, social policies, mortgage finances (e.g. Denmark, Sweden), fire/home insurance (e.g. Iceland) and expropriation (e.g. Spain).[5]

Although it is not necessary to have all this information for tax purposes, it is crucial for a well-functioning fiscal cadastre to have the necessary information to calculate tax obligations – not only for the recurrent taxes on immovable property but also for other taxes such as transaction taxes, capital gain taxation (e.g. Finland), net wealth taxation (e.g. Austria and Switzerland), water use taxation (e.g. Netherlands) and imputing the income derived from owner-occupied property (e.g. Italy, Netherlands).[6] Thus, the necessary information that a fiscal cadastre should have depends greatly on its purpose and, in case of recurrent taxes on immovable property, on the valuation method employed. Below there is a non-exhaustive list of items that fiscal cadastres may contain (not all information presented below should, in principle, be collected by the managers of the fiscal cadastre – it can be gathered through an integration with other cadastral systems managed by other levels of government or agencies):

1. Land use (e.g. business, rural, industrial or residential), since property tax rates and incidence may depend on it;
2. In case of residential properties, personal information, since property taxes' obligations may vary depending on the characteristics of the taxpayer (i.e. deferrals, allowances and exemptions are, in some cases, based on characteristics of the taxpayer such as his/her income, family size, etc.);
3. In case of non-residential properties, business information, since taxes' obligations may also vary depending on the characteristics of the corporate taxpayer such as revenues, number of employees, business sector, among others;
4. General property information that are useful for estimating a property's value, such as, among others, the year of construction, size, date and value of the last purchases, state of the building, number of rooms, etc.;
5. Geographical records that clearly delineate properties' boundaries and locate them with precision – agencies are increasingly using computerised Geographic Information System (GIS) and oblique aerial photographs of buildings to capture the current state of the building through the detection of physical changes (UN Habitat, 2013[10]);
6. Records of tax obligations and benefits, such as exemptions, deferrals and allowances.

Some types of property, such as public rights-of-way and routes of transportation (waterways, state-owned railroads, streets and roads), are often excluded from cadastres on grounds of administrative convenience (Almy, 2013[11]). That is, they are not considered a taxable asset since the administrative costs to register and value these types of property might exceed the tax revenues that stems from them. In such cases, policy makers decide to exchange cadastre completeness and horizontal equity for administrative convenience.

Up-front investments to keep records updated and accurate are worthwhile since they increase property tax revenues through a higher property coverage and taxpayer compliance

An effective fiscal cadastre increases property taxes revenues through both a higher coverage ratio and collection ratio (i.e. due to increased compliance), which tend to justify the need for a substantial up-front investment to have an accurate and complete cadastre. In other words, investments in fiscal cadastre management may bring positive returns in terms of tax revenues. In many cases, however, local governments don't have the necessary resources to make these investments, leading to a dysfunctional cadastre. In such cases, horizontal or vertical co-ordination might fill this gap (see Box 3.2 for Brazil's and Mexico's cases).

It is worth noting that although there is some overlap between the process of updating fiscal cadastres and the process of re-valuing properties, they are not the same activity. The former refers to keeping the property and taxpayer information updated, potentially increasing the number of properties to be appraised whereas the latter usually refers only to update of the information that is used to reassess properties' values. Most developed nations, when improving their property tax system, focus more on the update of the values of the property, since they usually have a high coverage ratio, meaning that their records already capture most properties. Nevertheless, this is not the case for some developing countries, which usually struggle to have a complete record of the taxable properties. More precisely, OECD countries have coverage ratios close to 100%, while developing and transitional countries can have ratios of only 40-60% (Kelly, 2012[2]). Therefore, collection-led property tax reforms may generate even more tax revenues for developing nations (or any nation with a low coverage ratio) in comparison to valuation-led reforms, although the latter is substantially more common worldwide.

The registration of informal settlements may generate more tax revenues and also be used as a policy tool to increase the access of poor dwellers to private and public services

Regarding cadastre coverage, one of the main problems in developing countries regards informal settlements, which are particularly challenging to register. This challenge is especially important for China, since its rapid urbanisation has created a number of houses with limited property rights,[7] normally situated on residual rural construction land that has been developed by rural collectives to meet the demand for low-cost housing (World Bank/Development Research Center of the State Council, the People's Republic of China, 2014[12]).

A Municipality in Brazil (Belo Horizonte) was able to alleviate this problem by carrying out field inspection and registering informal settlements, while giving possession certificates for tax purposes – this policy has been very well received amongst the benefiting communities, since these certificates have been the only legal document of their properties available to them, while the property tax charged has been very low or they are exempted (Junior, 2017[13]).

Smolka and De Cesare (2012[14]) argued that even if the property tax revenues from informal settlements are small, they may generate significant benefits to the community. First, they contribute to the creation of a fiscal culture. Second, they increase the completeness of the fiscal cadastre, which, as mentioned previously, is used for other purposes ranging from private activities such as mortgages and insurance to policy targeting. Third, the payment of property taxes may legitimise dwellers' right to use public services, potentially creating incentives for public officials to invest in urban improvements in the area. Fourth and lastly, access to credit of taxpayers might be facilitated since they have a property tax certificate.

Smolka and De Cesare (2012[14]) highlighted three reasons that might make it easier to register informal settlements. First, the benefits mentioned in the previous paragraph may help authorities to map these informal houses since dwellers might self-report their informal settlements to enjoy these benefits. Second, informal settlements tend to have vibrant property markets and, thus, valuation of properties might be feasible using similar methods to formal markets. Third, when only legal properties are taxed, potential taxpayers might be reluctant to regularise their properties in order to avoid tax obligations. In this light, the presence of informality might reduce the completeness of cadastre system only in case the cadastre policy neglects the fact that these informal settlements can actually be registered for tax purposes.

Box 3.2. Role of inter-governmental co-operation in cadastre management in Brazil and Mexico

Brazil is in a unique position with regard to recurrent taxes on urban property. Local governments have almost full autonomy to design their own tax systems with minimum interference of upper levels of government. From tax rates, exemption, reliefs and bases to tax administration matters, local governments are almost fully autonomous to design and manage their property tax systems. In a country with 5 570 municipalities (local governments), the 5th largest territory in the world, and substantial inequality within and across regions, Brazil's property tax systems work as a laboratory of practices that are employed under these different circumstances and environments.

Brazil's urban property tax (IPTU) is defined by municipal legislation and is applied to all taxable properties in each municipal urban area. It accounts for, roughly, 0.48% of GDP and, on average, 1.2% of local government's current revenues. Nevertheless, this aggregated number masks the fact that its distribution across local governments is rather unequal: although 60% of the Brazilian GDP is concentrated in 122 local governments, 60% of the urban property tax revenues is concentrated only in 22 local governments. This can be partially explained by asymmetries in administrative capacity. In Brazil, about 70% of municipalities have less than 20 000 people, and thus, municipalities may lack the scale to invest in technologies and human resources. For instance, only 38% of smaller local governments employed GIS technologies against 90% of capitals and local governments in metropolitan areas. Furthermore, in numerous small local governments, fiscal cadastres are not even digital. To make matters worse, in most cases all levels of government (federal, state and municipal/local) manage their own registers in an uncoordinated and unintegrated manner.

In order to overcome this problem, inter-governmental agreements are performed by local governments both with upper levels of government (vertical) or between themselves (horizontal). One of the most important vertical co-ordination arrangements is a programme for supporting local administrative capacity – PMAT (Modernization of Tax Administration Programme) – that was established in 1997 and has been implemented by the federal state-owned BNDES (Brazilian National Economic Development Bank). The programme consists of the provision of subsidised loans to local governments to fund projects aimed at tax modernisation. These projects are assessed and selected by the BNDES, which has the technical capability to aid local governments in designing and implementing the project. The flagship project of this programme involves fiscal cadastre update through digital mapping and, so far, it has been rather successful – a cross-section analysis revealed that own tax revenues of local governments that joined the programme was 30% higher than in municipalities that did not, and this difference reached nearly 100% for local governments that joined it more than nine years ago. The programme was also considered cost-effective since an average of one Brazilian Reais loan led to an extra of 1.8 Brazilian Reais of tax revenues. Despite this success, the coverage of the programme in terms of the number of local governments that joined the programme was unfortunately low. Since the programme requires debt clearance certificates, provision of collateral guarantees and credit approval under the Federal Senate and Municipal Councils, 89% of all local governments in Brazil were not eligible for joining the programme.

Aside from this programme that brings central support to local governments, some municipalities in Brazil also collaborate horizontally. Horizontal co-operation mechanisms are regulated by a Federal Law (No 11 107 of 2005) that defines requirements for any inter-municipal co-operation (not only for tax administration purposes). The co-operation is required to be formalised as a legal, private, or public entity registered under a notary instituted by a contract and approved by municipal councils. This Law requires, among others, that all members involved, its objective, execution times, mechanism of functioning, and share of each municipal government contribution must be defined in the agreement. This instrument has been widely used in Brazil and, in case of tax administration, there are cases in which the agreement encompasses a shared computerised register, infrastructure and human resources.

In **Mexico,** cadastre management is under the responsibility of state or local governments. Cadastral offices are in charge of functions related to the description of real estate such as the identification, location, demarcation, registration, mapping, valuation and update of cadastral values of real estates located within the territorial jurisdiction of the municipality.

Cadastral offices have autonomy in gathering and setting standards for this information and, as a result, there is a high level of complexity and variety in cadastral managing practices across the country. The main discrepancies between information contained in the cadastres derive from: 1) changes in the street names; 2) error measurements (i.e. related to physical references or calibration of instruments); 3) abbreviations used in names and surnames; 4) use of private contracts for transfer of ownership; and 5) constructions not declared to the municipal authority.

In order to set standards and to aid subnational governments in managing their cadastres, the federal government created the Programme for the Modernization of Public Property Registries and Cadastres (PMRPPC), which aims to improve cadastral administration institutions across the country through mainly modernisation of the cadastres and standardisation of processes. The PMRPPC offers Mexican subnational governments technical and financial support to improve the performance of these institutions. The programme includes the evaluation of robust and measurable parameters through the Comprehensive Model of the Public Registry of the Property and the Optimal Cadastre Model, in addition to promoting an integrated vision of cadastres.

In order to benefit from the programme, subnational entities develop a project to modernise their Public Property Registries complying with PMRPPC's proposed methodology from PMRPPC and these projects compete to obtain resources.

The methodology covers, among others:

1. *Professionalisation of the registry function*: Measures professional specialisation and constant training of registrars, operational and administrative officials in legal, administrative and technological concepts.
2. *Modernisation*: The use of paper, autograph signatures and conventional stamps should be eliminated and replaced by electronic signatures and digital stamps, which allows the use of databases as a means to guarantee the operations registered in them (instead of physical documents).
3. *Legal framework*: This component measures the adaptations to various legal systems in order to support the processes contemplated in the project, clarify attributions and responsibilities of the registry officials, and grant full legal validity to all electronic documents issued by the cadastral offices.
4. *Registry processes*: This component evaluates the processes carried out by cadastral offices, in light of a set of pre-established standards that are in accordance with the principles delineated in the legal framework.
5. *Institutional policies*: Evaluates the adequacy of cadastral offices institutional policies. Among the main policies are budget self-sufficiency, the promotion of registration culture, and the creation of cadastral-registry institutes with legal personality and own assets.
6. *Management and documentary collection*: Measures the adequate preservation, physical security and inviolability of the cadastre. Information technologies to digitise the collections and reforms to move from physical libraries to digital galleries are incentivised, which reduces the risk of illegal book manipulation.
7. *Participation and link with other sectors*: Analyses the existing degree of co-ordination between the cadastral institutions and various institutions related to the real estate management. Elements that are measured relate to the integration of information and the concentration of real estate related activities in a single institution. In addition, it analyses the relationships with other

relevant actors, such as notaries and the financial sector.

8. *Performance indicators*: This component assesses the operation and quality of services provided according to international standards, using indicators related to process efficiency, generation of operational statistics and agility of response.

The OECD worked along with officials from multiple levels of the Mexican government and enumerated four main elements that were crucial for an effective modernisation in cadastral management in Mexico. First, the existence of leadership and political support at the highest level of government and hierarchy, which was translated, among others, in the availability of financial resources. Second, inclusion of the staff that works directly with cadastral management in the modernisation process so as to create a shared vision and a sense of membership, both of which contributed to make the improvements robust and permanent. Third, the design of transparent and planned actions, with well delineated and achievable objectives. Fourth, the use of collaboration agreements between states and municipalities, which combined resources and experiences.

As a result of these modernisation programmes, some municipalities experienced significant improvements on their cadastral management. For instance, it is estimated that programmes funded by the National Bank of Public Works and Services (*Banobras*), which benefits municipalities with a minimum of 10 000 cadastral accounts, achieved a 30% average increase in property tax collection for the benefited municipalities. Mexico also used funding from other banks such as the Interamerican Development Bank (BID).

Sources: Junior (2017[13]) and Junior (2018[15]) for the Brazilian case, OECD (2012[16]) and information provided by Mexican authorities.

Property valuation

A non-functional valuation system may generate unfair assessments and horizontal inequities that may undermine the good properties of recurrent taxes on immovable property

Property valuation is considered to be among the costliest activity in property tax administration and is usually the task to which most attention is devoted. Without a proper valuation system, recurrent taxes on immovable property fail to have the expected outcome. A well-designed tax rate and base system may fail to have their intended outcome in case properties are assessed in an unfair and inequitable manner. In other words, even if nominal rates are identical for all types of property, effective rates can differ by property type if property valuation rules differ by type of property, causing horizontal inequalities. Moreover, the buoyancy of recurrent property taxes can only be sustained in a fair manner over time through frequented revaluations. Nonetheless, revaluations that lead to a significant increase in tax obligations are very unpopular and, thus, sometimes blocked politically. As a result, although a well-functioning property valuation process is crucial for the success of property tax reforms, the implementation of such a system is far from trivial and sometimes may suffer political resistance.

Good practices with regard to property valuation are described below – based on Rosengard (2012[17]), Franzsen and McCluskey (2012[18]) and Almy (2014[1]):

- All things being equal, it is generally preferred to align the relative value of properties with their “true” market values. In that manner horizontal and vertical inequities are minimised, improving the credibility of the tax system in the eyes of the taxpayers, which can increase compliance and reduce resistance for future investments on the property tax system.

- It is better to be approximately right than precisely wrong. It is worth highlighting that the purpose of property valuation is to calculate a tax levy and not to purchase a property and, thus, approximations are acceptable.
- It makes more financial sense to spend most of the administrative efforts on the types of properties that generate more tax revenues. The bulk of property tax revenues usually come from one or two types of properties. By trying to assess precisely the value of all properties, the valuation costs may skyrocket, damaging the net revenue raising capacity of the recurrent property tax.
- The tax administration should, when possible, avoid abrupt tax hikes from one year to another even in case property values did increase.[8] Since property values are based on the state of the real estate market, they might not be directly related to taxpayers' income. Therefore, abrupt increases on tax obligations might create liquidity problems. Such abrupt movements can be alleviated through frequent revaluations, indexation or linear increase of property values during the period in between property appraisals.

Capital values are by and large the most-used property value basis for recurrent taxes on immovable property in developed countries for numerous reasons: enough sales data, capital values can be used as a basis for other taxes and it is a buoyant tax base

The first step in property valuation refers to the definition of property value basis. Property values can only be estimated, and countries employ different measures of value. The three most common approaches in determining property values are the capital value,[9] the annual value and the notional value (i.e. usually based on properties' features such as area, region, etc.). The first refers to the net present value of future rents, and thus, in principle aims to estimate the market price of a property assuming a perfect market. The second, on the other hand, uses only a single year's rental value as a proxy for the value of the property. The third is less employed and regards the notional value, which aims at estimating a value that can be used in an adequate manner to calculate tax obligations – it may not be consistent with capital or rental values. In all cases the tax rate is multiplied by the value estimated and, as a result, the definition of the tax rate is heavily dependent on the definition of the tax basis for property values. Table 3.1, below, summarises the main advantages and disadvantages of each value basis.

Table 3.1. Features of property value basis

Basis	Advantage	Disadvantage
Annual rental values	• Particularly efficient when there is a vibrant rental market and, in this situation, mass appraisal can be used for similar properties • Rental payment is a better relative measure of the benefits a taxpayer receives in the course of a fiscal year than a property's capital value	• Vacant and owner-occupied properties may create difficulties in estimating rental values • Rental values are usually not consistent with the values used in the computation of other capital taxes
Capital values	• Particularly efficient when there is a vibrant property market, from which sufficient evidence of market prices can be obtained • This value basis is shared with other taxes such as capital, inheritance and transaction taxes, leading to economies of scope for tax departments • Capital values are buoyant when values are updated frequently.	• Depends on the availability of accurate data • Costly to implement in small scale • Requires relatively high level of expertise
Area based values	• Simple to administer since it requires significantly less data • Can be used regardless of market activity	• Can be unfair since desirable/high-end properties may pay the same or less amount of taxes than other properties • Tend to be less buoyant than value-based systems unless there are frequent changes to tax rates and adjustments that should reflect the real estate market

Source: Based on Franzsen and McCluskey (2012[18]) and Almy (2014[1]).

By and large capital values are the most used value basis for recurrent taxes on immovable properties. Figure 3.1, below, reveals that in 21 out of 39 countries capital values are the sole value basis for recurrent taxes on immovable property. In 12 countries multiple value basis are used while only in 3 countries an area basis and annual value basis are used alone. One potential explanation for this prominence of capital value basis is that some of the benefits from property taxation can only be reaped when the tax base is value-based. Value-based tax bases: 1) have a stronger link to taxpayers' income, enhancing progressivity; 2) are more sensitive to the level of economic development, which greatly affects the revenue-raising capacity of the tax in the long run, without resorting to unpopular increases in tax rates; 3) can be more effectively used as a tool to reduce the volatility of house prices since the higher the volatility the higher its effect on property values; 4) are less distortionary and more equitable than area-based taxes (Thomas, 2021[19]); and 5) are also used as a tax base for other taxes such as capital, inheritance and transaction taxes, leading to economies of scope for tax departments.

Despite these benefits, capital value basis can only be effectively employed when real estate markets are sufficiently well developed because capital values are commonly estimated using data on recent property transactions. As real estate markets have developed over a number of decades, OECD and partner countries have been able to gradually shift toward capital value basis for their recurrent taxes on immovable property (Almy, 2014[1]).

Figure 3.1 Value basis of immovable property taxes in OECD and partner countries

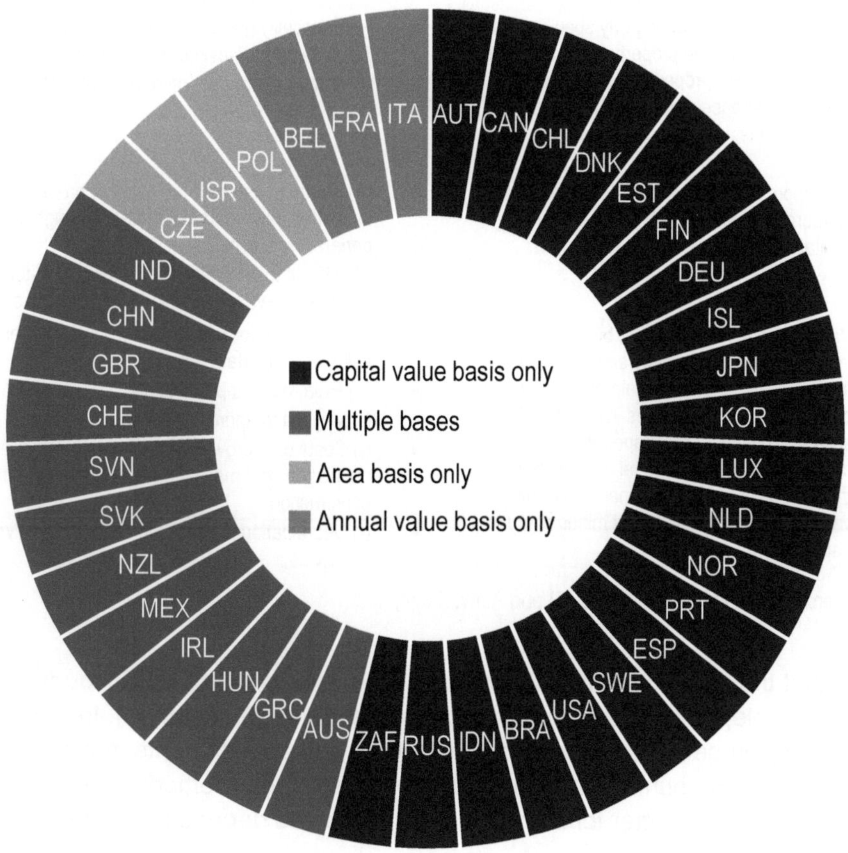

Source: Adapted based on Almy (2014[1]).

Sales comparison is the most used method to estimate property values across OECD countries, nevertheless other methods might be particularly useful for some types of properties for which there is not enough sales data available

The second step in designing a property valuation system is the definition of the method employed to estimate properties' value. The three most common valuation approaches are sales (or rent) comparisons, income capitalisation and cost approach. In general, the approach selected usually depends on the type of property being appraised. The income approach is especially employed for expensive income-producing properties, such as office buildings, hotels and retail malls, for which it is less challenging to forecast a property's future cash flows. Properties for which there is a substantial amount of data on sales, such as small offices, retail, and most residential properties, are commonly appraised through the sales comparison approach. Lastly, specific properties for which there is almost no sales or no easy way to forecast their income, such as factories, industrial properties, and transport infrastructure, are commonly valued using the cost approach. The rule of thumb is that for the cases in which there is sales data available, the preferred approach is sales comparisons, since it directly estimates the capital value (when, as in most cases, the capital value basis is used). The Table 3.2, below, summarises the main features of these three approaches.

Table 3.2. Features of property valuation approaches

Method	Description	Advantages and Disadvantages
Sales comparisons	Uses recent sales and property specific data in order to compare the property being appraised with other similar properties, adjusting for property differences related to, among others, improvements, location, size, property type, etc.	• (+) Especially good for mass appraisals • (+) Suitable for most common types of properties • (-) Heavily dependent on data availability
Income capitalisation	This approach estimates the net present value of future incomes through either a direct capitalisation or a discounted cash flow.	• (+) Useful to estimate the value of properties for which there is almost no sales data but there is enough data on its revenue generation activity • (-) Difficult to apply since involves a long-term cash flow forecast and cash flows are volatile in times of crisis
Cost	Values both the land and the building (i.e. improvement) of a property separately, and then combines them to obtain an estimated property value. Land values involves factors such as location, area, shape, physical characteristics, and potential improvements that would sell in the open market. Building value is the reproduction cost minus accrued depreciation.	• (+) Can be employed in cases for which there is no comparable sales or rental data • (+) Relatively simple to apply • (-) May fail to approximate market values • (-) Costs of improvements change over time and, thus, the replication cost may differ significantly from the actual cost of the construction • (-) Depreciation is difficult to assess objectively

Source: Adapted from Franzsen and McCluskey (2012[18]) and Almy, (2014[1]).

Figure 3.2 reveals that the sale comparison method is the most used in OECD countries (23 out of 24 of the countries in the sample, being the sole approach employed in 13 countries). Ireland, which is the sole exception, relies heavily on self-assessment (for the role of self-assessments in property valuation check Box 3.3). Furthermore, in ten countries a combination of these three methods is employed, which reflects the fact that some methods are better for some types of properties depending on their sale and rental data availability.

Figure 3.2 Valuation approaches employed by countries

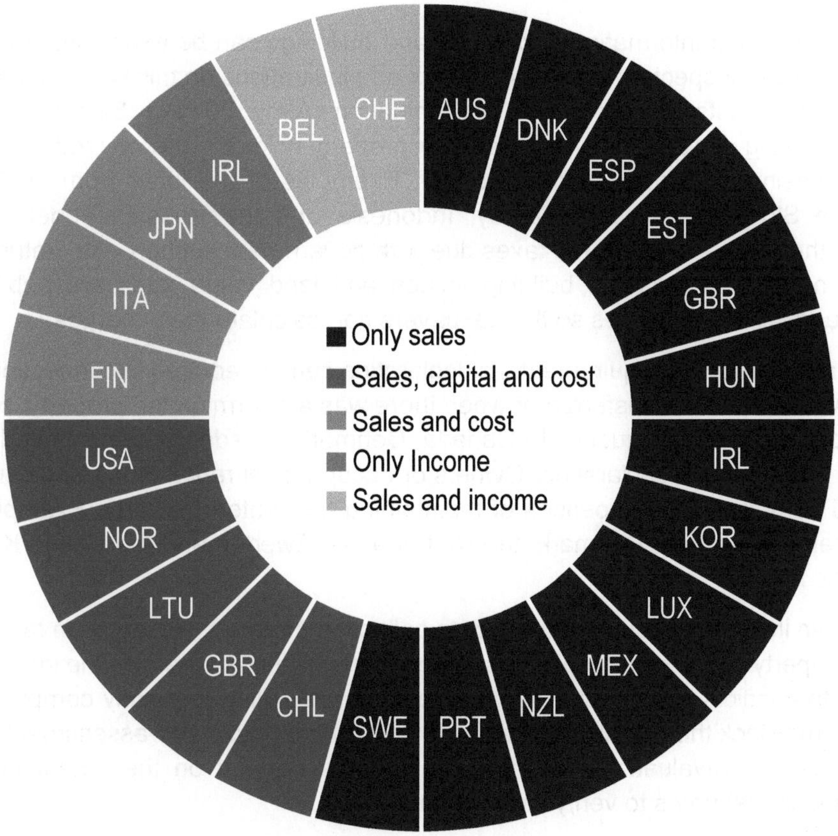

Source: Responses from OECD Survey on Recurrent Taxes on Immovable Property

It is worth highlighting that there are also other less employed valuation methods such as property value banding, used, for instance, in the United Kingdom and Ireland (Slack and Bird, 2014[20]). The general idea is to classify properties into different categories (in general from five to a dozen categories) that represent their value. As a result, the valuation task is heavily simplified at the cost of precision. The discrete nature of this system may create unfair valuations, especially to taxpayers located in a boundary of a band.

Another consideration regards taxable properties that are not being used in a manner that maximises their market values. In many situations, restrictions on use imposed under regulatory regimes (including zoning) influence market values, and any property valuation method can take these restrictions into account in determining assessed values (for tax purposes). For instance, buildings of architectural or historic interest have limited uses other than their existing use, but the site may well have a high value due to the location of the property (Franzsen and McCluskey, 2012[18]). Another example regards land that can only be used for agricultural uses, especially when this land is located near or in metropolitan areas. In this case, the basis for determining assessed value is the use value of the land (e.g. New Zealand employs this approach for agricultural land).

Box 3.3. The role of self-assessments in property valuation

Collecting and maintaining information about land and buildings can be expensive. In some countries (e.g. the United States), inspectors from property tax administrations do this work. Such work accounts for about 75% of the costs of assessment and valuation (Almy, 2014[1]). Elsewhere, taxpayers are required to help by filing declarations that detail their property holdings, thereby reducing administrative costs (while increasing their compliance burdens). Examples of the latter from OECD and partner countries include Slovenia, Sweden, Turkey, Indonesia and the Russian Federation. In Turkey, taxpayers figure their valuations and the taxes due with government support – tax return forms contain the information needed to calculate building values and land value rates are published in books available in tax administration offices so that taxpayers can calculate their charges.

In addition to general reporting requirements, a declaration can be required in connection with an event, such as when ownership was transferred or when there was a reform on the property; or only when the tax administration or cadastre requests. In Canada, Denmark, Sweden and the United States, buyers can be required to file a sales declaration. Owners or occupants of rental properties can be required to report rents and sometimes the expenses of maintaining the rented property. Examples of countries with such requirements include Denmark, the Netherlands, Sweden and the United Kingdom (for the Uniform Business Rate).

Several factors can influence decisions about data collection methods. Reliance on taxpayers to gather information on property values can reduce costs. Nonetheless, the accuracy of the information provided can be low due to conflicts of interest. Even if taxpayers are willing to supply complete and accurate information, they may lack the technical expertise to do so. As a result, self-assessments tend to reduce the budgetary costs of revaluations, but their net effects depend on the extent to which the tax administration needs resources to verify assessments.

Source: Almy (2014[1]).

Frequent revaluations are crucial as indexing leads to unfair assessments in longer term

One of the main difficulties in property tax management is to keep values updated. In many of the OECD reviewed surveys, severely out-of-date assessed property values are highlighted as a serious obstacle to boosting revenues from property taxes. These include Estonia, Finland, France, Germany, Greece, Indonesia, Mexico, Portugal and Sweden (Hagemann, 2018[3]). Revaluations tend to be not only expensive, but also unpopular. When a country doesn't update property values for a couple of years or decades, there often is substantial popular resistance against revaluations since they may increase abruptly and significantly tax obligations. Thus, the more property values are outdated, the more opposition there is to re-valuate them. Another problem regards the fact that when property valuations are defined by law (i.e. a law is required to trigger a revaluation process), the popular resistance can be especially efficient to block revaluations since in this case the valuation process depends on a political rather than technical decision. Sometimes even when legislation specifies a revaluation schedule, revaluations are not performed.

When property values are not reassessed frequently, recurrent property tax revenues may not increase with economic activity. That is, the increase in tax revenues resulting from an increase in cadastral values caused by appraisals will not occur. Nevertheless, it is possible to not reassess property values and still maintain some buoyancy. There are two commonly employed solutions, the first one is indexing. Indexing refers to the update of property values by some index or factor, such as the inflation rate or other price index more related to property prices. In that manner, cadastral values are going to increase in line with an index, potentially making tax revenues buoyant in case this index is correlated with economic activity. A second solution is to increase tax rates. When tax rates increase in line with the economic activity, tax revenues will follow.

It is worth noting that these two solutions increase buoyancy at the cost of fairness because they fail to capture the asymmetrical growth in property values and, thus, if used extensively without revaluations, they will create distortions. For instance, in many jurisdictions, especially cities, property values rise rapidly in some areas (e.g. due to gentrification) and stagnate or even decline in others. Without re-evaluation, the effective tax rates of households in locations where values appreciate would be smaller than the relative effective rates of households in areas with stagnating values. If, as is often the case, higher income households live in value-appreciating areas, the net result is an increase in the tax regressivity. As a result, in the long run, indexing and uniform increases in tax rates can have a similar distortionary effect as the non-revaluation of properties.

Figure 3.3 depicts the methods used to update property values across OECD countries. In most cases (19 out of 24), revaluations are used alone. In three countries (Spain, Finland and Norway) revaluation and indexing are used jointly. In five countries only indexing is used. Although, in principle, most countries rely on revaluations of property to keep the values current, in some cases properties are not re-valued for decades. Belgium, for instance, plans to re-value properties once every ten years but the last valuation was in 1975. In Germany, the last valuation occurred in the first half of the last century. In the United Kingdom, bands for residential property were established and have not been changed since 1991. The last valuation in Estonia was in 2001.

Figure 3.3 Method used to update property values

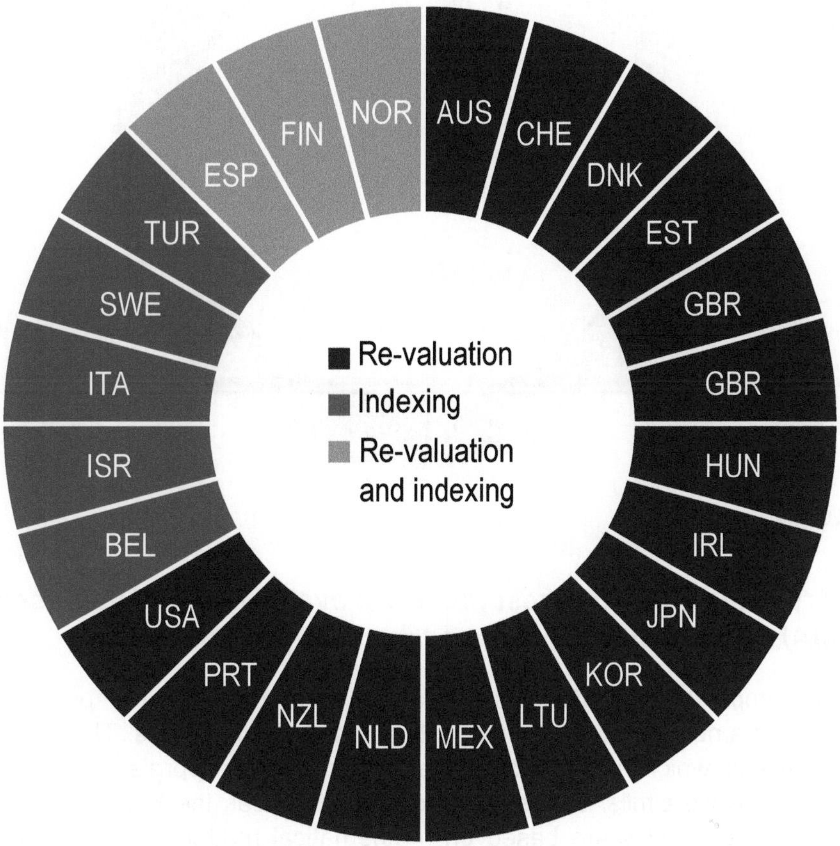

Source: Responses from OECD Survey on Recurrent Taxes on Immovable Property.

In a number of countries, though, properties are updated frequently. In Hungary, Korea, Mexico, Netherlands they occur every year; in Australia, Japan, New Zealand and Portugal every three years; in Chile every four years; Lithuania every five years; in Norway as the general rule every 10 years but varies (main residence valued every year if valued according to a model based on market value). Most of these countries follow IAAO (2017[21]) guidelines that recommend that property characteristics should be reviewed and updated at least every four to six years. The IAAO (2017[21]) suggest three ways to achieve this goal: 1) Re-inspection of all properties at periodic intervals; 2) Re-inspection of properties on a cyclical basis (e.g. one-fourth or one-sixth each year); and 3) Re-inspection of properties on a priority basis as indicated by ratio studies or other considerations while still ensuring that all properties are examined at least every sixth year.

In the United States, the frequency of reassessments depends on the state and, in some cases, on local governments. Higginbottom (2010[22]) revealed that most states follow IAAOs recommendations and reassess properties at least once every six years. More precisely, 26 states reassess property values at least once every six years[10] while 10 states do it annually. Two notable exceptions are the state of New York and California – they reassess properties only when new improvements are made or ownership is changed, respectively. Figure 3.4, below, summarises the minimum requirements for frequency of property reassessment imposed by American states – see Higginbottom (2010[22]) for details.

Figure 3.4 Frequency of reassessments in the United States

Source: Higginbottom (2010[22]).

When high-quality data and human resources are available, computer assisted mass appraisals (CAMA) can significantly reduce the costs of valuations

In many countries, computer assisted mass appraisals have changed the process of property re-appraisals, leading to, in a number of cases, a substantial reduction in costs. The term "mass appraisal" refers to the procedure in which a group of properties are jointly appraised, following standardising procedures and testing. While similar to a single property appraisal, the key difference is its scale and methods. Usually, mass appraisals are based on mathematical modelling (most commonly a multiple regression analysis).

Due to its heavy data reliant nature, mass appraisals are better implemented when aided by computer assisted valuation techniques, which is then referred to as CAMA or automated valuation model (AVM). The International Association of Assessing Officers (2018[23]) defines AVM as follows:

> *"A mathematically based computer software program that market analysts use to produce an estimate of market value based on market analysis of location, market conditions and real estate characteristics from information that was previously and separately collected. The distinguishing feature of an AVM is that it is a market appraisal produced through mathematical modelling. Credibility of an AVM is dependent on the data used and the skills of the modeller producing the AVM. AVMs should be developed by appropriately qualified market analysts, e.g. appraisers/valuers, who use statistically based applications to analyse data and select the best simulation of market activity for the analysis of location, market conditions and property characteristics from previously collected data. AVMs are designed to generate value estimates for properties at specified points in time (retrospective or prospective dates as required by client)."*

In order to set up a mass valuation system many steps are required. The International Association of Assessing Officers (2018[23]) suggests the following nine steps: creation of a scope of work, identification and acquisition of property data, exploratory data analysis, stratification, determination of data representativeness, model specification and feature selection, model calibration, quality assurance and model application and value review. Among these nine steps, two steps are highlighted here. First, regarding data gathering, it is worth noting that a CAMA system requires a substantial amount of high-quality property data (i.e. physical attributes of the property), locational data (i.e. market demographics, traffic, land-use policies and other geographic factors), and market data (i.e. sales, income and replacement cost information).[11] It is crucial that the data represents all types of properties whose values are being modelled. In some cases, this data can be obtained in the private sector. A second point that is worth highlighting is the quality assurance. The performance of the model should be compared with a minimum set of standards regarding accuracy and uniformity. That is, it is important for modelers to check whether the values given by the model to comparable properties are similar and whether the error terms are correlated with property values.

CAMA systems perform even better when integrated with a Geographic Information System (GIS), which is used for input, storage, processing and retrieval of spatial data. The integration of both is particularly valuable because the location of a property and the properties in its vicinity are important elements of a property price. Combining GIS with CAMA might significantly increase efficiency and reduce staff costs (see Box 3.4 for an example of a well-functioning CAMA system integrated with a GIS in China). According to Almy (2014[1]), the cost of operating a system which uses CAMA (in combination with GIS) is about EUR 20 (based on experience in Canada, Netherlands and the United States) compared to EUR 50 per property of a comprehensive revaluation, which is about one-tenth of the cost of an appraisal of a house for mortgage purposes.

Mass appraisal has a lot of benefits (McCluskey et al., 2013[24]): 1) valuates properties in a standardised and accurate way; 2) can provide a large number of valuations in a short scope of time; and 3) is a system that gets better accuracy and consistency over time (if given proper attention). Despite these benefits, mass appraisal is not recommended for all governments due to constraints and limitations. Mass appraisals require staff with technical expertise and high-quality data on property features, location and transactions. The modelling maxim "garbage in, garbage out" also applies to CAMA – when the data has poor quality, so the model outcomes. Problems in the model may generate mass horizontal (in case similar properties are valued differently) or vertical (in case high end values are valued as a lower percentage of the "true" market value than low end properties) inequities. The number of properties analysed should be sufficient to cover the up-front investment necessary to design a CAMA – at least in the longer term. In this light, similarly to the discussion on fiscal cadastre, local governments with limited capacity can make co-operative arrangements with other governments in order to fund a proper CAMA system[12] (see Box 3.8).

Almy (2014[1]) raised another (solvable) issue with mass valuation systems: they might be too complex to explain to the average taxpayer. The author suggested two approaches to communicate better model outcomes to taxpayers: 1) strive for simpler models that can be presented with ease, highlighting how features of their properties affect the assessed value; and 2) convert multivariate models into a series of tables that display prices per unit of area for different classes of properties. Although not trivial, some countries have successfully implemented and communicated model outcomes to taxpayers, and they have a small appeal rate. For instance, the Netherlands made models public and taxpayers can request a valuation report that includes valuation data for several comparable properties (see more on the Dutch case in Box 3.9, at the end of this chapter).

Box 3.4. Shenzhen's CAMA

Shenzhen is a southern Chinese city that has more than 12 million inhabitants. In 2003, the Chinese central government selected six cities to serve as pilots in an experiment aimed at appraising properties, with Shenzhen being one of these six cities. In collaboration with the Lincoln Institute of Land Policy, the Shenzhen Assessment Centre—a municipal statutory agency that was established to assist the collection of taxes on real estate sales and transactions—has developed a state-of-the-art CAMA system.

After fifteen years of progress, Shenzhen's CAMA is able to valuate properties using numerous indicators such as location, number of rooms, floor space, recent market prices, among others. The impact of the location on the price considers the value of being near to specific valuable services providers, such as schools and transport infrastructure, such as a metro station. In addition, Shenzhen's CAMA system models properties in three dimensions, which allows the valuation process to consider elements such as a property's view and the amount of sunlight it gets. Furthermore, the valuation assessment also encompasses the effects from noise on a property's value. For instance, a property facing busy traffic is estimated to have a lower value than a property facing a quiet street, all other things being equal. All these characteristics put together can amount to a 20% difference in value between two units in the same building.

This technology is not common in most countries or cities. Although there are no recurrent taxes on residential properties in Shenzhen, the system is being used to estimate values for the property transaction taxes. The number of properties valued amounted to 10 million, of which only 27 106 appraisals were challenged and only 282 assessments had to be readjusted (as of January 2017).

Despite this impressive system, Shenzhen's CAMA faces numerous challenges. The privatisation of urban housing is recent in China – it started in the late 1990s. As a result, the market is not as dynamic as in many cities in OECD countries that have had private markets for centuries, which forces the system to operate with a relatively limited amount of data. As discussed throughout this report, one of the main if not the key challenge of having an effective CAMA system is data availability. Furthermore, since the data that the system is based upon is also used to calculate transaction tax obligations, taxpayers tend to report artificially small values for their transactions in a manner to avoid taxes. The high rate of growth of the city is also an obstacle. As long as Shenzhen continues to grow at such a rapid pace, the fiscal cadastre administration will face an immense challenge to keep track of all the new buildings and properties. These challenges are caused by characteristics that most Chinese cities have in common. Nevertheless, Shenzhen's CAMA system and its fiscal cadastre management can be used as a benchmark for other Chinese cities.

Source: Nunlist (2017[25]).

Collection and appeal systems

Transparency and convenience are two important elements in collection and appeal systems that tend to maximise taxpayer compliance and, as a result, tax revenues

After having the taxable properties registered in a cadastre along with an estimation of their values, the third and last step is to effectively collect tax revenues, giving room for taxpayers to contest the assessed value of their property, in case they consider it to be inaccurate. These activities are the ones that determine the collection ratio, which is the ratio of the tax revenue collected versus the total tax billed for a fiscal year. The collection process encompasses mainly four main activities: 1) assessment of tax liability for each taxable property; 2) proper delivery/billing and accounting of tax obligations; 3) reinforced taxpayer compliance; and 4) administration of appeals.

For tax revenue maximisation, all these activities should be performed in a manner that taxpayer compliance is maximised. For such, the following set of principles are generally followed – based on Kelly (2012[2]):

1. The process should be transparent. Ideally timely information should be available for taxpayers, so the process is as predictable as possible;
2. Procedures should be as seamless and convenient as possible to minimise governmental and compliance costs;
3. Computer assistance and automation can be used to treat taxpayers in an equitable and fair manner and to minimise employee workload and costs; and
4. Ideally taxpayers should be previously educated on the tax policies and payment process – fiscal culture is considered an important aspect for increasing voluntary compliance.

An essential component of a good property tax system is an accessible and responsive appeal system

In regard to the appeal system, differently than other taxes, the taxable value of property taxes is notional – that is, exists only in theory and, thus, should be estimated. It contrasts heavily with, for instance, a transaction tax in which the value of the property is an element of the transaction. Therefore, the tax authority and taxpayers might disagree with regard to estimated property value and appeals are key to ensure a balance between them. In order to be as fair as possible, appeals usually are judged by multiple institutions/committees in a hierarchical structure. Initially appeals are head by assessors, then by committees (sometimes partially composed by ordinary citizens) and, lastly, by specialised tribunals/courts (Almy, 2013[11]).

Following the good principles mentioned in this section, the appealing system should be as transparent and as convenient as possible, stating in which conditions, when and how can the taxpayer appeal to his/her tax obligation so the whole appeal process is done smoothly and predictably. It is worth noting that appealing against valuation rules is normally different than appealing against a single property-specific appraisal. The tax department can organise the appeal process in a manner that appeals against the valuation method occur in a different period than appeals against property assessments in order to avoid the simultaneous judgment of multiple appeals of different nature, which may reduce the operational effectiveness of the appealing system.

Nevertheless, as important as having an efficient appeal system is to reduce as much as possible the number of appeals. For that avail, taxpayer education and transparency are important but are not the only strategies. Some countries only allow appeals in case the alleged error is higher than a certain threshold (e.g. 20% for Estonia).[13] Others use information from taxpayers not only to improve data collection but also as a manner to legitimise the appraisal and, thus, reducing the number of appeals (e.g. Netherlands, explored in Box 3.9, found at the end of this chapter). Lastly, conservative valuations (that is, that aims at estimating a value slightly below property value) might also significantly reduce appeals since when taxpayers believe that the assessed value is below market values they are less likely to appeal. The last practice is found in Denmark (who aims to produce values that are about 5% less than actual market prices) and in some Canada and US states, which aim to estimate values up to 10% lower than those of the market (UN Habitat, 2013[10]).

Figure 3.5 illustrates the responses from a questionnaire handled by Dobay et al. (2019[26]) about property tax appeal process in some OECD countries, Singapore, South Africa, and Australian states, Canadian provinces and US states.

Figure 3.5 Characteristics of appeals process in tax administrations across states/countries

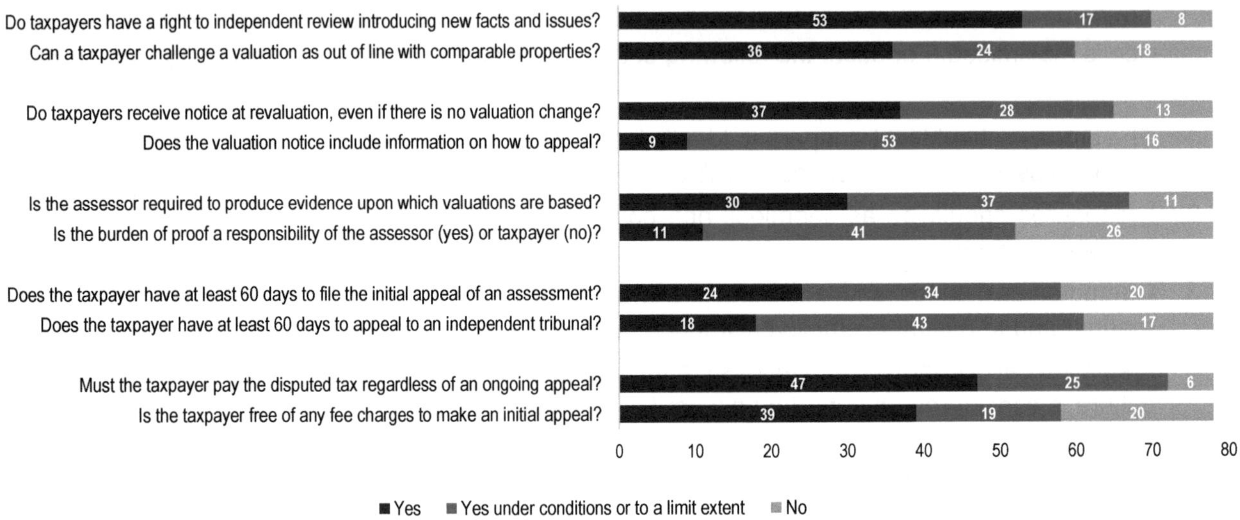

Note: Countries/States covered: Australian Capital Territories/AUS, New South Wales/AUS, Northern Territories/AUS, Queensland/AUS, South Australia/AUS, Tasmania/AUS, Victoria/AUS, Western Australia/AUS, Alberta/CAN, British Columbia/CAN, New Brunswick/CAN, Newfoundland and Labrador/CAN, Nova Scotia/CAN, Ontario/CAN, Quebec/CAN, Saskatchewan/CAN, England/UK, Northern Ireland/UK, Scotland/UK, Wales/UK, Alabama/US, Alaska/US, Arizona/US, Arkansas/US, California/US, Colorado/US, Connecticut/US, Delaware/US, District of Columbia/US, Florida/US, Georgia/US, Hawaii/US, Idaho/US, Illinois/US, Indiana/US, Iowa/US, Kansas/US, Kentucky/US, Louisiana/US, Maine/US, Maryland/US, Massachusetts/US, Michigan/US, Minnesota/US, Mississippi/US, Missouri/US, Montana/US, Nebraska/US, Nevada/US, New Hampshire/US, New Jersey/US, New Mexico/US, New York/US, North Carolina/US, North Dakota/US, Ohio/US, Oklahoma/US, Oregon/US, Pennsylvania/US, Puerto Rico/US, Rhode Island/US, South Carolina/US, South Dakota/US, Tennessee/US, Texas/US, Utah/US, Vermont/US, Virginia/US, Washington/US, West Virginia/US, Wisconsin/US, Wyoming/US, New Zealand, Singapore, South Africa, Spain, The Netherlands.
Source: Authors based on data from Dobay et al. (2019[26])

Regarding the right to appeal, it is common for property tax administrations to grant to taxpayers a right to review their assessments and introduce new facts that could change the assessments (53 out of 78). Nevertheless, some tax administrations impose restrictions on assessment reviews or do not fully provide an independent court for the judgment. For instance, in the state of New York/US the appeal right only applies to small assessment review claims. In Indiana/US appeals are judged by the Indiana Board of Tax Review, not the Tax Court. Rarely can the taxpayer not challenge valuations on the grounds that they are out of line with comparable properties (18 out of 78). However, in most cases challenging on such grounds can only be made under certain conditions, or if more information is provided. For instance, in the Netherlands only residential properties can be challenged on these grounds. In Alabama/US, additional evidence on the top of a difference in assessed values is required.

When it comes to notification, in most cases (62 out of 78) some information regarding the appeal process comes in the valuation notice. In some cases, the appeal form comes together with the note as well (e.g. in many Canadian states and in four US states). In some US states the state does not require that such information is given in the valuation notice, but some counties do include (e.g. Alabama/US). In the most complete case, the notice letter includes all the details and also the instructions of how to appeal but not the appeal forms (e.g. Spain, Florida/US, Kansas/US, the Netherlands, among others). In a small number of cases the notice does not include any specific information on appeal, but the information can be found elsewhere (e.g. in Oregon/US the information can be found in counties' websites).

Only a few tax administrations do not send a valuation notice in case there is no valuation change (only 13 out of 38 do not). 37 do send such notices – for instance, Spain, Singapore and South Dakota/US send annually while many US states (e.g. Virginia/US, Texas/US, among others) send always when there is a revaluation even if there is no significant change in cadastral values. In other cases, the note is only sent in case the value changes (e.g. Kentucky/US), increases (e.g. Delaware/US) or increases above a certain threshold (e.g. 15% in Louisiana/US, USD 1 000 in South Carolina/US,[14] among others).

Concerning the evidence used for analysing appeals, in most cases (67 out of 78) assessors produce evidence upon which valuations are based. Most tax administrations provide appraisal reports upon request (e.g. the Netherlands, Virginia/US, among others). In some cases, the complete information is given only during the appeal process (e.g. Louisiana/US, Missouri/US, Northern Ireland/UK, among others). In some rare cases the information is either not given (e.g. Ohio/US, New York/US, among others) or only given after the taxpayer has provided supporting evidence (e.g. England/UK).

When it comes to the burden of proof, the balance is a bit more skewed towards the taxpayers – they have to generate evidence in 26 cases (out of 78), against only 11 cases in which assessors bear the burden of proof. The most common situation, though, is in between – in 41 cases both the taxpayer and the tax administration bear some burden of proof. That is, equal weight is generally given to evidence provided by both parties, however, the burden is on the taxpayer on a preponderance of evidence basis (e.g. Scotland/UK, England/UK, Idaho/US, among others). In some exceptional cases, this definition depends on the type of property (e.g. in Kansas/US the burden of proof is on the appraiser, except for leased commercial and industrial property, where it is on the taxpayer by preponderance of the evidence).

With reference to appeal deadlines, the most common situation is when taxpayers have between 30-59 days to file the initial appeal assessment or to appeal to an independent tribunal. Notably tax administrations in the United Kingdom tend to give taxpayers more than 60 days to file appeals. Most tax administrations grant at least 30 days. The tightest deadlines are generally given by some US states and are, roughly, 13-15 days (e.g. Vermont/US, Kentucky/US, among others).

Regarding the costs, in most cases there is no fee requirement to file an initial tax appeal (39 out of 78). In some cases, some fees might apply at a later stage or only under certain conditions. For instance, in Scotland there is no fee for submitting an appeal to the tax administration, but fees are payable for appeals to the Lands Tribunal for Scotland. In Wisconsin/US, fees are only applicable for state assessed manufacturing property. Often they are also progressive – the higher the value of the property the higher the fee. For instance, in New South Wales/AUS there is no fee for the initial objection, but on a later stage appeal fees range from AUD 336 to 1 912. In Northern Ireland fees are 1% of the pre-appeal value to a max of GBP 15 000. When they are fixed, they tend to be small. In Vermont/US it is USD 75 and USD 30 in New York/US.

In most cases (47 out of 78) an appeal submission does not suspend the obligation to pay the property tax bill (e.g. Spain, New Zealand and most US, Canadian, British and Canadian states). Not rarely only a portion of the tax obligation should be paid. For instance, in South Carolina/US 80% of the disputed tax must be paid if an appeal is likely to extend beyond the end of the fiscal year. In Maine/US the undisputed amount must be paid to advance an appeal in case the case's value is greater than USD 500 000. In the

Netherlands it depends on the case – the municipal tax administration can grant a suspension of payment for the assessment that is contested, but it may charge interest if the objection is dismissed.

Many lessons can be drawn from the experience of these countries. First, it is important to grant to taxpayers a right to challenge assessments and, ideally, an independent institution (in most cases a tribunal) should be involved in the judgment. Second, the valuation notice is a very effective and widely used tool to convey the necessary information for taxpayers to appeal. A good practice is to send the appeal form with the notice or, at minimum, instructions on how to appeal. In that light, sending revaluation notices frequently (even when the value assessed does not change) can provide greater transparency. Third, evidence used to appraise properties is normally provided to taxpayers in case they request. Nevertheless, in most cases further evidence is necessary for taxpayers to be able to appeal. Pieces of evidence have, in principle, equal value regardless of who is providing them. Fourth, most tax administrations give at least 30 days for taxpayers to file an appeal, but rarely more than 60 days. This seems sufficient for taxpayers to prepare an appeal case. Fourth, typically there are no required fees to make an initial appeal. In case there are, they can be made progressive or small, so they do not represent a significant burden to taxpayers. A fair system should allow all taxpayers to appeal in case they deem necessary. Fifth and lastly, an appeal submission typically does not suspend the obligation to pay the property tax bill. Two potential reasons for this are to not incentivise appeals just to postpone payments and to maintain a predictable inflow of tax revenues.

Billing: measures aimed at increasing payments convenience and improving communication can improve the compliance rate

One way to facilitate the payment process is through the provision of multiple payment methods. Examples include cash, e-banking and credit/debit cards though commercial banks, regional tax centres and post offices (Kelly, 2012[2]). When payments can be made in conjunction with other bills such as mortgages and utility, compliance tends to increase (for instance, in the case of Netherlands, the payment is made together with the charges from the Real Estate Tax Water board). For that purpose, some innovative methods have been employed recently, such as the Irish case of allowing property taxes to be deducted at source from salary or occupational pensions (for more on the Irish case see Box 4.1 in the next chapter). Payment in instalments is also a good practice to help illiquid taxpayers to make the payment – usually instalments are offered along with an option of an early lump payment with a discount to encourage compliance (see Box 3.5).

The billing process can also be used to increase transparency. So as to make the process more transparent, the tax bill notification may serve as a communication channel, in addition to other channels such as television, newspapers and posters advertisements. It is important for taxpayers to know the role of the property tax in funding public services, the billing and appeal processes and channels (e.g. website, telephone) for gathering further information. Box 3.5 covers how the compliance rate can be improved through better communication with country examples.

Box 3.5. Improving the compliance rate

The content and format of tax notifications can have a significant impact on compliance rates

In Lima, Peru, Carpio (2014[27]) found evidence that disclosing information on the compliance rate of property taxes can have a large positive impact on compliance (20% on average). In contrast, mentioning the average level of municipal enforcement did not raise compliance significantly. A similar conclusion was drawn from a by Hallsworth et al. (2017[28]) , as cited by the World Bank (2019[29]), analysing data from the United Kingdom. The payment of declared tax liabilities was boosted by up to 5.1 percentage points when the average number of people who pay on time was informed to taxpayers. Thus, disclosing positive behaviour of other taxpayers seems to have a significant impact on compliance.

Letters with simplified messages also tend to increase compliance. As cited by the World Bank (2019[29]), Behavioural Insights Team (2012[30]) found evidence in the United Kingdom that letters that clearly delineated the actions required to pay the tax saw a 15 to 30% higher response rate than other types of messaging. In Belgium, Neve et al. (2020[31]) found evidence that simplifying communication by the tax administration and including deterrence messages consistently improves tax compliance. Similarly, in the Pampas/Argentina, Castro and Scartascini (2015[32]) found evidence that deterrence messages increased the property tax compliance by roughly 5%.

Mentioning what public goods are funded with the tax was found to increase compliance. In Rwanda messages indicating that the taxes are used to fund education, healthcare and safety led to a persistent increase in tax compliance (Mascagni, Nell and Monkam, 2017[33]).

Communicating sanctions are also found to increase compliance. For instance, In Washington State/United States, Iyer, Reckers and Snaders (2010[34]) concluded that mailed letters that enhanced perceived detection risk and/or raised penalty awareness resulted in an increase in tax compliance.

Finally, in an overarching study covering five countries (Costa Rica, Guatemala, Poland, Latvia and Kosovo), the World Bank (2019[29]) found evidence that slight changes in communication policy can produce a significant increase in compliance rate. Nevertheless, countries differ and the tone in the message and mean used to send it (e.g. e-mail, letter) have a different impact depending on the country. Thus, the tax administration can test different messages to tune the message tone and format to its specific audience.

Increasing the number of instalments can affect positively the compliance rate

Compliance rates can also be increased when taxpayers can pay their property tax obligations in multiple instalments. Waldhart and Reschovsky (2012[35]) investigated the relationship between the number of annual payment instalments and the property tax delinquency rate using five years of data from Wisconsin municipalities. Their analysis indicated that an increase in the number of instalments from two to three per year reduces the delinquency rate by nearly half. Nevertheless, increasing further the number of instalments did not lead to a statistically significant reduction in delinquency. As a result, it seems that increasing the number of instalments has a positive effect on compliance. Nevertheless, this effect is non-linear and can cease to exist when a certain number of instalments is reached. Of course, this number can change depending on the region and, thus, a tax administration can test which number of instalments work best for it. In addition, in order to select this number, other elements should be considered such as the impact of an increase in the number of instalments in government finances.

Source: World Bank (2019[29]).

In addition to convenience and transparency, another tool to increase compliance is the penalisation of non-compliant taxpayers. In general, the most common penalties are the imposition of fines and tax liens, incidence of interest rates on the arrears, impediment of the use of certain government services, "shaming" through the publication of delinquency list and, ultimately, property seizure (Kelly, 2012[2]). In order to avoid penalising taxpayers unfairly, such more extreme non-financial penalties can be employed only in case of a lasting delinquency (typically ranging from one to three years), stipulated beforehand. The tax system is considered fairer when penalties are transparent and predictable. For instance, in the specific case of property seizure, the taxpayer should be informed of the deadlines of all steps in advance, such as demand notice, warnings, periods to respond to each demand, judgement, release period and sale/auction.

Figure 3.6 reveals practices employed by property tax administrations across countries with regards to collection, transparency and penalisations. Concerning due dates for property tax filling and payments, in most cases (43 out of 78) the country/state defines the due date. Due dates vary widely and can be as early as January 31 (e.g. Singapore) or at as late as December 31 (e.g. for the 2nd instalment in Oklahoma/US). Usually instalments are apart from one another by roughly 3-6 months. Due dates can also vary by property type (e.g. in Wisconsin/US and Wyoming/US). Some tax administrations (18 out of 78) have limited freedom to set their own filing and payment dates. For instance, in Western Australia/AUS, payment dates for Land Tax are consistent across tax administration but not the payment dates for the Council Rates. In Spain, local governments can choose the date, but the taxpayer must have at least two months to pay. Lastly, in a minority of states/countries due dates are not consistent across jurisdictions (17 out of 78).

Figure 3.6 Characteristics of collection process in tax administrations across states/countries

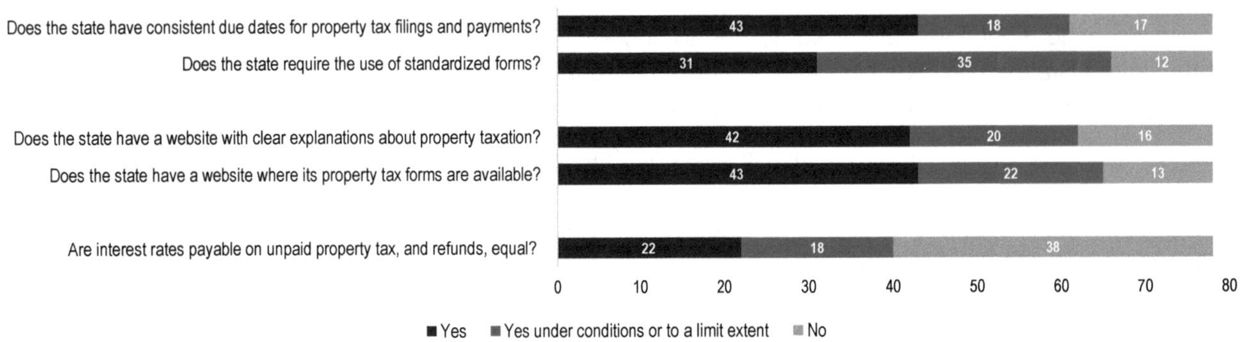

Note: State here may refer to the immediate upper level of government (e.g. in the United Kingdom, England, Northern Ireland, Scotland and Wales; in the Netherlands and New Zealand the central government). Countries/Jurisdictions covered: Australian Capital Territories/AUS, New South Wales/AUS, Northern Territories/AUS, Queensland/AUS, South Australia/AUS, Tasmania/AUS, Victoria/AUS, Western Australia/AUS, Alberta/CAN, British Columbia/CAN, New Brunswick/CAN, Newfoundland and Labrador/CAN, Nova Scotia/CAN, Ontario/CAN, Quebec/CAN, Saskatchewan/CAN, England/UK, Northern Ireland/UK, Scotland/UK, Wales/UK, Alabama/US, Alaska/US, Arizona/US, Arkansas/US, California/US, Colorado/US, Connecticut/US, Delaware/US, District of Columbia/US, Florida/US, Georgia/US, Hawaii/US, Idaho/US, Illinois/US, Indiana/US, Iowa/US, Kansas/US, Kentucky/US, Louisiana/US, Maine/US, Maryland/US, Massachusetts/US, Michigan/US, Minnesota/US, Mississippi/US, Missouri/US, Montana/US, Nebraska/US, Nevada/US, New Hampshire/US, New Jersey/US, New Mexico/US, New York/US, North Carolina/US, North Dakota/US, Ohio/US, Oklahoma/US, Oregon/US, Pennsylvania/US, Puerto Rico/US, Rhode Island/US, South Carolina/US, South Dakota/US, Tennessee/US, Texas/US, Utah/US, Vermont/US, Virginia/US, Washington/US, West Virginia/US, Wisconsin/US, Wyoming/US, New Zealand, Singapore, South Africa, Spain, The Netherlands.
Source: Based on data from Dobay et al. (2019[26]).

Upper levels of government often standardise the forms that local governments provide to taxpayers (31 out of 78). Occasionally upper levels of government do not provide a form for local governments (12 out of 78). It is, however, more common for standard forms to be provided by upper levels, but not required to be used – in this case localities may use their own preferred forms and the forms sent by upper levels work as a suggestion (35 out of 78).

With regards to transparency, websites are a widely used tool to both provide general explanations and information about property taxation and to provide forms to taxpayers. The majority of state/central governments (42 out of 78) have a centralised website in which standard forms can be found and further information is provided. For instance, in the Netherlands the Council for Real Estate Assessment has a website that gives comprehensive details about property tax assessment. In Northern Ireland/UK, The Land & Property Services (LPS) website (part of ni.gov.uk) provides links to other sites providing property tax information. In South Africa the Cooperative Governance Traditional Affairs website provides an explanation of the rates system, valuation, rate setting and the appeal process. In most cases (43 out of 78) these websites also provide the forms to taxpayers. In some cases, though, not all forms are provided on the same website. For instance, in New South Wales/AUS, Objection forms are on the state website while forms for rebates and exemptions are on the individual Council websites. Exemption forms are not provided by some tax administrations in their websites (e.g. Arkansas/US, Kentucky/US and West Virginia/US).

Lastly, with regards to interest rates payable on unpaid property tax and refunds, the largest group of tax administrations (38 out of 78) applies a higher rate to unpaid property tax than to tax refunds. Annual interest rates applied to unpaid property taxes range from less than 2% (e.g. Oregon/US) to 15-18% in some US states (e.g. 15% in Alaska/US, 16% in Arizona/US, 18% in Wyoming/US). On the other hand, interest rates applied to tax refunds (overpayment) are generally lower than 2% and their values are equal or similar to rates applied to underpayment in a minority of countries/states (22 out of 78). Some states/countries work with a variable interest rate (e.g. in Ohio/US, the interest rate applied to both over and under payment is 1/12th of the federal short-term rate per month).

Many lessons can be drawn from the experience of these tax administrations. First, country/state-wide standardisation with regard to due dates and forms is relatively common, which reveals that the upper levels of government do have some role in setting guidelines for lower level of government's procedures. Second, there is no clear period of the year in which tax obligations are paid but, in general, multiple instalments tend to be spaced by 3-6 months. General guidelines can be given to establish a minimum period for payment (e.g. Spain). Third, websites are a widely used tool to increase transparency and to provide forms in a convenient manner. Commonly states/countries have a centralised website that provides general information and forms to the taxpayers. Websites can provide a wide range of information with regards to rates system, valuation, rate setting and the appeal process. Fourthly and lastly, interest rates are commonly used to penalise taxpayers given that interest rates applied to underpayment tend to be higher than market rates and the rate applied to overpayment. It is worth noting that a penalisation of underpayment can also be achieved with a fee plus an interest rate in line with market rates.

Responsibility for property tax administration across levels of government

Local governments often have the autonomy to set property tax rates within limits

There are multiple reasons to give SNGs some autonomy over tax rate setting. First, much of the economic and political benefits of decentralised public finance come from the ability of SNGs to make their own decisions about taxation. That is, SNGs should be autonomous enough to define its taxation in line with the level of spending that they deem necessary to provide public services for its citizens. Without that discretion, SNGs cannot be fully accountable for a fiscal crisis or poor-quality public services since they are not able to raise the necessary revenues to balance their budgets or to improve public services. As Ahmad (2017[36]) puts it, *"direct linkage between taxes and spending, especially at the local and city level, is critical for both accountability and good governance and sustainable development"*. Second, tax bases are unevenly distributed across regions and, thus, when the tax rates are set by the central government, local governments would not be able to compensate for their regional differences, creating regional asymmetries in terms of revenue capacity. Thus, tax rate and relief settings are considered a key element of subnational autonomy (Dougherty, Harding and Reschovsky, 2019[37]), without which hardly one can consider a government autonomous. Some authors, such as Ahmad (2017[36]), consider the control over rates at the margin even more important than the decentralisation of the tax collection.

Despite this important role of tax rate and base setting for subnational autonomy, an excessive discretion over elements of a subnational property tax policy poses some risks. First, it is common for inter-governmental grants' systems to have an equalisation component that provides more funds for SNGs that have, in comparison to other jurisdictions, less own revenues[15] and, as a result, SNGs might be tempted to use their tax power to under-tax their own citizens[16] since their losses in tax revenues will be compensated (partially or fully) with higher equalisation grants. Second, SNGs might use their tax power to minimise the tax burden on their citizens and maximise the burden on citizens from other jurisdictions, such as by setting lower tax rates for residential properties and higher tax rates for business properties, which can lead to tax exporting. Third and lastly, asymmetrical tax bases and exemptions across jurisdictions leave room for horizontal inequities within a country – that is, taxpayers in some jurisdictions might be disproportionately taxed in comparison to taxpayers from other jurisdictions. Sizeable differences of tax burden across jurisdictions can affect behaviour and lead to distortions. Thus, although subnational autonomy to set tax rates and bases is desirable, granting too much autonomy to SNGs can also be problematic.

Box 3.6. Israeli case of different effective tax rates across jurisdictions when local governments have little autonomy to change tax rates

Israel has 257 local governments, whose primary source of its own revenues come from the Israeli property tax (*Arnona).* This recurrent property tax accounts for approximately 80% of all local taxation, while this share is roughly 33% in OECD countries (see Figure 1.5). The *Arnona* has some similarities and dissimilarities with other recurrent property tax systems of OECD countries. Regarding similarities, first, the same tax levies on both residential and non-residential properties; second, tax reliefs are given to certain groups of households such as low-income families and the elderly. Concerning dissimilarities, first, the tax base for the Israeli recurrent property tax is unusual: the *Arnona* is based on the size of a property (territorial area in square meters), whereas in most OECD countries capital values are used; second, the autonomy granted to local governments to set tax rates is very limited; and third, annual increase in tax rates are linked to the inflation rate. Rates are typically higher for non-residential than residential property and vary substantially by type of non-residential property.

In this situation, it would be expected that the very limited local discretion over tax rates would make the effective tax rates similar across jurisdictions. Nevertheless, this is not the case in Israel. Since *Arnona* rates vary by the type and use of properties and since local governments are, to some extent, in charge of property classification, tax rates can differ across regions if the same type of property is classified differently across jurisdictions. Although the central government has defined only 13 main classes of property, local governments can establish their own set of subclasses. As a result, local governments have created thousands of subclasses, and they differ substantially across local governments. The myriad of subclasses contributes to economic inefficiency, horizontal and vertical inequities, and conceal the effective tax rates that are applied across jurisdictions. In effect, local governments use their control over properties' sub-classification as a way to gain more control over local effective tax rates. This situation could be avoided if the central government established a standard classification system or if local governments were given more autonomy to set tax rates.

Source: OECD (2021[8]) and Thomas (2021[19]).

When limiting subnational autonomy to set tax rates, it is important to also limit local autonomy to change effective tax rates through tax administration policies, otherwise SNGs may seek ways to overcome these restrictions as a means of asserting more local fiscal control (see Box 3.6 in the Israeli case).

For instance, SNGs can influence effective tax rates by 1) under/over-valuing some types of property; and 2) classifying properties in a manner that the desired statutory tax rate is applied to them (in case there are a myriad of tax rates depending on the type of property). Tax policy can be (and often is) decentralised in a manner that SNGs have control over their tax policy while horizontal inequities and distortions are minimised.

Box 3.7. Piggybacking on national taxes in some OECD countries

Piggybacking refers to a mechanism in which lower levels of government can levy a supplemental rate on an upper level of government's tax base, which reduces the costs of the tax administration (through economy of scale) and simplify the tax system in comparison to the case in which each jurisdiction can define and operationalise their own tax policies (i.e. setting tax rates and reliefs). Piggybacking may also cover tax reliefs and have bands for the piggybacking rates. In countries using piggyback taxes, rates are generally low, but these taxes provide a substantial amount of revenue because of the large size of the taxable base. Undoubtedly the control at the margin of the tax rates can provide some degree of autonomy and accountability to lower levels of government.

In the most extreme case, upper levels of government administer the whole tax system and transfer the collected tax revenues to each jurisdiction considering the supplemental rates accordingly. Such a system is similar to tax sharing, the main difference being the fact that lower levels of government enjoy an additional autonomy. As a result, piggybacking suffers from one of the same disadvantages of tax sharing arrangements: upper levels of government might not have the proper incentives to collect tax revenues effectively since they are not accrued to them.

Many countries supplement upper levels of government taxes with piggybacked rates from lower levels of governments. In **Sweden**, personal income taxes administered by the central government are subject to piggybacked rates levied by municipalities that tend to be lowest in rich suburbs of large cities and higher in the rural north and municipalities suffering from industrial decline. Similar situations occur in other Nordic countries such as **Denmark**, **Finland** and **Iceland**. A group of local governments in the **United States** also levy supplements to state individual income taxes and retail sales taxes. In **Switzerland**, local governments may levy supplements to canton (i.e. state/regional level) personal income taxes. In **Canada**, for the harmonised sales tax and corporate income tax, the provinces or territories may select their rate but must use the national base.

In the **United Kingdom**, since 2009 piggybacked rates are levied by local governments and applied to business property taxes, which are paid into a central pool and distributed to local governments. Local governments are required to consult with taxpayers that are liable to the tax before implementing the supplement. The supplement is, thus, subjected to the approval by these taxpayers, which vote in a referendum. In addition, the supplementary rate cannot be higher than 2% of rateable values. The funds may be spent locally on economic development. The City of London, for example, levied a 2% business rate supplement on businesses in the area of the Crossrail to help pay for the Crossrail.

Sources: Mikesell (2012[38]) and Slack and Bird (2014[20]).

One option is to give SNGs only the control over tax policies that have limited impact outside their jurisdictional borders (i.e. over recurrent taxes on residential properties, while tax policy regarding recurrent taxes on business property is assigned to upper levels of government). A second option is to limit the potential differences in tax rates across jurisdictions so these differences will be unlikely to cause a change in taxpayers' behaviour. In the latter case, small differences in tax obligations would be outweighed by other factors that are relevant in the decision-making process and, thus, distortions would be minimised. A third option is to grant to upper levels of government the responsibility of providing tax reliefs and/or exemptions. A fourth and last option is to increase subnational autonomy in the form of supplemental rates on an upper level of the government's tax base (see Box 3.7 on piggybacking in some OECD countries). There is room for adopting multiple options simultaneously.

In OECD countries, it is common for local governments to have a limited discretion over tax rate, base and exemptions of their recurrent taxation on properties. Usually local governments 1) can set tax rates within bands set by the upper levels of government; 2) can only create exemptions in a limited manner; and 3) have no or little discretion over tax bases. It is worth noting that these tax rates' bands can be used to limit not only discrepancies across jurisdictions but also discrepancies between different tax bases within a jurisdiction (i.e. business and residential properties). As mentioned above, when tax bases differ widely in terms of tax rates, taxpayers might try to avoid taxes by concealing the true nature/use of their properties.

Table 3.3 reveals the degree of decentralisation of property taxation policy in multiple countries. In most countries in the sample (31 out of 35) local governments have some autonomy over tax rate setting (usually subjected to limits) whereas only in a few (5 out of 35) they can define tax bases. Regarding exemptions, in less than one third of them (10 out of 35), local governments have discretion over exemptions and reliefs.

Table 3.3. Recipients of revenue from recurrent taxes on immovable property by level of government and local government discretion over property tax policies

Central, regional & local	Central & local	Regional & local	Local only
Spain (R)	Norway (B, R)	Switzerland (B, R)	Hungary (I, B, R, E)
	Israel (R, E)	France (R, E)	New Zealand (I, B, R)
	Brazil (I, B)	United States (R, E)	Colombia (R, E)
	Iceland (R)	Australia (R)	Estonia (R, E)
	United Kingdom (R)	Mexico (R)	Lithuania (R, E)
		Russia (R)	Netherlands (R, E)
		Denmark (I)	Poland (R, E)
			South Africa (R, E)
			Austria (R)
			Canada (R)
			Czech Republic (R)
			Finland (R)
			Germany (R)
			Ireland (R)
			Japan (R)
			Korea (R)
			Luxembourg (R)
			Portugal (R)
			Slovak Republic (R)
			Slovenia (R)
			Latvia (E)
			Turkey (N)

Legend:

Countries with the same colour have the same SNG classification

"B" means discretion over the base

"E" means discretion regarding certain exemptions and relief measures

"I" means discretion over whether to impose a tax

"N" means no local discretion regarding rates (or other features of the tax)

"R" means some discretion in setting tax rates (usually subject to limits)

Note: This table should be read in the following manner: in Spain, revenues from recurrent taxes on immovable property accrue to the central, regional and Span's SNGs have discretion over tax rates only.

Source: Based on data from Almy (2013[11]).

China and rate setting

In China, local government's expenditure as a share of general government expenditure has been increasing while, at the same time, their tax revenues as a share on general government tax revenues has been decreasing. As a result, the vertical fiscal gap is widening (CDRF, 2020[39]), which can have many adverse effects (this topic was discussed in detail in the first chapter).

Moreover, China's local governments have little to no discretion over a great portion of their revenues, which hinders local fiscal policy to adapt to local needs and conditions. Liu (2021[40]) explains that a tax-sharing system currently in place in China in which local taxes are collected and fully retained by local governments while some taxes are collected by the central government and shared in a predetermined proportion with lower levels of government. In this system lower levels of government have autonomy only over small local taxes.

In these conditions, it may be difficult to hold local authorities accountable for their fiscal outcomes given that they cannot choose the necessary level of taxation to fund public services. In addition, Ahmad and van Rijn (2020) suggest that when subnational governments have little to no revenue sources over which they can exert control, subnational fiscal rules are not credible and funding through a municipal bond system or the use of public-private partnership are impaired. In this light, if China were to follow the most adopted practice of giving to local governments some autonomy in tax rate setting for recurrent taxes on immovable property, local governments' autonomy would be improved, with overarching positive consequences throughout the intergovernmental fiscal system. As explored in the first chapter, since recurrent property taxes tend to generate a substantial amount of revenue, often being the most important local tax in OECD countries, the impact on local autonomy can be significant.

Tax policy and administration are closely intertwined and often involve a trade-off between greater technical capacity at the central level and better incentives for revenue collection at the local level

After having discussed decentralisation of tax design, it is worthwhile to discuss decentralisation of tax administration. In principle taxes need not be administered by the government that levies them. There are multiple examples of taxes for which tax revenues are accrued to one level of government but tax administration is assigned to another level of government. The choice of the level of government responsible for tax administration generally involves a trade-off between technical capacity and incentives (Mikesell, 2012[38]).

On the one hand, upper levels of government tend to have more resources to fund a better technical capacity and they may also enjoy economies of scale and scope. Economies of scale are obtained, in the case of property taxes, mostly by using the same fiscal cadastre and mass valuation systems and they can not only reduce costs but also improve the scope and quality of fiscal cadastres and valuations. On the other hand, lower levels of government tend to have more incentives to collect tax revenues that are accrued to them, which can affect all phases of revenue collection, from cadastre management to settle disputes over regional interests. According to Mikesell (2012[38]), slow and inaccurate payment has been a common complaint among localities in the United States when local governments depend on taxes that are administered by state governments. The same author also mentioned that when US states have budget problems, they sometimes delay scheduled payments to their local governments. Another advantage of having local tax administrations refers to the fact that local governments tend to have more information on the local conditions due to their licensing and regulatory responsibilities, which may help them to run a property tax administration system and to create a fiscal culture, necessary for compliance. The case for federalism as a "laboratory for democracy" works in tax administration as well: effective tax systems in place in some jurisdictions can be "exported" to different regions,[17] promoting innovation across jurisdictions. Lastly, economies of scale can also be obtained through inter-governmental co-ordination arrangements (see Box 3.8 on the US case).

Box 3.8. Economies of scale and scope in property taxes: examples from the United States

In the **United States**, usually state governments determine guidelines for property valuation and tax collection while local governments execute these activities under the state oversight. Since US local governments differ significantly in size, with some local governments with a low administrative capacity, it is common for them to make co-operative arrangements to reduce costs related to these activities.

In 2013 the International Association of Assessment Officials (IAAO) conducted a survey on assessment offices in these two countries. The survey identified nearly 8 700 agencies and received 500-700 valid responses to each question. The survey found a strong positive (nonlinear) relationship between the number of parcels in a jurisdiction and staffing levels, pointing towards a clear economy of scale in the assessment function. More precisely, for the average size jurisdiction (about 15 000 parcels), a 10% increase in the number of parcels is associated with a 0.9% decline in the average cost per parcel for counties and a 0.8% decline for cities and townships. IAAO believe that this reduction is likely due to the fact that a 10% increase in parcels at the mean is associated with a 2.8% increase in the number of parcels per employee for counties (3.0% for cities and towns).

In addition, the type of agency also seems to significantly affect the costs per parcel. The median budget per parcel in agencies that work for a single county, municipality and township was USD 21.85, 30.79 and 23.71, respectively. When agencies work with multiple jurisdictions or for a state/province the necessary budget reduces. Public agencies, private agencies and state agencies working for multiple have a median budget per parcel of USD 17.35, 12.53 and 24.05. These agencies that cover multiple jurisdictions also tend to have better access to technology such as aerial image, GIS, cell phones in field inspection, electronic distance measuring device used in field inspections, real-time remote access to assessment data used in field inspections, among others. Indeed, the adoption of technology advancements is related to the parcel count that an agency is responsible for assessing.

Source: Walters, L. C. and International Association of Assessing Officers Research Committee (2014[41]); OECD (2021[8]).

Country-specific conditions, such as SNGs' typical size and structure, and the scope for vertical and horizontal co-operation are important factors in determining the degree of tax administration decentralisation

Tax administration involves multiple activities and only some portion of them can be decentralised, which generates a myriad of possible administrative arrangements depending on how the distribution of activities across levels of government is organised. China, for instance, has a strong central tax department (the State Administration of Taxes, SAT) that defines the guidelines and oversees the tax administration that is performed by subordinated SNGs tax departments. The revenues are accrued to upper levels of government and, then, partially shared with lower levels of governments through an inter-governmental transfer system and revenue sharing system. With these systems, the discretion for setting tax policies are centralised and, thus, to a great extent also the tax policy accountability.

Regarding recurrent taxes on immovable property, the delineation of activities involves the distribution across levels of government and agencies of the main steps discussed throughout this chapter: fiscal cadastre, property valuation and tax collection. Although there is no arrangement that is superior to others in all possible criteria, it is paramount for the different levels of government and/or agencies involved in the process to co-operate and communicate efficiently. The data that is gathered for the fiscal cadastre is the data used in the property valuation step and both the valuation and the fiscal cadastre data are used for billing. Thus, data flows should be smooth and integrated across levels of government/institutions. Moreover, in case guidelines and policy aspects are defined by upper levels of government and lower levels of government only execute the policy, there is a need for a supervisory or monitoring activity.[18]

Box 3.9, found at the end of this chapter, shows the Dutch case, which is a good example of an effective property tax administration that applied these principles.

Fiscal cadastres are generally managed at the central level in European countries, contrasting heavily with the decentralised cadastral management in the United States.

In European countries, fiscal cadastres are normally managed at the central level (UN Habitat, 2013[10]), provides country-specific information on fiscal cadastres). European central governments usually either consolidate the data obtained through self-assessments or assessments done by SNGs or gather the data themselves through subsidiaries. For instance, according to UN Habitat (2013[10]), in Belgium, Denmark, Italy, Latvia, Lithuania, Norway, the Slovak Republic, Spain, Sweden and Turkey there is a central agency or department responsible for maintaining property records; Germany is a noteworthy exception as fiscal cadastral systems are managed by state governments; in Hungary both local government agencies and a central government ministry are involved in the cadastral maintenance; in the Netherlands, municipalities are required to continuously update the sales register, which is managed at the central level by a cadastral agency.

This situation heavily contrasts with the United States, where fiscal cadastres are administered at the subnational level, resulting in a wide variety of cadastral procedures and standards across the country. Nevertheless, since all other activities related to property tax administration are also performed at the subnational level, for the sole purpose of recurrent taxes on immovable property administration, there is no need for federal integration.

It is worth noting that China already has in place a decentralised property cadastre management system. In this situation, special attention should be given to asymmetries in local capacity and harmonisation of cadastral procedures and standards. Local capacity is sometimes an issue for local governments that don't have the necessary scale to operate a fiscal cadastre efficiently. This problem can be tackled with intergovernmental co-operation – horizontal or vertical (Box 3.2 and Box 3.8 covered this topic). Regarding oversight, China's upper levels of government already have the role of ensuring that cadastres are coherent with one another and sufficiently accurate and complete.

Subnational governments are typically involved in property valuation, either alone or jointly with upper levels of government – the latter case requires co-ordination across levels of government

Concerning the responsibility to assess property values, there is significant variation not only regarding the level of government responsible for it but also regarding the type of agency that performs the valuation. In a sample of countries, Almy (2014[1]) identified that the central government is responsible for valuation in 12 countries; regional governments in 3; local governments in 7; and mixed arrangements in 10. Regarding the type of agency responsible for property valuation, the same author identified that a tax or revenue agency was responsible for that task in 12 countries; a cadastral agency in 7; a standalone agency in 1; and mixed arrangements in 5. Figure 3.7, below, reveals how OECD and partner countries assign valuation responsibilities.

Figure 3.7 Level of government and type of agency responsible for valuation in OECD and partner countries

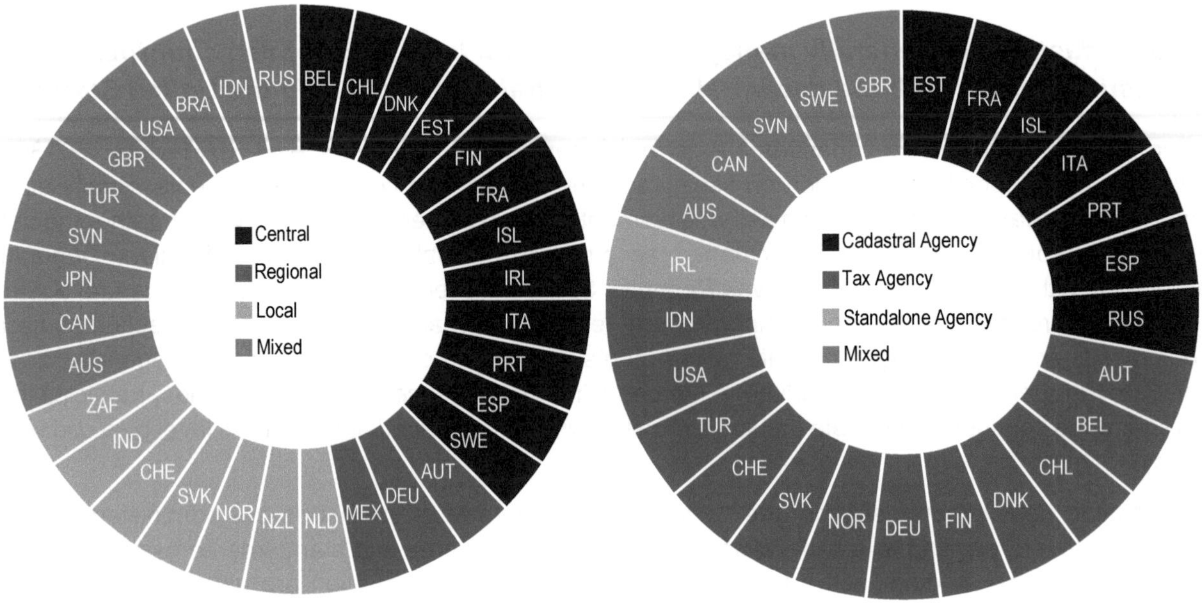

Note: In the United States valuation is overwhelmingly the responsibility of local governments – only two states have responsibility for valuation.
Source: Based on data from Almy (2014[1]).

In all countries that are among the 15th largest in terms of territory (i.e. Australia, Brazil, Canada, India, Mexico, Russia, the United States), and thus, with a territory size closer to China's, SNGs are involved in property valuation.[19] In large countries, differences between regions tend to be wider, making the familiarity of subnational administrations with regional and local conditions especially relevant.

Co-operative arrangements can also be used in property valuation as a way to increase local capacity. Scope of these co-operative arrangements vary widely (Mikesell, 2012[38]). For instance, a co-operative agreement might not necessarily involve all types of properties. Non-residential properties that have an illiquid market – such some specific industry factories, football stadiums, and transportation infrastructure like train stations – are challenging to appraise and co-operative arrangements can be made to deal only with these more complex properties.

Figure 3.7 also revealed that in 10 countries different levels of government are involved in the valuation process. In some cases, this involvement is voluntary but in others it is mandatory. In these mixed arrangements a good delineation of activities coupled with inter-governmental co-ordination might combine the benefits of a larger fiscal capacity with the local familiarity of conditions and local autonomy, resulting in more uniform and precise valuations. In these arrangements upper levels of government are typically involved in the definition of valuation standards and guidelines, while local governments perform the valuations based on these guidelines.

Billing and tax collection are commonly managed at the local level since property tax revenues are often accrued to local governments

Billing and tax collection are usually decentralised to local governments. These activities can be assigned to local governments through a central/federal legislation that provides local governments with the authority to levy and collect property taxes. In no country in the sample of OECD and partner countries state/regional governments are responsible for collecting recurrent taxes on immovable property. Figure 3.8 reveals that in 18 out of 31 countries in the sample local governments are the sole responsible for these activities and only in 7 countries central governments are the sole responsible for them.

Figure 3.8 Level of government responsible for tax collection in OECD and partner countries

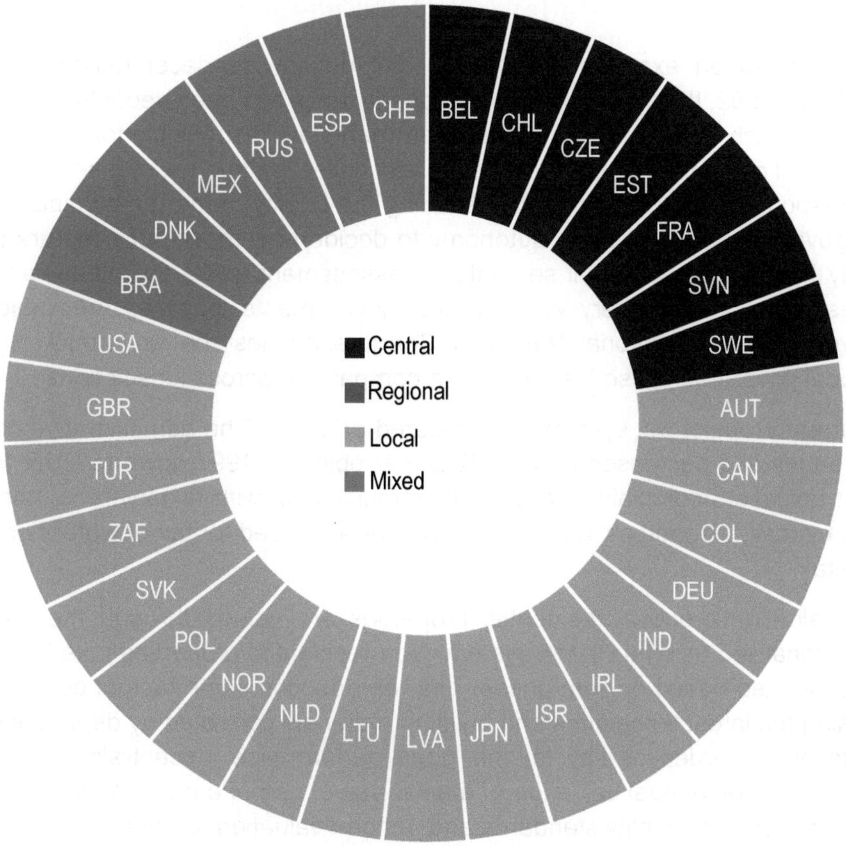

Source: Based on data from Almy (2014[1]).

There are multiple reasons for this prominent role of local governments in the administration of billing and tax collection activities. First, recurrent taxes on immovable property revenues typically accrue to local governments, which put local governments at the level of government that has the highest stake in their collection. Second, tax billing and collection involve important definitions that directly impact cash flow management such as regarding the distribution of the receipts over time in a given fiscal year (i.e. that is, in which months the parcels must be paid) and regarding the trade-off between increasing compliance at the cost of a higher discount for up-front payments.

Nevertheless, central administration of tax collection and billing activities also has its advantages. When central governments administer the billing and collection systems, the same enforcement system can be used across jurisdictions, which enhances the overall consistency of the tax policy and reduces costs. Central administration can also centralise communication and collection of multiple taxes, making it more unlikely for taxpayers to get confused about which tax department he/she should contact in case of necessity.

It is worth mentioning that since recurrent taxes on immovable property often generate a substantial amount of revenues, China's local governments might have more incentives to invest in local tax administration in case they are in charge of the collection of property tax revenues. Today China's local governments are in charge of multiple minor taxes,[20] which, alone, cannot be used to raise their local revenues substantially through only an improvement in tax administration. In this regard, recurrent taxes on immovable property can play an important role to boost investments in local tax administration, also helping to create a fiscal culture.

Box 3.9. The Dutch recurrent property taxes on immovable property

The Netherlands offers an example of a successful nationwide decentralisation of property tax administration. Since 1992, the administration of property taxes has been decentralised from the central government to 399 Dutch Municipalities. Local governments are responsible for activities related to the maintenance of fiscal cadastres, property valuation, tax collection and tax rate setting while the central government is responsible for controlling and levelling the quality of the tax administration across the country. Local governments have some autonomy to decide how these activities are performed – for instance roughly half of them use civil servants for assessment, while the other half employ private firms. Properties are re-valued every year by local governments, but they are subjected to central government oversight. The National Valuation Board examines the uniformity of the valuations performed by local governments, so the values are comparable across jurisdictions.

The Dutch recurrent property tax system is considered effective. The administrative costs are around 1.5% of tax revenues and decreased from EUR 22 per object in 1997 down to EUR 16 in 2017. Only roughly 1.4% of taxpayers complain or appeal. Communication with taxpayers is mostly online (80% online and 20% by mail). Properties' assessed value are also used for tax of water boards, income tax and inheritance tax.

Regarding the valuation process, residential properties are valued through the sales comparison approach, operationalised using a CAMA system. Non-residential properties take the highest value of market value (estimated based on rent prices) and reproduction costs (actual costs of rebuilding the same object, using the latest techniques and building materials corrected by depreciation, aging, etc.). Seven elements are regarded as key for this good performance: decentralised valuation process, centralised quality control, annual valuation of market value, use of a mass appraisal system, uniform working procedures, uniform quality standards and uniform valuation reports.

Dutch mass valuations use information from the System of Register Database, information from real states adds, specific information collected by Municipalities, and specific information from interaction with taxpayers. Characteristics of properties' buildings such as improvements' quality and maintenance can be provided by taxpayers (in some cases even the size and the year of construction are self-reported) through online questionnaires or in the form of complaints and appeals. Other pieces of information that are not gathered automatically are collected through fieldwork (e.g. location features) or from aerial photo/street view. Data on cadastral registration, registration of buildings, registration of addresses, registration of inhabitants, registration of foreigners, registration of companies, large scale base maps and value of real estate are shared between governments.

The appealing system involves opposition procedure at the municipality, appeal proceedings at the District Court, legal recourse (second appeal) at Appeal Court and cassation at the Supreme Court. Municipalities have to prove the correctness of the appraised value and procedures are the same for every tax (national or local).

Source: Mikesell (2012[38]) and Dutch authorities.

References

Ahmad, E. (2017), *Political economy of tax reform for SDGs Improving the Investment Climate; Addressing Inequality; Stopping the Cheating*, https://www.g24.org/wp-content/uploads/2017/09/Political_Economy_of_Tax_Reform_for_SDGs.pdf. [36]

Almy, R. (2014), "Valuation and Assessment of Immovable Property", *OECD Working Papers on Fiscal Federalism*, No. 19, OECD Publishing, Paris, https://dx.doi.org/10.1787/5jz5pzvr28hk-en. [1]

Almy, R. (2013), "A Global Compendium and Meta-Analysis of Property Tax Systems", *Lincoln Institute of Land Policy Working Paper*, https://www.lincolninst.edu/sites/default/files/pubfiles/almy_wp14ra1-v2.pdf. [11]

BIT (2012), *Applying behavioural insights to reduce fraud, error and debt*, Technical report, Behavioural Insights Team, Cabinet Office, UK. [30]

Carpio, L. (2014), *Are the Neighbors Cheating? Evidence from a Social Norm Experiment on Property Taxes in Peru*, Working Paper Princeton University, Princeton, NJ. [27]

Castro, L. and C. Scartascini (2015), "Tax compliance and enforcement in the pampas evidence from a field experiment", *Journal of Economic Behavior & Organization*, Vol. 116, pp. 65-82, http://dx.doi.org/10.1016/j.jebo.2015.04.002. [32]

CDRF (2020), *Background document on China's property taxation*, China Development Research Foundation. [39]

Dobay, N. et al. (2019), *The Best (and Worst) of International Property Tax Administration: COST-IPTI Scorecard on the Property Tax Administrative Systems of the US States and Selected International Jurisdictions*, Council on State Taxation (COST). [26]

Dougherty, S. and K. Forman (2021), "Evaluating fiscal equalisation: Finding the right balance", *OECD Working Papers on Fiscal Federalism*, No. 36, OECD Publishing, Paris, https://dx.doi.org/10.1787/253da2b8-en. [42]

Dougherty, S., M. Harding and A. Reschovsky (2019), "Twenty years of tax autonomy across levels of government: Measurement and applications", *OECD Working Papers on Fiscal Federalism*, No. 29, OECD Publishing, Paris, https://dx.doi.org/10.1787/ca7ebc02-en. [37]

Enemark, S. (2004), *Building Land Information Policies*, UN, FIG, PC IDEA Inter-regional Special Forum on The Building of Land Information Policies in the Americas, Aguascalientes, Mexico. [9]

Forman, K., S. Dougherty and H. Blöchliger (2020), "Synthesising good practices in fiscal federalism: Key recommendations from 15 years of country surveys", *OECD Economic Policy Papers*, No. 28, OECD Publishing, Paris, https://dx.doi.org/10.1787/89cd0319-en. [6]

Franzsen, R. and W. McCluskey (2012), "Value-Based Approaches to Property Taxation", in *A Primer on Property Tax*, Blackwell Publishing Ltd, Oxford, http://dx.doi.org/10.1002/9781118454343.ch2. [18]

Hagemann, R. (2018), "Tax Policies for Inclusive Growth: Prescription versus Practice", *OECD Economic Policy Papers*, No. 24, OECD Publishing, Paris, https://dx.doi.org/10.1787/09ba747a-en. [3]

Hallsworth, M. et al. (2017), "The behavioralist as tax collector: Using natural field experiments to enhance tax compliance", *Journal of Public Economics*, Vol. 148, pp. 14-31, https://doi.org/10.1016/j.jpubeco.2017.02.003. [28]

Higginbottom, J. (2010), *Fiscal Fact: State Provisions for Property Reassessment*, https://files.taxfoundation.org/legacy/docs/ff223.pdf. [22]

International Association of Assessing Officers (2018), *Standard on Automated Valuation Models (AVMs)*, International Association of Assessing Officers, Kansas City. [23]

International Association of Assessing Officers (2017), *Standard on Mass Appraisal of Real Property: A criterion for measuring fairness, quality, equity and accuracy*, International Association of Assessing Officers, Kansas City. [21]

Iyer, G., P. Reckers and D. Sanders (2010), "Increasing Tax Compliance in Washington State: A Field Experiment", *National Tax Journal*, Vol. 63, pp. 7-32, http://dx.doi.org/10.2307/41791100. [34]

Junior, P. (2018), *Panorama do IPTU: Um Retrato da Administração Tributária em 53 Cidades Selecionadas*, https://www.ipea.gov.br/portal/index.php?option=com_content&view=article&id=34366&Itemid=433. [15]

Junior, P. (2017), *Property Tax Performance and Potential in Brazil*, http://hdl.handle.net/2263/62689. [13]

Kelly, R. (2012), "Property Tax Collection and Enforcement", in *A Primer on Property Tax*, Blackwell Publishing Ltd, Oxford, http://dx.doi.org/10.1002/9781118454343.ch6. [2]

Liu, Z. (2021), "Municipal finance and property taxation in China", in *Local Public Finance and Capacity Building in Asia: Issues and Challenges*, OECD Publishing, Paris, https://dx.doi.org/10.1787/73c69466-en. [40]

Mascagni, G., C. Nell and N. Monkam (2017), "One Size Does Not Fit All: A Field Experiment on the Drivers of Tax Compliance and Delivery Methods in Rwanda", *ICTD Working Paper*, No. 58, https://dx.doi.org/10.2139/ssrn.3120363. [33]

McCluskey, W. et al. (2013), "Computer Assisted Mass Appraisal and the Property Tax", in *A Primer on Property Tax: Administration and Policy*, John Wiley & Sons, Inc. [24]

Mikesell, J. (2012), "Administration of Local Taxes An International Review of Practices and Issues for Enhancing Fiscal autonomy", in *Primer on Property Tax: Administration and Policy*, John Wiley & Sons, Ltd, pp. 89-124, http://dx.doi.org/10.1002/9781118454343.ch4. [38]

Neve, J. et al. (2020), "How to Improve Tax Compliance? Evidence from Population-wide Experiments in Belgium", *The Warwick Economics Research Paper Series*, No. 1252, University of Warwick, Department of Economics (TWERPS), https://ideas.repec.org/p/wrk/warwec/1252.html. [31]

Nunlist, T. (2017), "Virtual Valuation: GIS-Assisted Mass Appraisal in Shenzhen", *Land Lines*, Lincoln Institute of Land. [25]

OECD (2021), *A Review of Local Government Finance in Israel: Reforming the Arnona System*, OECD Multi-level Governance Studies, OECD Publishing, Paris, https://dx.doi.org/10.1787/a5bc4d25-en. [8]

OECD (2020), *Tax Policy Reforms 2020: OECD and Selected Partner Economies*, OECD Publishing, Paris, https://dx.doi.org/10.1787/7af51916-en. [7]

OECD (2015), *OECD Economic Surveys: Belgium 2015*, OECD Publishing, Paris, https://dx.doi.org/10.1787/eco_surveys-bel-2015-en. [4]

OECD (2012), *Mejores prácticas registrales y catastrales en México*, OECD, Paris, https://www.oecd.org/centrodemexico/publicaciones/OCDE%20(2012)%20Mejores%20pr%C3%A1cticas%20registrales%20y%20catastrales%20en%20M%C3%A9xico.pdf (accessed on 13 December 2021). [16]

OECD (2005), *OECD Economic Surveys: Austria 2005*, OECD Publishing, Paris, https://dx.doi.org/10.1787/eco_surveys-aut-2005-en. [5]

Rosengard, J. (2012), "The Tax Everyone Loves to Hate: Principles of Property Tax Reform", in *A Primer on Property Tax*, Blackwell Publishing Ltd, Oxford, http://dx.doi.org/10.1002/9781118454343.ch7. [17]

Slack, E. and R. Bird (2014), "The Political Economy of Property Tax Reform", *OECD Working Papers on Fiscal Federalism*, No. 18, OECD Publishing, Paris, https://dx.doi.org/10.1787/5jz5pzvzv6r7-en. [20]

Smolka, M. and C. De Cesare (2012), "Property Tax Collection and Enforcement", in *A Primer on Property Tax: Administration and policy*, John Wiley & Sons. [14]

Thomas, A. (2021), "Reforming the taxation of housing in Israel", *OECD Taxation Working Papers*, No. 53, OECD Publishing, Paris, https://dx.doi.org/10.1787/83fd48ad-en. [19]

UN Habitat (2013), *Property tax regimes in Europe*, UN Habitat. [10]

Waldhart, P. and A. Reschovsky (2012), "Property Tax Delinquency and the Number of Payment Instalments", *Public Finance & Management*, Vol. 12/4, pp. 316-330. [35]

Walters, L. C., & International Association of Assessing Officers Research Committee (2014), "Staffing in assessment offices in the United States and Canada: Results of 2013 survey", *Journal of Property Tax Assessment & Administration*, Vol. 11/2, pp. 5-62. [41]

World Bank (2019), *Behavioural Insights for Tax Compliance*, eMBeD brief, World Bank, Washington, DC. [29]

World Bank/Development Research Center of the State Council, the People's Republic of China (2014), *Urban China: Toward Efficient, Inclusive, and Sustainable Urbanization*, World Bank. [12]

Notes

1 See Walters and of Assessing Officers Research Comittee (2014[41]).

2 See Almy (2014[1]).

3 This dependency on the tax administration for the collection of tax revenues is not exclusive for recurrent taxes on immovable property.

4 Topic explored in more detail in the Fiscal Cadastre section.

5 Almy (2014[1]).

6 Almy (2014[1]).

7 According to CDRF (2020[39]), this refers to the situation in China in which farmers sell their houses to urban residents, which is not recognised and protected by the law – rural residential land is collectively owned, and villagers only have the right to use the land. As a result, dwellers cannot apply for land-use certificates, property ownership certificates, tax deed certificates, etc. Through an on-going national programme, it is estimated that more that approximately three-quarters of rural, collectively owned land has gone through a land ownership registration process.

8 It is worth mentioning that calculations of market value should be independent from decisions about property tax revenues. Tax hikes can be avoided without changes in tax rates. Some tools implemented for that purpose are discussed in depth in the fourth chapter on property tax reforms.

9 In the case of capital values, it is important to know the taxable items since valuations aim at estimating only the values of these items. As shown in Figure 2.1, in the previous chapter, taxable items refer to land and improvement. In most OECD countries (26 out of 31 in the sample) both lands and buildings are taxed; only three OECD countries feature a pure land tax; and only two a pure land tax. Having both land and improvements as taxable items make it easier to use a property's market value, which captures both land and improvements simultaneously.

10 Four every two years, five every three years, eight every four years, seven every five years and two every six years.

11 For instance, in case the cost approach is used.

12 This topic will be covered in more detail at the end of this section.

13 Country examples based on Almy (2013[11]).

14 This is what the South Carolina/US Law requires but often the note is also sent even in the absence of such an increase in assessed property values.

15 Revenue equalisation systems are often based on revenue capacity. Nevertheless, it is not uncommon for countries to assess revenue capacity with actual tax revenues (Dougherty and Forman, 2021[42]).

[16] It is worth noting that tax benefits can also be granted through valuation policies (e.g. not updating property values, deliberately under-valuating properties, etc.).

[17] This occurs frequently in the United States due to their heavily decentralised tax system.

[18] Note that these recommendations of clearly delineating responsibilities and enhancing inter-governmental co-ordination apply to many other aspects of fiscal decentralisation, as explored in Forman, Dougherty and Blöchlinger (2020[6]).

[19] Although only India has a comparable population to that of China, aside from Australia and Canada, all these countries are among the 10th largest in terms of population.

[20] Business tax and urban construction tax (some industries excluded), city and town land-use tax, farmland conversion tax, land appreciation tax, property tax, vehicle and vessel tax, deed tax, slaughter tax, feast tax and tobacco tax (CDRF, 2020[39]).

4 Reforming recurrent taxes on immovable property

Recurrent taxes on immovable property tend to be unpopular among taxpayers for numerous reasons, including their visibility, indirect relation to income, perceived regressivity, potential for tax hikes and lack of sensitivity to economic growth. These challenges can be addressed through a combination of having frequent property reassessments, coupling tax reform to improvements in local services, allowing payment in instalments, provision of tax benefits and taxpayer education. It is also crucial to consider the impact of the reform across regions and levels of government – these reforms may exacerbate regional inequalities, which can be minimised with changes to equalisation systems. Gradual introduction of the reform can also be valuable to avoid abrupt and distortionary changes in tax obligations, as well as bundling the property tax with the reform of other related taxes. Lastly, timing can be crucial, with booming housing markets often being an ideal period to put forward such a reform.

Key messages

1. Recurrent taxes on immovable property have six main characteristics that usually create resistance for reforms: their visibility, presumptive nature, erratic volatility, indirect relation to income, perceived regressivity and lack of sensitivity to economic activity. These issues can be approached by specific design features.
2. The most promising approaches used to deal with unpopular features of recurrent taxes on immovable property include: payment in instalments, withholding tax at source, allowing payments to be made in conjunction with other payments, tax deferrals for seniors, tax reliefs for low-income households, taxpayer education and consultation, accessible appeal process, frequent reassessments, phased increases and indexing.
3. Certain countries employ solutions that, despite solving the underlying issue, create other distortions that can cause more harm than good. These potentially problematic approaches are assessment limits, property tax capping, banding, classified tax rates and self-assessments.
4. Bundling is a powerful tool that is commonly employed in recurrent property tax reforms as a way to overcome political resistance through compensation of losers and improvements in distributional effects. For instance, occasionally property tax reforms are bundled with inter-governmental fiscal relations reforms to alleviate problems related to the distribution of revenue across and within levels of government.
5. Engaging a wide range of stakeholders, obtaining a consensus on a reform's broad long-term goals and focusing the discussions on the systematic rather than individual impact of the reform are good communication strategies that can be adopted to reduce resistance to a tax reform.
6. Transitional measures can be useful to alleviate short-term effects of a tax hike, nevertheless reformers need to design and implement these measures in a manner such that the full implementation of the reform is secured so the reform can achieve its initial goals.
7. Timing is crucial in tax reforms. In general, most property tax reforms are made during economic upswings since governments tend to be in a better financial situation to compensate losers and since a potential reduction in house prices would lead to a stabilisation rather than an attenuation of price movements.

Introduction

Tax reforms in OECD countries are seldom implemented with ease and without political and/or popular opposition. Often tax reforms are discussed for years and yet they fail to reach the Congress/Parliament floor (Brys, 2011[1]). Sometimes they stall in the proposal phase. In other situations, the implemented reform differs significantly from the initial drafts. In the latter situation the reform may fail to accomplish the intended goals. Making tax reforms happen in a manner that it fulfils its goals is a challenge.

A successful tax reform normally takes into consideration potential conflicting public finance, economic, administrative, institutional and political factors and objectives. A tax reform is never completely neutral or Pareto optimal since at least a small group of actors will be worse off after its implementation. Even when the "losers" of the reform form a small group, they tend to organise themselves and, sometimes, have substantial political power. Conversely, people who benefit from the tax reform tend to be significantly less vocal (Blöchliger and Vammalle, 2012[2]). Concessions unrelated to the purpose of the reform at hand might be necessary to secure its approval and, therefore, other topics not directly related to the specific tax being reformed are commonly involved in the tax reform's discussion (Brys, 2011[1]).

Usually the reasons for reforming recurrent taxes on immovable property are to build on its strengths or ameliorate its shortcomings. To recap, at the local level, recurrent taxes on immovable property are particularly good for boosting local revenues, improving local autonomy and accountability and reducing vertical fiscal gaps. With regard to the tax system, neutral shifts towards recurrent taxes on immovable property can improve economic efficiency and, depending on the tax design, distribution of income. Other reasons to implement these taxes refers to their role in reducing the volatility of house prices and underpinning land-use policies. Reforms focused on the administrative process of the recurrent property tax system can be made so as to reduce costs and inequities generated by unequal treatment of taxpayers and to increase compliance.

Most tax reforms typically face common obstacles in addition to tax-specific hurdles. Factors that can undermine a reform's implementation are, among others, the impact on the revenue of multiple levels of government, the popularity of the tax, uncertainty about their distributional consequences, transitional costs and timing – Brys (2011[1]) and Slack & Bird (2014[3]). In general, efficiency gains, whose effects are mostly felt in the long term, are less of a concern while, in contrast, distributional effects that are felt in the short-term can generate resistance from the groups that become worse off (Brys, 2011[1]). Besides, regarding the particularities of recurrent taxes on immovable properties, special attention should be given to features that makes it unpopular, such as their salience, liquidity constraints, perceived regressively, erratic volatility, presumptive nature and small buoyancy (Slack and Bird, 2014[3]).

This chapter's goal is to analyse general guidelines/good practices that are followed/employed in OECD countries to reform recurrent taxes on immovable property. It is divided into three sections. The first section focuses on the specific hurdles to reforms of recurrent taxes on immovable property; the second discusses common strategies that are used in all types of tax reforms; and, lastly, the third examines how specific problems related to fiscal federalism and inter-governmental relations can be handled.

Hurdles in reforms of recurrent taxes on immovable property

Recurrent taxes on immovable property have six main problems that create resistance for reforms: their visibility, presumptive nature, erratic volatility, potential non-relation to taxpayers' income, perceived regressivity and small buoyancy (Slack and Bird, 2014[3]). The first five make these taxes unpopular among taxpayers while the last affect governments. This section explores solutions employed by OECD countries to approach these problems. Table 4.1, below, summarises potentially successful and problematic strategies to deal with these issues.

Table 4.1. Strategies for property tax reform

Issues and Problems	Promising Approaches	Potentially Problematic Approaches
Salience: property tax is more visible than other taxes	• Couple tax reform with improvements in local services • Tax paid in several instalments • Withhold tax at source/payment in conjunction with other payments	• Assessment limits • Property tax capping • Banding • Classified tax rates • Self-assessment • Sole use of indexation
Liquidity constraints: tax is a burden for the housing-rich but income poor, especially seniors	• Tax deferrals • Tax reliefs • More payment options	
Perceived regressivity: Taxes can be higher as a percentage of income for low-income taxpayers	• Progressive tax rates[1] • Tax reliefs • Bundle with other tax reforms	
Presumptive tax: tax base is inherently arbitrary	• Taxpayer education • Consultation • Accessible appeal process • Conservative valuations	
Erratic volatility: potentially sudden large swings in taxes for some taxpayers	• Frequent reassessment • Indexing between reassessments • Phased increases	
Small buoyancy inelasticity: taxes do not increase with economic growth	• Frequent reassessments • Indexing between reassessments	

1. This solution is not recommended by some authors, such as Slack and Bird (2014[3]). Among other problems, levying progressive rates alone can aggravate the problem of asset-rich income-poor households.
Source: Authors, primarily based on Blöchliger (2015[4]), Slack and Bird (2014[3]) and UN-Habitat (2013[5]).

Salience improves accountability and transparency at the cost of popular resistance

Recurrent taxes on immovable property are very salient and transparent, unlike most other taxes. The most relevant taxes in terms of revenue-raising capacity are levied on income, consumption or payroll (i.e. mostly as social security contributions). All these taxes are, in most cases, collected automatically through payments and/or withheld at source, which requires the taxpayer to take no additional action to pay them. In contrast, in most cases taxpayers need to take action to pay their recurrent property taxes. Furthermore, taxes levied on income, consumption and payroll are paid "continuously" throughout a fiscal year whereas the recurrent taxes on immovable property are often paid in a (a couple of) relatively larger lump-sum payment(s).

On one hand this salience and transparency can improve efficiency and government accountability but, on the other hand, they create fierce opposition to tax hikes. In principle it is good for taxpayers to be aware of their tax payments so they can demand an appropriate supply of public service. Since recurrent taxes on immovable property are usually accrued to local governments and since public local services tend to be more visible than public services provided by upper levels of government, it is possible to directly link payments to a visible improvement in the supply of public services. There is evidence that when taxpayers can visualise the benefits that they receive from paying taxes, they are more willing to pay them (Slack and Bird, 2014[3]).

Offering the option for taxpayers to pay the tax in several instalments, withholding the tax at source and coupling the tax reform with improvements in local services are among the most common solutions to overcome the problem related to property tax salience. Although payment in instalments neither reduces the tax burden nor the transparency, the payment in multiple instalments reduces the value of each payment, which reduces its salience. Withholding the tax at source or coupling the tax payment with other payments can also help in reducing its salience but in this case at the cost of a reduction in transparency. For instance, property taxes can be paid in the same bill as mortgages and utilities. In some cases, it can also be withheld directly from income (e.g. see Box 4.1 in the Irish case). Lastly, coupling the tax reform with improvements in local services follows the benefit principle of taxation in which the tax payment serves as the payment of a public service, improving accountability. Nevertheless, it is also the most difficult to implement because it depends on activities beyond the scope of tax policy and because service improvements often require some time to become apparent whereas tax levies are immediate.[1]

Liquidity: the imperfect link between property values and income can create liquidity problems

Unlike other taxes, taxes levied on properties are often based on a stock rather than a flow. Although the value of properties is indeed correlated with the income of taxpayers, these two numbers are not perfectly associated. Thus, the tax obligation might be particularly large as a proportion of taxpayers' income for asset-rich income-poor households. Usually pensioners are in that group, which might be one of the reasons why they tend to oppose recurrent property tax reforms.

Not only pensioners suffer this problem though – other taxpayers that lose either temporarily or permanently their source of income may also have liquidity problems to pay their property tax obligations. In 2020 this problem occurred in many countries due the COVID-19 outbreak. The outbreak reduced the income of some households but not the value of their properties (at least in the short term), creating a temporary mismatch between their property tax obligations and their financial situation. To cope with this problem, some countries decided to defer or even exempt a portion of property tax payments, such as Chile and Italy (OECD, 2020[6]).

There are multiple ways to solve this problem such as by granting: deferrals for seniors, tax exemptions or rebates based on income and more payment options. The case for deferrals is strong since they do not change the tax obligation, they only match the tax obligation payment with the period in which the taxpayer is expected to have a better ability to pay for it. Nevertheless, such schemes are not particularly popular among taxpayers and are thus not popular politically, given that the elderly, which compose the group of asset-rich income poor households, typically wish to leave their property for their heirs without substantial amounts of obligations (Slack and Bird, 2014[3]). As a result, taxpayers might be disinclined to take advantage of tax deferral programmes, which don't solve the problem of the mismatch between property tax liabilities and current income. For these reasons, which could be the most economically efficient solution has limited power to weaken the resistance of the elderly against recurrent taxes on immovable property. Countries usually handle this problem through tax reliefs programmes. Some focus directly on pensioners (e.g. in Australia, Chile, Estonia, the Slovak Republic and some U.S states) while others on low-income households (e.g. in Estonia, Italy, Japan, Portugal, the Slovak Republic and the United States).[2]

Box 4.1. Irish property tax reform of 2013: A tax reform from scratch

Ireland levies two separate types of recurrent property taxes, one mainly on commercial property (Commercial Rates and non-Principal Private Residence Tax – NPPR) and the other on residential property (Local Property Tax – LPT). This box discusses the latter type.

The levy on residential property was introduced in a phased manner. In 2012, Ireland introduced an annual lump sum household charge (EUR 100 per house regardless of size) but only for one year. In 2013, the annual household charge was replaced by the residential property tax. Specifically in 2013 the property tax applied only for half of the year (since it was implemented in July) and from 2014 onwards it started to apply on a full-year basis. The Irish case has interesting peculiarities that makes it relevant for countries that aim at implementing a reform nearly from scratch.

The tax base of the LPT is wide: it is liable on any residential property. For LPT purposes, residential property is defined any building or structure which is in use as, or is suitable for use as, a dwelling and includes any shed, outhouse, garage or other building or structure and any yard, garden or other land, appurtenant to or usually enjoyed with that building, save that so much of any such yard, garden or other land that exceeds one acre shall not be taken into account for the purposes of this definition. Even residential portions of business premises are taxable. Exemptions include charities, properties situated in unfinished housing estates, nursing homes, properties vacated by their owners due to illness, diplomatic properties and property purchased, built or adapted to make it suitable for occupation by a permanently and totally incapacitated individual.

Regarding tax rates, they are progressive and the level of government responsible for setting them changed throughout the years. The LPT started as a central tax but, in 2015, new powers were conferred to local authorities. The incremental reform of 2015 let local governments vary the annual rate by up to 15%. The goal of this incremental reform was to boost local autonomy.

One of the main problems that the Irish had to overcome regards the fact that property values were not updated since 1845 – the Irish government relied on a banding system and self-assessments, both potentially problematic approaches. A banding system with 19 bands was used to determine properties' values in conjunction with self-assessments, which were planned to be used in the first three years of the implementation. Taxpayers (i.e. in this case property owners) must select a band based on their own estimation of their property market value. In order to increase the accuracy of taxpayers' estimations, the Irish government provided at least three options for determining a property's value: 1) An online interactive guide that gives data on market values of properties in a given locality, considering property's characteristics such as age, type of property (e.g. apartment, house) and others; 2) The use of the value of the property registered for the purpose of the stamp duty; and 3) Hire a professional valuer. The central government can raise cadastral values in case it is believed that the valuation was not accurate enough.

To deal with the unpopularity of property taxes' salience, the Irish government allowed the LPT to be deducted at source. Property owners were given the choice of 1) paying their tax obligations in one single payment; or 2) having the tax deducted at source from salary or occupational pensions. The Irish government required employers and pension providers to make this second option available. As a result of these measures, the compliance rate for 2013 was nearly 90%.

Efforts were also made to solve the issue of the asset rich cash poor households (i.e. with income below a threshold) by letting taxpayers opt to defer, or partially defer, LPT's payment to when the property is sold. This threshold varies with, for instance, whether the taxpayer took out mortgages at the height of the property boom. Interest at a rate of 4% per annum is charged on deferred amounts.

Source: Slack and Bird (2014[3]), OECD Revenue Statistics and OECD Survey on Recurrent Taxes on Immovable Property.

Perceived regressivity of recurrent taxes on immovable property can be minimised with tax rate progressivity, tax reliefs to low-income households and bundling strategies

Recurrent taxes on immovable property are normally perceived to be regressive. As discussed in the second chapter, the empirical research on tax incidence suggests that the property tax can indeed be anything from progressive to regressive because the redistributive effect of property taxation hinges on various factors, such as the distribution of home ownership and tax design. In addition, recurrent taxes on immovable property are considered to have a smaller impact on the income distribution than other important taxes, notably income taxes. As a result, recurrent property taxation can be seen as regressive even if their impacts are not necessarily so.

Most countries aim at making their recurrent taxes on immovable property more progressive/less regressive by either levying progressive tax rates or by granting tax reliefs or exemptions to low-income households (to recap see Figures 2.4 and 2.5) It is worth noting that, in the latter case, the problem of asset rich and income poor households is also alleviated. Progressive rates can indeed increase the progressivity of a property tax system but, in some situations, it can aggravate the problem of asset rich income poor households.

Another potential solution is bundling a reform of recurrent taxes on immovable property with other taxes (e.g. income tax, wealth tax and inheritance tax) in a manner that the overall impact of the reform improves the income distribution even if the impact of the reform of recurrent property taxes alone would not. Property tax reforms can also be bundled with policies outside the realm of taxation – for instance, the reform can be bundled with an income-transfer programme targeted to the poor and, thus, although the property tax will not be progressive, the overall fiscal system will be (Kitchen, 2012[7]) or with provision of other public services, such as education (Ahmad, 2021[8]). Cash transfers to low-income households tend to be among the best tools to reduce income inequality (see Chapter 2).

In China's case, recurrent taxes on the ownership of properties tend to be more progressive than for other countries. As discussed in the second chapter, since real estate represents most of the wealth of Chinese households, recurrent taxes on immovable property can have a greater effect in reducing income inequalities (OECD, 2019[9]). This prominence of real estate in household wealth can be highlighted in the discussions about the reform, potentially raising its popular appeal. Linking the reform to the provision of public services can have, though, greater redistributive effects.

The presumptive nature of recurrent taxes on immovable property can lead to unfair assessments or perception of unfairness – both of which can be mitigated with a good tax administration

Property values are a relative concept – different buyers may value the same property differently and, thus, rarely can one estimate a value for a property that is considered fair by everyone. In recurrent taxes on immovable property, property values have to be estimated to serve as a basis for the tax obligation. This problem does not occur, for instance, in transaction taxes in which the taxable value is the value agreed between the buyer and seller. The necessity of having an estimation of the tax basis can lead to the situation in which taxpayers believe that the value of their properties is not being correctly assessed. can contribute to the tax being perceived as unfair, which may create problems in property tax reforms (see Box 4.2 on Latvia's case).

Multiple tools can be put to use to reduce the perceived unfairness in property assessments – for instance, taxpayer education, involvement of the taxpayer in the valuation process, accessible appeal process and conservative valuations. All these solutions involve a continuous effort from the tax administration. A transparent administrative process that timely makes information available to taxpayers is crucial for the tax system to be perceived as fair. For that purpose, tax bill notifications may serve as a communication channel, in addition to other channels such as television, newspapers and posters advertisements.

Communication can focus not only on explaining the process of the tax collection but also on explaining the role of the property tax in funding public services (Box 3.5, in the previous chapter, covered this issue in more detail). Communication should also occur both ways, by giving room for the taxpayer to ask questions and query the tax department, potentially leading to changes in assessments if the taxpayer has a strong point.

Lastly, conservative valuations[3] (i.e. that aim at estimating a value slightly below properties' values) might also significantly reduce appeals since when taxpayers believe that the assessed value is below market values they are less likely to appeal. Although this practice can reduce tax revenues,[4] it can also increase compliance and reduce the appeal rate, both of which are costly to the tax administration.

Box 4.2. Latvia's property tax revolt

Latvia is one of the three Baltic states located in the Baltic region of Northern Europe with an estimated population of 1.93 million as of 2018. The country introduced recurrent taxes on immovable property (Real Property Taxation – RET) in 1997 and has been incrementally improving their design and administration since then.

RET accrues to local government but its administration is shared across levels of government

RET administration is shared across levels of government and agencies. The Ministry of Finance is responsible for defining the general principles. The Ministry of Justice was responsible for defining guidelines for property valuation, cadastre, and ownership registration. An Executive body (State Land Service) is responsible for the maintenance of the cadastre, cadastral valuation and surveying buildings. Local governments are the executive body and beneficiary of the RET, being responsible for revenue collection in their jurisdiction, determination of land use for taxation purposes, development of local and spatial planning documents and issuance of building permissions. In addition, local governments can set tax rates and grant reliefs for residential estates of "politically repressed persons" (up to 50% of the tax obligation) and for vulnerable groups (up to 90%).

The RET levies on land and buildings (different tax rate may apply to both) and exempts government buildings, property owned by a foreign state, graveyards, property owned by religious organisations, land in special natural reserves, transport infrastructure, among others. The incidence is on owners or persons with possession rights and users of state or municipal real property.

Recent reforms have increased RET's tax burden

The fiscal crisis of 2008 led local governments to improve their fiscal sustainability through, among other measures, a property tax hike. From 2008 until 2016 many incremental reforms increased the property tax burden. In 2010 rates applied to land increased from 1.0% to 1.5%; in 2011, a housing tax was introduced and some types of residential property that were previously exempted (e.g. detached houses, apartments, summer cottages) became taxable. In 2012 tax rates applied to housing were doubled. Since 2013, a rate of 1.5% has been applied to vacant residential buildings.

The legislation gives local governments room for applying different tax rates to different types of property, and since 2014 this flexibility has been used by many Latvia's municipalities with the purpose of attracting residents through the offer of tax reliefs (usually 50%) on owner occupied dwellings. In addition, tax rates differ for an owner's inhabited and uninhabited properties. Higher tax rates are also applied to second homes regardless of taxpayers' income. The purpose of these tax treatments is to reverse Latvia's shrinking population by incentivising people to move to inhabited houses, whose share as a percentage of total houses approached 20.6% in 2011. This high rate is explained by the fact that many people own several residential properties and that the house ownership rates reach 80% (one of the highest numbers in Europe).

For instance, in Latvia's capital, Riga, the RET rate applied to buildings in unoccupied properties increased, in some cases, sevenfold. At the same time, the municipality of Riga offers RET discounts to persons that own only one property. This policy achieved the desired results in the capital: the number of Riga's residents in 2015–2016, for the first time in many years, showed a growth tendency. As a result, other municipalities of the agglomeration of Riga later followed Riga's example.

Public resistance and protests

Despite the success of these reforms in increasing the number of dwellers, they were heavily criticised by a group of taxpayers. One of the reasons for the criticism is not directly related to this specific reform but to the fact that cadastral values supposedly did not reflect market values, as suggested by reports and audits. Thus, issues in property valuation eroded taxpayers' confidence and brought resistance to the tax reform, regardless of its noble objective.

The unpopularity of the reform has led Latvia to freeze cadastral values until the Ministry of Finance develops a solution for this problem. It is worth noting that although the group that is against the property tax reform was very vocal, the activity of the group in social networks and the volume of protest activity were limited, suggesting that the group was not very large. This makes sense considering that only 2% of all properties were heavily affected by the tax hike since the boost in tax rates were accompanied by discounts for more vulnerable groups (e.g. poverty stricken, families with three children, poverty-stricken pensioners, politically repressed persons). Furthermore, increasingly often opinions are voiced that RET is a necessary disciplinary tax and that taxpayers agree that higher RET rates should be applied to second homes.

Conclusion

Despite reform's noble objectives (i.e. to increase local government revenue and to reverse a shrinking population) and their progressive features (i.e. taxing more second and vacant homes and granting reliefs to vulnerable groups), Latvia's recent property tax reform faced a vocal opposition. Although the group that opposed the reforms is not numerous, its resistance was sufficient to make the government freeze cadastral values, at least temporarily. The resistance movement was helped significantly by the fact that cadastral values were considered unfair in the eyes of taxpayers. Indeed, it seems that the process of property revaluation was not adapted on time to keep up with the changes in legislation.

This case offers interesting lessons. First, despite achieving a reform's objectives (i.e. Riga was successful in increasing its population) and despite the fact that most taxpayers pay a low tax rate, a small but vocal opposition can influence and damage a reform's implementation. Second, when cadastral values are unfair in the eyes of taxpayers, the opposition of a tax reform is inflated (see also Box 3.1 that showed how horizontal inequities can lead to a complete discontinuation of a property tax). Third, taxpayers' education can boost popular support and help the implementation of reforms.

Source: Barvika (2020[10]).

Erratic volatility: tax obligations can vary abruptly when cadastral values are rarely updated, creating resistance against property revaluations

Although property values tend to change over time, unless they are updated in the fiscal cadastre, tax obligations are not going to reflect properties' value. The longer the period in between reassessments, the greater the mismatch. And the greater the mismatch, the greater the tax hike when properties are reassessed. Abrupt tax hikes are unpopular. The end result is a reinforcing feedback loop, in which the more cadastral values are outdated, the more likely for their update to be unpopular, reducing the likelihood of a reform's approval and implementation, perpetuating distortions.

Tax hikes caused by property revaluations are also not uniform: shifts in taxes depend on the movement in housing prices that can differ markedly by region or even neighbourhood. Thus, even if the average house has not appreciated much, the tax hike can be significant for some taxpayers. And, again, since income and property values are not perfectly linked, this increase in tax obligation can lead to liquidity problems and face fierce opposition, as was the case in many reforms (Slack and Bird, 2014[3]).

In principle, the best solution for this problem is to keep cadastral values updated. This requires frequent reassessments that can be costly. Indexing between reassessments can also help but if used alone may lead to distortions since indexing, by definition, uses an index that represents an overall price change and house prices' movements are asymmetrical by region, infrastructure, among others. Therefore, indexing can be used as a palliative solution but, if used alone, will lead to horizontal inequities and, in the long run, a tax hike for houses that experienced a greater increase in their market values in comparison to their cadastral values may still lead to abrupt tax hikes. Phased increases can also help but, again, should be very well structured to not create distortions (see Box 4.3 on Denmark's case).

On the one hand, inelasticity with regard to the cycle can create a mismatch between tax revenues and government expenditures but, on the other hand, can serve as a cushion in times of crisis

The fact that property tax bases are relatively inelastic with respect to economic activity can create long-term mismatches between property tax revenues and government expenditures. Belinga et al. (2014[11]) estimated the buoyancy of different types of taxes in OECD countries and concluded that, with regard to property taxes, their short-run buoyancy is the only one that is not statistically significant, and that their long-run buoyancy is the lowest among other taxes (i.e. personal income tax, social security contributions, corporate income tax, and good and service tax). This can be explained by three factors: 1) the imperfect link between property values and economic activity; 2) the mismatch between house prices and cadastral values; and 3) local policy makers in some countries (more notably in the United States) often reduce statutory tax rates when properties' market values are raising in order to not increase the tax burden on dwellers while maintaining their property tax revenues.

Despite these factors, policy makers and tax administrators can make property taxes more buoyant through different means. First, regarding the imperfect link between property tax bases and economic activity, policy makers can select a more "buoyant tax base" – property taxes applied to capital and rental values tend to be more buoyant than area-based ones, since the latter has no significant link with the economic activity while it is expected that a booming economy would increase house prices and rents (Almy, 2014[12]). Second, the mismatch between house prices and cadastral values can be minimised if cadastral values are indexed in-between reassessments and/or properties value are reassessed frequently (see Figure 3.3, in the previous chapter, to see examples of countries that implemented such measures). Third, tax rates should, ideally, not be reduced in times of house price booms.

This last recommendation is disputable and it is worth digging into it further since inelasticity with regard to the economic cycle reduces the impact of crises on property tax revenues. As a result, all other things held equal, the higher the share of recurrent taxes on immovable property revenues in government revenues, the less they are impacted by economic crises – see OECD (2020[13]). Given that local governments tend to have less access to financial markets than central governments, which raises their vulnerability to liquidity crisis, this feature of recurrent taxes on immovable property is especially valuable for them.

In that light, Belinga et al. (2014[11]) suggested that municipalities might aim at keeping property tax revenues stable, regardless of what happens to GDP (and house prices). Norregaard (2013[14]) showed that even in periods of very rapid property price appreciation, property tax buoyancy still remains low.

Lutz (2008[15]) performed empirical research for US states and concluded that the elasticity of property tax revenues with respect to home prices equals 0.4, indicating that statutory tax rates are probably adjusted downwards when house prices rise, reducing the tax buoyancy and stabilising property tax revenues. Norregaard (2013[14]) also found that SNGs in the United States tend to compensate for revenues losses in times of crisis by increasing property tax rates. In this situation, property tax rates tend to behave counter-cyclically – they increase in times of crisis and decrease during economic upswings.

Despite these benefits that stem from having a stable revenue source, it cannot be overstated that the main goal of a tax is to raise revenues for governments. Taxation is the main means through which governments can fund public services. Thus, the long-run buoyancy of property taxes should, ideally, not be very small. Very small long-run buoyancy would reduce the capacity of property taxes to raise revenues and, thus, would harm the funding of essential public services. In case other taxes are adjusted upwards to offset this small buoyancy of property taxes, there will be a neutral shift towards these other types of taxes, changing the properties of the tax system, potentially in an undesired manner since this change was driven only by the necessity to raise more revenues. The use of a more buoyant tax base and frequent property revaluation (possibly with the use of indexed cadastral values between revaluations if they are not frequent enough) are, thus, recommended.

Box 4.3. Denmark's ending the property valuation freeze in place since 2002

In 2001-02, the Danish Government implemented a "tax freeze" policy with the goal of controlling public spending by freezing tax revenues. The tax freeze applied to multiple types of taxes. For taxes that are stated in percentages, their rates were capped, while for taxes that are stated as nominal amounts, their amounts were frozen. In the case of recurrent property taxes (i.e. Denmark levies a land tax, commercial building tax and a residential property tax), the increase in cadastral values was capped at 5% of the 2001's values.

Nonetheless, in addition to the intended effects of controlling expenditure, the property tax freeze also impacted the housing market in a negative manner. With cadastral values capped, property taxes failed to alleviate the abrupt increase in house prices that occurred in the mid-2000s, potentially leading to a more volatile economic and financial cycle. Furthermore, a tax deduction for mortgage interest rates also encouraged house purchases, contributing to the housing market boom of that decade. As discussed in the second chapter of this report, favourable tax treatment of owner-occupied housing can create distortions in investment allocation, favouring housing investments over others.

In order to alleviate these undesirable effects, Denmark recently made significant changes to its housing taxation. From 2021 onwards, cadastral values – for the property value tax and for the land tax – are expected to reflect market values, thereby ending the property valuation freeze in place since 2002, which has led to falling effective tax rates for houses experiencing increases in value. These changes can lead to an abrupt tax hike and, thus, can significantly affect taxpayers. To alleviate this expected increase in tax obligations, Denmark coupled the cadastral values updated with other changes in its property tax system. First, statutory tax rates will be lowered. Second, a tax rebate will be granted to taxpayers in order to compensate for increases in tax obligations. Third, in an effort to protect homeowners from tax increases while they occupy their own home, increases in tax obligations can also be deferred until the property is sold.

In essence, Denmark is bundling the de-freeze with other property tax measures, creating, to some extent, a "phased-in" reform. As a result, Denmark will be able to lift its property tax freeze that was in place for nearly two decades, which is typically unpopular and politically challenging. Although the property tax revenue might be mildly affected in the short-term, the reform will reduce horizontal inequities and inefficiencies generated by the tax freeze.

Source: OECD (2018[16]), Smidova (2016[17]) and OECD (2005[18]).

The use of assessment limits, property tax capping, banding, classified tax rates and self-assessments can create distortions that, in the end, might cause more harm than good

Some countries employ solutions that do solve one of these specific problems but at the cost of creating others. Caution is advised when employing these palliative solutions. Among them there are the imposition of assessment limits, property tax capping, banding, classified tax rates, use of self-assessments for property assessments and the sole use of indexation for updating cadastral values. The reasons are provided below – based on Slack & Bird (2014[3]):

- Assessment limits (i.e. restrictions to how much properties' cadastral values can increase) and property tax capping (i.e. restrictions to how much tax obligations can increase) both aim at cushioning property tax hikes and, thus, they also have a role in reducing the chances of causing liquidity problems to taxpayers when tax obligations increase. Nevertheless, these benefits come at the cost of horizontal inequities. By capping increases in property values, some properties are going to be undervalued in comparison to others (see Box 4.4 on the Californian case). More specifically, properties whose values are growing rapidly will be undervalued in comparison to properties whose values are either stable, growing slowly or decreasing. As a result, taxpayers that are having their assets appreciating the most are the ones who benefit the most from these restrictions, which may create distortions that reduce the progressivity of the tax.
- A similar outcome occurs when tax obligations are capped: taxpayers who should be taxed the most are those with higher property values and, thus, they benefit the most from tax capping. Moreover, capping taxes obligations, either directly or through limits on assessments, are also capping tax revenues. In the long run, limits to tax revenues can create mismatch between tax revenues and government expenditures. In addition, paradoxically, because such measures reduce the elasticity of property tax revenues, they likely increase the pressure for future property tax reforms (Slack and Bird, 2014[3]).
- Banding, which is used, for instance, in the United Kingdom and Ireland, can alleviate the impact of property value hikes and reduce administrative costs since banding systems are rather simple to understand and to administer. Nevertheless, banding creates horizontal inequities caused by the impossibility of valuing properties in such a discrete manner – the range of values (or values per square meters) of houses vary markedly, which is not captured by the small number of bands (e.g. eight values in the United Kingdom and nineteen in Ireland).[5] This discrete nature of this system is particularly perverse for taxpayers located in a boundary of a band, leading to appeals and discontent.
- Self-assessments are useful for dealing with the presumptive nature of the property tax and also for reducing administrative costs but these benefits come at the cost of precision. Self-assessments should not be confused with consultation. The former regards the situation in which taxpayers provide the value of their property whereas the latter refers to the case in which taxpayers provide additional pieces of information that are used in the appraisal. Consultation is a good tool to gather data in a relatively cheap way while improving the credibility of the appraisals in the eyes of the taxpayers given that they participate in the valuation process. Self-assessments can also be useful when employed temporally, but when employed permanently and as the only means to gather properties' information, they are likely to lead to inaccurate estimates of property values, with a tendency toward under-estimation[6] (Slack and Bird, 2014[3]). In case governments are to audit self-assessments to handle these issues, they might significantly increase costs and create discontent, defeating the purpose of setting a self-assessment system.
- Classified tax rates (i.e. the situation in which multiple tax rates are applied to different "classes" of properties) can be used to increase progressivity in case tax rates vary with variables linked to income. When varying tax rates apply to different properties whose incidence rests on taxpayers

in a manner that the higher the rate the higher taxpayers' ability to pay, in theory, we have a progressive tax system. Nevertheless, classification of properties can significantly increase the complexity of the tax system and create room for arbitrary classifications (see Box 4.4 on the Ontario's case, below, and Box 3.6, on the Israeli case, in the previous chapter). The higher the complexity of the tax system the lower its transparency and the higher its compliance costs, and the higher the room for governors/policy makers to classify properties and to define tax rates to each type of property, the more the tax system can be exploited to benefit some taxpayers due to political reasons, generating horizontal inequities.

- Indexation, as discussed throughout this section, can yield good results if used in between frequent reassessments. It does increase buoyancy and it also averages out strong tax hikes. Nevertheless, the sole use of indexation will create horizontal inequities in the long term since the effect captured by the index represents an average and not individual house prices. House prices' movements vary markedly depending on many aspects of a property such as its region, neighbourhood, infrastructure, among others and, thus, cadastral values that were only updated though indexing will lead to unfair assessments in the long term.

Box 4.4. The cases of California/United States and Ontario/Canada

Ontario's classified property tax system

In 1998 the province of Ontario, Canada, implemented a significant fiscal reform, which involved a property tax reform along with a fiscal reform that covered the delineation of responsibilities across municipal and provincial governments, the state-local transfer system, and a reduction in the number of municipalities from 800 to 445. The property tax reform had two pillars: a uniform assessment system based on properties' market values and a classified tax rate system. Municipalities were allowed to levy different tax rates on seven classes of property (residential, multi-residential, commercial, industrial, pipelines, farms and managed forests). At the same time, they could 1) establish additional classes in case they wish so (e.g. new multi-residential, office buildings, shopping centres, parking lots, large industrial properties); 2) reduce tax rates for specific subclasses of property (e.g. vacant commercial, vacant industrial, farmland pending development, theatres); 3) create more subclasses for some specific classes (i.e. commercial and industrial) depending on properties' values; and 4) establish progressive tax rates within classes. The final outcome was that there were dozens of classes of properties and the respective tax rates could vary across classes, across properties' values and across the 445 municipalities in Ontario.

In subsequent years, Ontario introduced new pieces of legislation to reduce the burden of property taxes on housing and business. For instance, tax deferrals, phase-ins, caps on tax increases and claw backs were introduced. The valuation cycle was enlarged from annual to every four years. All these measures in conjunction made Ontario's tax system very complex and inefficient with regard to revenue-raising capacity.

California's tax limits and horizontal inequities

The classic example of a property tax limitation arising from a tax revolt is Proposition 13, which was passed by referendum in California in 1978 and remains in place. Proposition 13 is an amendment of the Constitution of California aimed at limiting property taxation burden on residential and commercial properties. Among other elements, it limits the tax rate for real estate to 1% and restricts annual increases of cadastral values to inflation, limited to an annual increase of 2%. In the cases of change in ownership or completion of new construction the property can be fully reassessed (i.e. the transaction price becomes the cadastral value in case of a sale), updating the cadastral values with the new reassessed values. It is worth noting that California house prices have grown much faster than inflation – a house price index for California estimates that house prices have grown by a multiple of seven from 1980 to 2020.[1] As a result, Proposition 13 granted huge tax benefits for properties whose ownership did not change throughout the years.

Proposition 13 was successful in providing the desired tax burden stability for taxpayers who stay in their homes. Nevertheless, this came in exchange for economic efficiency and fairness. Under Proposition 13, virtually identical properties can have a vastly different tax burden depending on a property's last transaction date. The transaction date is not correlated with taxpayers' ability to pay and, thus, in some circumstances, Proposition 13 can have strong regressive impacts. In addition, it discourages property transactions that are necessary to improve the allocation of resources. For instance, a family might decide not to move closer to its work because of the higher property tax obligation, which causes an increase in their commuting time and transport costs, negatively impacting the traffic and the environment. Similar situations also apply to business. Moreover, Proposition 13 limits the revenue-raising capacity of the property tax, resulting in reductions in local spending.

Despite these issues, Proposition 13 remains popular. Proposition 15, which would have switched commercial property value assessments to market value, was narrowly defeated in the 2020 election. It is likely that repealing Proposition 13 altogether would be even less popular.

1. See https://fred.stlouisfed.org/series/CASTHPI (accessed on 20 February 2021)

Source: Slack and Bird (2014[3]) and McCluskey and Franzsen (2012[19]).

General strategies in tax reforms

A successful implementation of a tax reform usually involves a sound plan that takes into consideration not only the design aspects of the tax but also operational and political aspects such as timing, a transition phase and communication (Brys, 2011[1]). Without a sound strategy, the ability of special interests to influence the reform or administrative problems can create impediments to a reform's full implementation. This section discusses strategies that can be employed to most tax reforms (i.e. not restricted to recurrent taxes on immovable property) given that regardless of the type of tax, tax reforms face a set of similar challenges.

Brys (2011[1]) explored multiple challenges and strategies related to tax reforms, several of which are summarised here. First, the approval of fundamental reforms depends greatly on the political context of a given period. Usually, policy makers discuss and prepare a reform in a given time and wait for the proper timing to put it forward. Second, the impact of a tax reform can change over time – the losers at the initial phase of a reform might be winners at a later stage. Furthermore, efficiency gains usually arise only in the medium to long term while distributional impacts can be immediate. As a result, for some time a reform can leave many people worse off and a phased reform or transitory measures might be necessary to alleviate these impacts. Third, a reform can greatly affect the tax administration process, and, therefore, a reform's pace should depend on the pace in which the tax administration can implement it. Fourth, communication is crucial to minimise changes in a reform's design throughout its approval and implementation phases. A proper communication can greatly improve a reform's success likelihood through, among others, explicitly establishing its priorities, reduction of uncertainty about its effect and creating public awareness of and support for the reform. These challenges and strategies are approached in more detail throughout this section.

Timing: economic upswings and booming housing markets can create an opportune moment for putting forward a property tax reform, yet reforms following downturns can also be successfully implemented

Kingdon (2014[20]) created a theory that explains the process through which a policy is designed and implemented – the Multiple Streams Framework. This framework outlines that a solution to a problem in the format of a policy is only implemented when three different streams come together at the same moment: the problem, policy and political streams. The problem stream refers to the public and media attention given to a specific problem. The policy stream refers to the existence of solutions to address this particular problem. The political stream regards the policy makers' motivation to implement a project with such a solution. Therefore, according to this theory, a policy is only implemented when, at the same moment, the people/media are giving attention to a particular problem for which there are available solutions that can solve the issue and the policy makers have incentives to turn at least one proposed solution into an implemented policy. This moment when these three streams come together is called a policy window.

Policy windows are not necessarily created in a spontaneous manner Kingdon (2014[20]). In fact, "policy entrepreneurs" are actors whose role is to create policy windows so a policy can be successfully launched into the political arena. Tax reforms are no different. Tax reforms that are well-designed to solve the underlying issue and that are backed by the general public and policy makers have greater chances of approval. As a result, it is crucial to put the reform forward only when these elements are in favour of the tax reforms. For these reasons, reforms are prepared in advance and usually wait for a good timing to be put forward (Brys, 2011[1]). Besides, there are multiple aspects of a reform that depend on timing such as when the reform is discussed with policy makers, when it should be discussed with the general public, when it should come into force, among others. Regarding the latter (the implementation), it is worth highlighting that the implementation of a tax reform can have multiple phases, and the implementation of each phase also depends on good timing to be successful. Not rarely reforms are phased and there is no support for the latter incremental stages of a reform, leading to an incomplete reform (see Box 4.6 on the Korean case at the end of this section).

Some particularly relevant issues for timing a property tax reform are the states of public finances, economy and housing market. Experience shows that it might be easier to implement fundamental tax reform when a country is running budget surpluses that could absorb possible revenue losses or could be used to partly compensate the "losers" from the tax reform (Brys, 2011[1]). Regarding the economy, due to the salience of property taxes, introducing revenue raising property tax reforms in economic downturns can harm households whose income have shrunk and, thus, not able to pay the taxes. In other words, the reform would not only have less compliance but could also have an undesired pro-cyclical effect. Therefore, there are incentives for governments to engage in property tax reforms in good times.

For instance, Blöchliger and Vammalle (2012[2]), in a study on fiscal federalism and subnational government reforms covering ten OECD countries (Australia, Austria, Belgium, Canada, Denmark, Finland, Italy, Portugal, Spain and Switzerland), found evidence that a reform succeeds if implemented at times of economic upswings and healthy fiscal conditions. As the authors put it *"while a few reforms were initiated when the economic situation was weak or driven by consolidation needs, implementation of virtually all reforms took place when central and – to a lesser extent – sub-central public finances were in good shape. A sound fiscal position allows the central government to compensate sub-central governments, while reform resistance tends to be stiffer and reform failure more likely without central government support."*

Concerning the housing market, evidence shows that recurrent taxes on immovable property can be used as a policy instrument for asset price stabilisation (Blöchliger et al., 2015[21]) and can also influence the share of housing investments in total investments through different tax treatment (Millar-Powell et al., 2022[22]). Rapid tax increases during a slowdown – or tax reductions during a boom – seem to make property taxation strongly destabilising (Blöchliger, 2015[4]). In that light, when the housing market is in a downturn, the potential contraction caused by revenue-raising property tax reforms can attenuate the contraction, which is undesirable. On the other hand, when the housing market is booming, a reduction in the growth pace can be desirable.

Despite this solid case for putting forward property tax reforms in economic upswings, downswings can also improve the political support for a tax reform through various channels (see Box 4.5 on the Italian case). Pro-growth reforms can gather more political and popular support in downswings since they can be employed to revert the situation. More specifically, recessions sometimes expose very clearly the weaknesses of the economy and, thus, the need for reforms, leading to a greater acceptance of the necessity of the reform from taxpayers and voters (Brys, 2011[1]).

The timing to start discussing with the general public and/or experts also varies greatly. One approach is to present the tax reform only when their main elements are already defined and there is little uncertainty about their impact. Combined with good communication, this strategy may increase the likelihood of a reform to resist political pressures due to the reform's maturity. Another approach is to start the discussion earlier and let the learning occur during the discussions. This approach is especially useful in the presence of high levels of uncertainty about the number of winners and losers and the extent to which they are (positively or negatively) affected by the tax reform. That is because in this situation policy makers might become more careful in making a decision to engage in tax reform (Brys, 2011[1]). Therefore, anticipating discussions can lead to a long period of debate with the purpose of answering the most difficult questions and criticisms. However, after this long period the reform may reach a maturity, leading to a quick implementation.

Administrative problems can also affect a reform's timing. In that regard, tax reforms in general have been most successful when they are least needed. Rosengard (2012[23]) explains that non-urgent reforms allow tax administrators to introduce new processes smoothly and, in that manner, the learning period for both taxpayers and administrators to familiarise themselves with the new system can last longer, enhancing the understanding of, and voluntary compliance with, the tax. Timing for taxpayers to familiarise with the tax is especially relevant for recurrent taxes on immovable property since taxpayers usually have to actively pay the taxes (in contrast to income or consumption taxes that are, in most cases, paid indirectly when receiving income or buying a product, respectively).

In light of this discussion, it can be stated that there seems to be no perfect time for putting forward a property tax reform. Despite that, we argue that introducing a recurrent levy on residential households in the near future can benefit China in many different ways. First, despite of COVID-19's contractionary effects, China is not facing a significant economic downturn – on the contrary, the Chinese economy is recovering at a strong pace, which is particularly important for the reform to not have pro-cyclical effects. Second, house prices in China have continued to rise throughout the last decade. Although the upswing movement was stronger in the early 2000s, prices are still growing in most regions. Third, the vertical fiscal gap is widening in China (CDRF, 2020[24]), and, thus, a new source of income could potentially revert this trend. Although Chinese local governments may not have the necessary income to compensate losers during the first phases of the implementation, these compensations can be temporarily made, if necessary, as a part of an agreement with upper levels of government. There are no guarantees that this positive outlook will continue in the coming decades and, thus, it is opportune for China to introduce recurrent taxes on immovable property relatively soon.

Box 4.5. Italy's case of property tax reforms in downswings

Italy has reformed its property tax system multiple times in the last decades. This section explores the two revenue-raising property tax reforms that occurred in 1992-93 and in 2011-12, both in times of crisis.

In Italy, the year of 1992 is known as the year of the Great Crisis. Investors' speculation against Italy's former currency (the Lira) led to its sharp devaluation. Between 1991 and 1995 the Lira lost almost a third of its external value on the foreign exchange markets and Italians domestic purchasing power decreased by one sixth (Rossi, 2010[25]). Rossi highlighted that a decrease in foreign investments was one of the reasons that led to the crisis.

As a part of a fiscal package to face this deep financial and economic crisis, the Italian government introduced a temporary levy on properties in 1992, which became permanent in 1993. The tax base was wide (residential, industrial and commercial buildings, and land both for agriculture and residential purposes) and local governments could set the tax rate within the range of 0.4-0.7% on cadastral values.

In 2008 the Italian property taxes suffered a hit: the government promised in an electoral campaign and honoured the promise of abolishing the levies on owner-occupied houses. This has led to a substantial loss in local revenues, in part counterbalanced by increased transfers from the Central Government.

In 2011-12, though, after the financial crisis of 2008-09, as a part of a major package of fiscal reforms aimed at improving fiscal sustainability, the Italian government again implemented a revenue-raising property tax reform. First, cadastral values that were outdated for more than 20 years were reassessed using a fixed multiplier that reflected market values. Second, primary residences were brought back into the tax base (it was excluded from it in 2008). Overall, the new measures resulted in a significant increase in property tax revenue (roughly 240%). It is worth noting though that in 2013, right after the adoption of these revenue raising reforms, the Italian government froze property tax obligations due to the unpopularity of this reform.

Longobardi (2013[26]) highlighted that these reforms had been discussed and prepared for a long time but were only implemented in times of acute crisis. Political consensus that could not be obtained in normal circumstances was obtained in difficult moments. Probably this political support was a consequence of the necessity of undertaking reforms to improve the fiscal sustainability of the government that was threatened by both financial crises. As a result, despite the solid case for implementing property tax reforms in economic upswings, political support might arise only in times of necessity.

Unfortunately, in the Italian case, the implementation of a revenue raising property tax reform in the aftermath of a severe crisis has made the tax unpopular, leading to further legislative changes in the following years aimed at substantially easing taxation of owner-occupied houses.

Source: Longobardi (2013[26]), Rossi (2010[25]) and Italian delegates.

Administrative hurdles: a collection-led strategy coupled with a focus on more valuable properties can help emerging economies to maximise tax revenues

Recurrent taxes on immovable property are among the taxes that depend the most on having an effective administration to translate tax laws and regulations into field realities (Slack and Bird, 2014[3]). In some cases, the scope of recurrent property tax reforms covers only administrative issues (e.g. in case of reforms focused on updating cadastral values). In other cases, the administration needs to be reformed to operationalise the design changes. Rarely a property tax reform does not include any administrative element.

Often administrative reforms involve costly changes that require time to mature, such as the development of digital systems and the training or hiring of human resources. In addition to these costs incurred by the tax administration, changes in tax administrations might also increase taxpayers' compliance costs, at least during the period when they are adapting to the reform (e.g. learning to fill new forms, understanding the new elements of the tax obligation, among others). In order to reduce such costs, reformers can implement the reform in a more gradual way through the use of a transition phase or through an incremental implementation of the reform (Slack and Bird, 2014[3]). Both strategies can be used to improve the link between taxpayers' and officials' learning curve with the reform's pace. When these strategies are employed, the reform is only fully implemented in the medium-term.

Especially for governments in developing economies that do not have the capacity to register, valuate and collect revenues from all types of properties in a short period of time, a particularly interesting gradual implementation strategy is to focus on properties that can raise more tax revenues (Rosengard, 2012[23]). Particularly in developing economies, the distribution of properties' values tends to be highly skewed, with a relatively small number of properties comprising the bulk of properties' values. As a result, narrowing a reform's focus to these small number of high-end properties can maximise tax revenues in the short term. In addition, administrative simplifications can be made in order to maximise net tax revenues from low valuable properties. For instance, self-reporting and a simplified CAMA can be employed for cheaper properties while individual valuations are only employed for more expensive real estate. This strategy can aid developing countries to raise tax revenues in a quicker manner. These revenues can then be used to provide the necessary local services to raise popular support for the reform and to finance the costs of the rest of the reform.

In China's case, administrative capacity is asymmetrically distributed across municipalities. For instance, Shenzhen already has an advanced property valuation system in place (for more on Shenzhen see Box 3.4). Shanghai and Chongqing already have some experience with recurrent property taxes on residential properties since they already have introduced this levy in a small scale due to a pilot programme. In this situation, the central government can allow local governments to implement the reform in different moments – the greater the administrative capacity, the earlier the levy can be introduced in a municipality. For municipalities that do not have the capacity to implement the reform, Liu (2019[27]) suggests that a financial incentive programme in the form of an inter-governmental transfer aimed at rewarding municipalities that make substantive efforts to roll out the new property tax can incentivise the introduction of the tax and help boost capacity. In addition, the implementation in each municipality can also be phased, with a stronger focus on high-end properties at first.

Another interesting option is to use a relatively simple tax base at the time of the introduction of the reform, when fiscal cadastres are not yet completed, and the administrative apparatus has not yet matured. Along these lines, Ahmad (2021[8]) suggests that China could introduce a recurrent tax on residential properties that uses area as the tax basis. Such a tax is relatively easy and cheap to implement, as it is not necessary to assess properties' values and, if combined with a linkage between revenues and local expenditures, could still increase the overall redistributive effects of China's fiscal system. This approach could be valuable for some regions and municipalities in which data on property transactions and characteristics are not available. By following this approach, the tax could be introduced sooner and, therefore, raise own revenues for SNGs sooner than waiting until property values are fully assessed. It would be important to clearly announce that the simplified approach is a transitory one, with the longer-term objective to use a value basis. Over time, then, depending on the maturity of the regional/local property tax administration and on the quality of the data collected on properties, the local/regional tax administration could move towards a value-based approach.

Transitional measures can be useful to alleviate short-term effects of a tax hike, nevertheless reformers need to design and implement these measures in a manner that the full implementation of the reform is secured in the long term

Tax reforms can change the status quo to which taxpayers have already adapted, leading to undesirable disruptive effects. In the case of a salient levy as recurrent property taxes, a sudden tax hike can catch households unprepared and may increase delinquency (Slack and Bird, 2014[3]). Furthermore, a sudden tax hike can also impact the real estate market in case tax obligations are capitalised into prices, potentially destabilising the state of the real estate market (Blöchliger, 2015[4]). As Slack and Bird (2014[3]) put it, "*failure to allow adequately for transitional problems and to cushion burden shifts adequately can be a fatal defect*". In addition, property tax reforms may change the relative tax power across jurisdictions and, in case they are revenue neutral, can cause a reduction in revenues in some jurisdictions. Examples of (temporary) transitional measures include reduction in tax rates and the provision of tax benefits/reliefs such as tax credits, tax deferrals, among others (Box 4.3, presented in the previous section, gives interesting examples of transitional measures employed by Denmark).

Blöchliger and Vammalle (2012[2]) in an overarching study on fiscal federalism and subnational government reforms covering ten OECD countries found that transitional compensation is almost always necessary. The target of these measures can be stakeholders or jurisdictions. In the cases analysed by these authors, the central government usually funded these transitional costs and opt-out clauses were provided. For instance, the Swiss established transitional "cohesion funds" to ensure that SNGs would suffer no losses in financial terms in the next 28 year after the reform.

One option to cushion the impact of a reform on taxpayers is by keeping effective tax rates low until the tax administration can have a good coverage (Rosengard, 2012[23]). When fiscal cadastres are not yet complete, properties' values were not assessed or the tax collection is not working properly in some specific regions, tax obligations across properties will shift greatly only due to administrative obstacles. In case this transitional period lasts long, these inequities may start to influence taxpayers' behaviour, creating economic distortions. Keeping effective tax rates low may minimise this risk.

Although cushioning the impact is desirable to avoid disruptive effects, measures employed for that purpose are neither costless nor risk free. First, the longer the cushioning mechanism stays in place the longer it takes to move to the desirable tax system. Second, some planned changes might never be put into place and, in numerous cases, temporary solutions are perpetuated (see Box 4.6 in the Korean case at the end of this section). Thus, although transitional measures might be politically important for the approval of a reform, reformers need to design and implement these measures in a manner that the full implementation of the reform is secured so it can achieve its initial goals (Slack and Bird, 2014[3]). One way to increase the chances of a full implementation is to include in the original legislation the expiry date of the transition period or the date in which incremental changes will enter into force (i.e. sunset provision or clause). In that manner, groups that benefit from the transitional measures would have to work harder to maintain their special treatment since it would require a change in the reform's plans, which were made transparent and were legitimised in the legislation (Brys, 2011[1]).

Two specific elements of the Chinese tax system are worth mentioning in the context of transitional measures. First, China already levies transaction taxes on immovable property and, thus, right after the introduction of recurrent taxes on residential property, taxpayers might feel that the new obligations are unfair since they just paid their transaction taxes. Second, Liu (2019[27]) pointed out that due to the very low carrying costs of housing investments in China, many households own multiple properties, and, in this case, the introduction of a recurrent property tax applied to these households could create a disruption. In order to alleviate this sense of unfairness and to give room for investment portfolio adjustment, transitional measures can be employed. Liu (2019[27]) and Brys et al. (2013[28]) suggested that authorities can mitigate these problems by phasing-in the property tax reform, granting a temporary high basic tax-free allowance for the recurrent taxes on immovable property and/or starting with a wide tax base and very low tax rate. In case the reform is bundled with a reduction of the levies on properties transactions, a tax credit can be given to taxpayers who recently paid transaction taxes so that the new recurrent levy on residential properties is not considered unfair to these taxpayers. Such a levy needs to be temporary and, ideally, phased-out gradually over a few years.[7]

Communication strategies for tax reforms: engaging a wide range of stakeholders, obtaining a consensus on a reform's broad long-term goals and focusing the discussions on the systematic rather than individual impact of the reform

Communication, when employed effectively, can help sustain the necessary political and popular support to ensure that the reform will be introduced and implemented in full. Slack and Bird (2014[3]) suggest that both policy makers and taxpayers are more likely to buy into a reform if they have been consulted and feel that their issues have been properly heard. In this light, a consultation previous to the announcement and implementation of the reform can reduce popular opposition.

A communication strategy that engages multiple stakeholders such as business, unions, special interest groups, academics and the broader public can create a feeling of ownership and reduce resistance (Brys, 2011[1]). Blöchliger and Vammalle (2012[2]) highlighted that external expertise can be particularly useful since they can provide impartial and unbiased scrutiny, raising the credibility among the public. These authors showed how external expertise was fruitful in reforming elements of the fiscal policy in several OECD countries such as Finland, Australia and Canada. It is worth noting that the language spoken by these experts are often different from the language spoken by the average citizen and officials. These authors found evidence that creating a credible independent panel consisting of experts and professionals who know how to communicate with non-experts can help the interpretation of the reform package by the general public.

Blöchliger and Vammalle (2012[2]) emphasised that although consultation is clearly beneficial, too much consultation can inflame opposition. From the cases analysed by these authors, the most successful consultation strategy involved parsimony with numbers related to the short-run impacts of the reform and a focus on discussing a reform's overall/long-term goals. In other words, the long-term objectives were the focus of the communication instead of short-term distributional impacts. These long-term benefits can be communicated to the general public through promotional slogans such as "better services" and "more autonomy". It is worth noting that although it is beneficial to highlight long-term benefits, reforms issues should not remain hidden – successful reforms often emphasise the long-term benefits without concealing negative impacts (Blöchliger and Vammalle, 2012[2]).

In the same vein, Brys (2011[1]) highlighted the importance of obtaining a consensus on these broad long-term goals of a reform and explored how this can be achieved through a clear communication focused on long-term objectives and trade-offs involved. Accepting specific constraints to the reform might also facilitate the reform's implementation since stakeholders are now aware of what is negotiable and what is not. In the absence of broad strategic consensus, the same author suggests that governments can reduce uncertainty and begin to guide debates by announcing aspirational tax reform's goals before presenting specific proposals. This announcement can 1) bring support to the reform from groups that are benefited by the reform; and 2) create a reputational cost for the government to change the reform's goals after an announcement.

Lastly on communication, Alt et al. (2010[29]) argue tax reforms should not be discussed in isolation. The general public often lacks understanding about the interplay between the tax being reformed and fiscal policy's goals and, thus, can make wrong assessments about the impacts of the tax reform. Keeping a narrow focus on an individual tax hinders comparisons and makes it easier for opposing groups to attack the reform by showing its negative impacts without comparing them to the impacts of other available options. For instance, according to these authors, one of the reasons for the abolition of the estate tax in the United States (i.e. inheritance tax) was a narrow-focused communication, which helped the organisation of opposing groups that focused the debate only on the tax's problems and not on its overall effect on the progressivity of the tax system and on its revenue-raising capacity that can raise funds for the provision of additional public services.

Bundling is commonly employed in recurrent property tax reforms as a way to overcome political resistance through compensation of losers and improving distributional effects

Bundling multiple reforms together is a good strategy to offset or alleviate negative impacts of individual reforms with the impact from other reforms. It is worth noting that bundling is not the same as transitional compensations as bundling may involve elements outside the original scope of the property taxation reform and in a permanent way. A bundling strategy can be designed in a manner to overcome political resistance and build popular support for the implementation of the reform. According to Olofsgård (2003[30]), bundling reforms may be especially useful in case there are many actors whose support is crucial – for instance, when multiple groups have veto power because each group should be satisfied in order for the reform to pass and, under these circumstances, bundling the reform with elements that satisfy each of these groups can secure a reform's approval. Blöchliger and Vammalle (2012[2]), on the other hand, although they recognise that bundling is typically employed and often fruitful, it can lead to an excessive focus on satisfying stakeholders, detracting the reform from its efficiency-enhancing aspects.

Brys (2011[1]) explored two important benefits that come from bundling. First, it may make it easier to address distributional issues, especially when a tax is bundled with measures from the expenditure side that have substantial impact on the income distribution, such as cash transfers to the poor (Joumard, Pisu and Bloch, 2012[31]). Second, bundling tax reforms with improvements in service delivery can increase the overall acceptance of and compliance with the tax being reformed – see Simonsen & Robbins (2003[32]). For the latter strategy, it is particularly interesting to phase in tax changes over several years so the pace at which services can be improved is linked to the pace at which citizens are being taxed.

In OECD countries it is common for countries to bundle reforms in recurrent taxes on immovable property with other tax reforms and with changes in the inter-governmental fiscal framework.[8] For instance, in 2005 Korea introduced a comprehensive real estate tax together with a reduction in property transaction taxes and with an introduction of a grant inversely related to property tax raising capacity (i.e. as a compensation for local revenue losses). Another example is Finland, which has, in less than 3 years, 1) reformed its property tax system; 2) increased the share of corporate income tax that is allocated to municipalities; and 3) discontinued its revenue equalisation transfer system (see Box 4.7 in the Finnish case for more details).

Box 4.6. Korea's property tax reform: success and failures

In 2005, Korea introduced the central government's "comprehensive real estate tax" on immovable property, thereby complementing the existing range of local immovable property taxes. The tax base covers residential and business property with land and improvements as taxable items, which are assessed in conjunction by market prices. Tax rates are progressive with respect to property values and vary between 0.15% and 0.5% of the overall value of a property. Local governments must use the same tax base for their own property tax (Korea has a central and a local property tax) and are allowed to set tax rates individually but, in practice, all municipalities set the standard rate recommended by the central government.

After the introduction of the comprehensive real estate tax, local and central property tax revenues combined rose from 0.5% of GDP in 2005 to almost 1% of GDP in 2007, before declining to around 0.8% after 2009. Nevertheless, the comprehensive real estate tax is still, as a proportion of total property tax revenues, much smaller than the average OECD country (see Figure 1.2, in the first chapter of this report).

Improving the chances of a successful implementation

The reform aimed at making Korea's property tax system fair in the eyes of taxpayers. Until 2005, Korea could be described as having a "narrow-tax-base, high-tax-rate" property tax system, which used to offset the undervaluation of properties with high and excessively progressive tax rates. As discussed throughout this report, compensating an adequate valuation process with tax rate setting is very likely to lead to horizontal and vertical distortions, making the tax system unfair. The reform reverted this situation by 1) broadening the tax base; 2) reducing tax rates; and 3) improving fairness by establishing an isonomic and fair valuation system based on both land and improvements assessed in conjunction by market prices. The result was an increase in the assessed value of 60% of the dwellings in the urban area, where about 80% of the Koreans live. This increase more than compensated the reduction in tax rates, increasing tax revenues while simultaneously creating trust that the underlying rules of property taxation were fair, progressive and equitable. In addition, many strategies aimed to improve the chances of a successful implementation covered in this section were put to use by the Korean government.

First, regarding communication and the perceived regressivity of recurrent property taxation, the government openly supported a reduction in income inequality and the reform was openly one of the means used to achieve this goal. Despite the fact that property tax rates in place before the reform were progressive, their overall distributive effects were minimised by distortions on cadastral values. These distortions greatly reduced the tax burden in an unfair and regressive manner. To solve this problem, the reform improved the valuation system along with a reduction in tax rates. More specifically, the range of tax rates was reduced from 0.2-7% to 0.15-0.5% and many taxpayers were charged with the lowest possible tax rate.

Second, the timing of the reform was very good. As with many successful reforms, the introduction of the comprehensive real estate tax took place during a period of strong economic growth, which averaged almost 3% annually between 2003 and 2007. Real house prices rose by 5 to 10% per annum during the same period. Also, the government finances were in good shape. The timing was important to reduce the resistance against the property tax reform. Taxpayers were aware of the disproportionate increase in property values in some areas and were in favour of a tax system that distributes the tax burden in a more equitable fashion. It is worth noting that the reform seemed to have temporarily stabilised soaring house prices – after the reform implementation's there was an inflection in house prices that started to decrease slightly, picking up again afterwards.

Third, the property tax reform was bundled with other reforms, especially the reduction of property transaction taxes and a new inter-governmental grant. Transaction tax revenues were almost three times higher than recurrent tax revenues before 2005 and, after the reform, this proportion shrank to two. The comprehensive real estate tax was also coupled with the introduction of an inter-governmental grant inversely related to property tax raising capacity. This grant compensated local governments for losses in local revenue capacity because the new central tax affected other local taxes on property whose tax base became aligned with the new national tax. In addition, tax revenues from the new tax were distributed in favour of poor jurisdictions, doubling the channels through which the tax distributed income to the poor.

Conclusions

Korea offers a very interesting case of how an unpopular revenue-raising property tax reform can receive public support when the reform strategy is well implemented. The reform successfully improved Korea's property tax structure, which was based on unrealistically progressive rates with deliberate under-assessment of properties, which used to generate unfair charges. Having fair assessments, timing the reform well, bundling the reform with the reduction in transaction taxes and changes in the inter-government transfer system, and focusing on improving the distribution of income are all strategies that China can replicate to increase the popularity of such tax reform.

Nevertheless, despite this success, the reform was only partially implemented. The initial reform project foresaw an annual increase of the ratio of taxable to assessed property values by 3 percentage points each year until that ratio reached 100%, but this stepwise increase was soon abandoned, and the taxable ratio remained at 60% to 70% of assessed values. This example of transitional measures that last more than it should reveals the difficulties of securing the full implementation of phased reforms.

Source: OECD – Reforming Immovable Property Taxation in Korea (background note).

Leaseholds and collectively owned land can create problems for property tax reforms; nevertheless, these can be mitigated with bundling, communication and transitional strategies and with a clear distinction of the levies on land and buildings

When introducing recurrent taxes on immovable property in a country that has a leasehold system in place, taxpayers might oppose the reform on the grounds that they are being double taxed since they are paying both a lease fee and a recurrent property tax. Hong (2012[33]) raised interesting points, here highlighted, regarding the introduction of recurrent property taxes in such a context.

First, despite the convenience of combining all land related levies into one payment (i.e. lease and recurrent property taxes), taxpayers might confuse taxes with leasehold fees and, thus, these should be kept separate, so the taxpayer knows what he is paying for in each payment. The similarity of lessees and taxes payments without proper taxpayer education can create an expectation that the land is owned by the lessees. According to Hong (2012[33]) this has happened to some extent in Canberra/Australia and Israel, both of which have a leasehold system. In order to minimise this problem, lessees in Canberra must pay the entire leasehold value up front and the property tax afterwards on an annual basis (Neutze, 2003[34]). In addition to clearly separating the leaseholds fees and tax payments, taxpayers should be educated about property taxes and the leasehold system so they understand what the purposes of each charge are.

Second, when ownership of land and buildings are not the same (as in China, especially in the case of collectively-owned land), two different levies – one applied to buildings and other to land – can be created to tax these assets separately. These arrangements are not uncommon in OECD and partner countries.[9]

For instance, Hungary has a separate levy on land and improvements. Denmark and Slovenia have a separate land, building and immovable property tax. Greece, Ireland and the United Kingdom have a building tax plus an immovable property tax. Finally, Australia, Brazil, New Zealand, Poland and the Slovak Republic have a land tax plus an immovable property tax.

Third, as explored in the second chapter, tax liabilities can be capitalised into house prices[10] and, in case of taxes applied to leaseholds, this capitalisation can hurt leasing fees. In the most extreme scenario, the revenue obtained from recurrent property taxes can be fully offset by a reduction in leasing fees. Of course, the timing of the capitalisation is not immediate and depends greatly on many factors such as the date of leaseholds' renewals and the elasticity of supply and demand of properties. As a result, until the effect kicks in, it is possible for governments to use the revenues raised by the recurrent property taxes to improve the supply of public services and local infrastructure, among others. In that way, this improvement can also be capitalised into property prices, alleviating or potentially cancelling out the reduction in leasing fees. It also is worth noting that there is evidence that taxpayers are more inclined to pay property taxes when they rate the quality of public services highly (Simonsen and Robbins, 2003[32]).

Fourth, recurrent taxes on immovable property can be levied on the occupancy of the property – as suggested by Ahmad (2021[8]) – and, therefore, be interpreted as a tax on housing services or on capital or even as a fee for using land or local services. Although in essence the levy is applied to the same tax base, these different interpretations are particularly important in the context of leaseholds since some of these interpretations can minimise the impression of double taxation. Especially when property taxes are viewed as a fee charged to the occupant for using local services, this interpretation is implausible. That is because leasehold fees and local service fees clearly do not refer to the same charge. In that regard, one potential way to reduce the room for interpretation that recurrent taxes on immovable property lead to double taxation is to name the charge in a way that favours the interpretation of a fee for using local services. For instance, recurrent taxes on immovable property in the United Kingdom and in Australia are known as "council tax" and as "council rate", respectively.

As a result of the third and fourth points, a bundling strategy that combines the introduction of the levy on properties with improvement of local services may not only offset potential reductions in leasing fees but also makes it harder to interpret the levy as a form of "double taxation", reducing the resistance against the reform. In that context, Ahmad and Colenbrander (2020[35]) suggested that China could link property tax revenues with social benefits, such as free or subsidised transport for the elderly or support for basic education. These authors highlighted that this linkage could have many benefits such as: 1) improving the distributional impact of the tax; 2) enhancing accountability; 3) assuring a stream of funding for basic services; and 4) enabling access to private finance for investments. All these effects could increase the acceptability of the reform.

Fifth and lastly, the introduction of levies on leaseholds may be considered unfair to lessees who recently paid the entire leasehold fees, and thus, did not anticipate this future liability. In case leasing fees are reduced due to the introduction of the tax, this problem can become even more apparent. In that regard, transitional measures targeted at these taxpayers can be employed (the previous section covered this issue in more detail).

Tax reforms and fiscal decentralisation

Recurrent property tax reforms can affect the distribution of revenue across levels of government (vertically) and within levels of government (horizontally)

One last issue that is worth discussing in the context of property tax reforms regards their impacts on different levels of government and inter-governmental fiscal relations. As recurrent taxes on immovable property typically are an important source of revenue for subnational (mainly local) governments, property tax reforms can significantly affect the distribution of revenues across levels of government (i.e. vertically) and within the same level of government (i.e. horizontally). Therefore, in order to alleviate negative impacts on certain levels of government and/or jurisdictions, it is common for governments to bundle reforms on recurrent property taxation with reforms on inter-governmental relations (see, for instance, the Korean case in Box 4.6, above, and Box 4.7 and Box 4.8 on the Finish and Italian cases).

Regarding vertical relations, when recurrent taxes on immovable property accrue to SNGs, raising their share in total taxation will tend to increase the share of subnational revenues in general government revenues. This shift in the distribution of revenues across levels of government as a "by-product" of a property tax reform can be undesirable. In this situation, this relative increase in subnational revenues can be offset by a reduction in inter-governmental grants from upper levels of government. In case this shift is desirable, it might be convenient to reform other aspects of a country's fiscal federalism framework. As a result, it is common for property tax reforms to be part of a comprehensive package on fiscal federalism reforms (Box 4.7, on Italy's 2009 property tax reform, presents an interesting example of a joint reform of property taxation and fiscal federalism).

Box 4.7. Reshaping fiscal relations in Italy

Italy's 2009 fiscal federalism reform offers an example of how reforms on recurrent taxes on immovable property can be bundled together with fiscal federalism reforms. The main goal of Italy's 2009 reform was to increase both the efficiency and accountability of subnational governments through an increase in their own revenues and reduction in inter-governmental grants. The reform had four pillars: 1) alignment of subnational own revenues with their expenditures; 2) clarification of spending obligations; 3) equalisation of tax-raising capacity and costs; and 4) harmonisation of accounting principles.

Alignment of subnational own revenues with their expenditures: this reform entitled subnational governments to a set of own taxes and to shares in national taxes sufficient to cover their spending needs. Regions were entitled to 1) the tax on productive activities (i.e. a regional business-cum-value-added tax) and the personal income tax, with autonomy to set tax rates within pre-established limits; and 2) a share in the national value-added tax. Municipalities were entitled to 1) a recurrent levy on properties applied to properties that are not occupied by their owner; and 2) a share of the value-added tax and the personal income tax. These sources of revenue were granted to SNGs simultaneously with the discontinuation of inter-governmental grants. Only equalising grants and some special-purpose grants remained.

Clarification of spending obligations: responsibilities for public services at the subnational government level were divided into compulsory services (i.e. health care, education, social protection and local transport) and all other public services. While the central government has the responsibility of defining minimum standards for compulsory services, subnational governments are free to define standards and spending levels for the other services. All services not explicitly allocated to the central government level are of regions' responsibility.

Equalisation of tax-raising capacity and standard cost: two different equalisation systems were introduced: 1) equalisation of the cost for essential and compulsory services, to be fully equalised and based on standard cost instead of historical cost; and 2) equalisation of tax-raising capacity, for which the equalisation rate gradually increases by 5% every year to reach 100% in 2030, leaving SNGs an incentive to develop their economic and fiscal base.

Harmonisation of accounting principles: accounting principles for regional and local levels of government (such as accounting and budget rules, the treatment of publicly owned enterprises, depreciation rules, etc.) were harmonised, so that regional and local accounts will be truly comparable and "creative accounting" minimised.

Source: Blöchliger and Vammalle (2012[2]).

Revenue equalisation can be employed to offset differences in tax revenue capacity – in this case it is important that upper levels of government prevent local governments from gaming the transfer system

Regarding horizontal relations within levels of government, property tax reforms can lead to an asymmetrical distribution of tax revenues across jurisdictions. This asymmetry can start with the reform's implementation and may grow over time in line with regional/local characteristics such as the regional/local housing market and administrative capacity. For instance, Färber et al. (2013[36]) found evidence that a reform of the German property valuation system would considerably change the relative tax capacity across Germany's states. Similarly, Ahmad et al. (2019[37]) simulated the impact of the introduction of a recurrent property tax in China and concluded that the distribution of revenues would be asymmetrical across and within provinces with bigger cities, like Guangzhou and Shanghai, raising significantly more revenues than smaller ones.

Due to these differences in tax revenue raising capacity across jurisdictions, it is common for OECD countries to establish a or to enhance their existing fiscal equalisation system, for a detailed view in equalisation systems see (Dougherty and Forman, 2021[38])). Fiscal equalisation is a transfer of fiscal resources across jurisdictions with the aim of offsetting differences in revenue raising capacity and public service costs. This arrangement is adopted in most OECD countries. According to OECD (2020[13]), these funds, when considering both revenues and costs equalisation together, can amount to roughly 20% of the total subnational expenditure (e.g. in Japan, Austria, Ireland, Korea and Germany). In that regard, when property tax reforms create imbalances on revenue capacity, changes in the fiscal equalisation framework can be adapted to offset these re-distributional effects (see Box 4.7, above and Box 4.8, below).

Exemptions can also cause vertical or horizontal imbalances in property tax revenue capacity. In that case, exemptions granted by lower levels of governments should be treated differently than exemptions granted by upper levels of government. In the first case, the lower levels of government decided to give away their potential tax base and, thus, the potential tax base for equalisation purposes should include the exempted base (i.e. maintaining the revenue capacity of the SNG that granted the exemption identical to its revenue capacity before granting the exemption and, thus, keeping its equalisation fund share constant). In the second case, the exempted tax base should be excluded from the tax base used for computing the revenue capacity for equalisation purposes. That's because lower levels of government should not be harmed by a decision from upper levels of government, whose impacts are proportional to the asymmetrical distribution of tax-exempt properties across jurisdictions. In this manner, jurisdictions that are losing more revenue capacity are also going to be compensated more by the equalisation system. Lastly, exemptions granted by upper levels of government can also create vertical imbalances, creating resistance from lower levels of government to the exemption. For instance, in Poland local governments asked for compensation for their loss in property tax revenue capacity and demanded that the introduction of new centrally imposed exemptions should require local government consent (Swianiewicz and Lukomska, 2015[39]).

It is important for equalisation transfer systems to be designed in a way that they incentivise tax collection and prevent governments from obtaining a larger share of the equalisation funds than they deserve. In many countries, equalisation penalises tax collection (Blöchliger, 2015[4]) – that is, subnational governments can increase equalisation funds by under-taxing local taxpayers. Most countries minimise this issue by cutting the link between equalisation funds and actual subnational tax revenues through the use of revenue capacity instead of actual revenues in the equalisation formula. Some countries go even one step further by employing a system that rewards subnational governments for collecting more property tax revenue.

Some interesting examples of equalisation systems in which there are incentives for local governments to raise property tax revenues can be found in Norway, Germany, Ireland, among others. Property tax actual revenues of Norway's municipalities are not considered in the equalisation formula, while in Germany only 64% of municipal property tax revenues are included in the equalisation formula. In Ireland, a local property tax on residential properties (LPT) was introduced in 2013, in addition to the existing property tax levied commercial properties (commercial rates). 80% of LPT's revenues are retained locally for the funding of basic public services, while the remaining 20% are allocated to the equalisation fund (Slack and Bird, 2014[3]).

In case equalisation funds are based on revenue raising capacity, upper levels of governments should also hinder subnational governments to game the system by systematically under-assessing properties. One way to mitigate this problem is by ensuring that all jurisdictions maintain a specified average "assessed to market value ratios". Another way is to accept differences in this ratio and adjust the equalisation formula so that property values used for equalisation purpose take into account these differences. These measures minimise distortions in the equalisation base that are caused by differences in valuation policies.

Bundling property tax reforms with reforms in fiscal federalism can be challenging – characteristics of the fiscal system of the country should be carefully analysed

Lastly, despite the fact that bundling a property tax reform with reforms in fiscal federalism can yield benefits, the complexity of the reform can increase substantially. Fiscal federalism reforms are complex and need to be tailored to socioeconomic and institutional characteristics of a country[11] (Kim and Dougherty, 2018[40]). There are a myriad of fiscal federalism reforms, ranging from, for instance, a simple change in equalisation rules (e.g. Finnish case) to a more overarching change in subnational expenditure responsibilities and revenue assignments (e.g. Italian case). As a result, designing such a reform is far from trivial. It can also be a strategic choice to separate these two types of reforms (i.e. tax and fiscal federalism) in case this separation would facilitate the approval of important parts of the reform.

Box 4.8. The Finnish attempt to increase the role of recurrent taxes on immovable property

Recurrent property taxes in Finland

In Finland, the taxes on immovable property were introduced in 1993 when it replaced a set of small infrastructure and service-related local taxes. The tax base covers both land and buildings of residential and business properties. Agricultural land and forests are not taxed. While land is assessed on the basis of market prices, values of buildings are assessed on the basis of replacement cost and indexed to the national construction price index. The tax base is set by the central government, while municipalities set the tax rate within a lower and an upper limit. Tax rates are lower for residential buildings than for land and business estates. Municipalities have the option to tax vacant land at a higher rate; this is compulsory for municipalities in the metropolitan area.

Fiscal context

Finland is an unusual case with regard to fiscal decentralisation and property taxes. Finland has one of the most decentralised public sectors in the OECD (see Figure 1.7 in the first chapter of this report). Finnish municipalities enjoy ample fiscal autonomy and are responsible for providing a large array of public services, in particular education and health care. In order to finance these services, local governments can set a proportional tax rate on top of the progressive national income tax, which makes roughly 85% of their tax revenues. Most of the remaining 15% comes from property taxes and the local share in the corporate income taxes – both representing around 7% each.

Design and administrative aspects are relevant for explaining the reasons why property taxes in Finland generate relatively low revenues. First, the share of households that 1) are renting; 2) live in tax-exempt municipal houses; or 3) own a house in a property corporation where the residents pay the tax collectively is above 60%. Second, taxable values, which are updated by the Ministry of Finance, have tended to lag market values (Hagemann, 2018[41]).

In addition, Finnish local governments have more leeway in setting their local income tax rate than in setting their local property tax rates. Given that income taxes tend to generate substantially more revenues than property taxes, local governments can raise income more easily through an increase in tax rates that are applied to income rather than properties. Hagemann (2018[41]) pointed out that this system results in a counterproductive reluctance by municipalities to shift revenues toward immovable property taxation.

Recurrent property tax reforms in the last 10 years

The government has been trying to change these incentives and promote an increase in the role of recurrent taxes on immovable property in the country. Multiple reforms were implemented in the last ten years. Here most of their elements are highlighted. First, in 2010, 2016 and 2017 the government enlarged the limits at which local governments can set property tax rates. Second, governments have been updating cadastral values, which are expected to be fully updated in 2023. Third, in 2012 the property tax base was taken out of the inter-municipal equalisation system, with municipalities now fully benefiting from any effort to increase their tax base.

Source: Political Economy of Property Tax Reform in Finland (background note) and Hagemann (2018[41]).

In China's case, special attention should be given to vertical and horizontal disparities

Although China's regional and urban-rural disparities are declining, they are still significant and higher than the average OECD country. First, OECD (2019[9]) shows that regions differ substantially in many respects, such as medical staff per capita, infrastructure, and disposable income. Second, the Chinese tax system is designed in a manner in which tax yields tend to be more unequally distributed geographically than income. Third, in China vertical disparities between revenues and spending mandates are high, and the gap between own revenues and spending is the greatest at the lowest levels of government (OECD, 2019[9]).

Therefore, a reform that aims to introduce recurrent taxes on immovable property in China can be particularly important to reduce this vertical gap, but it needs to take into consideration these large regional disparities so as to not to further increase them. Such a reform can increase regional inequality for at least two reasons. First, richer local governments are more likely to succeed in the implementation of a well-functioning property tax administration structure that, as was explored throughout this report, has a fundamental importance for collecting property tax revenues. Second, property values are higher in richer jurisdictions, which directly affects their tax revenue capacity. Therefore, in case a fully decentralised property tax system is implemented and local governments do not have the necessary support from upper levels of government, such a tax reform is likely to increase regional disparities in local revenues.

Despite this challenge, OECD countries offer valuable examples of strategies that can be employed to deal with regional inequality. Based on OECD countries' experience, at least two strategies can be implemented by China: a boost in equalisation transfers and the provision of central support to SNGs. Although China already has in place a substantial equalisation system, the introduction of recurrent taxes on immovable property are likely to increase the disparities in revenue capacity across jurisdictions and, thus, an increase in equalisation funds can be necessary to offset that. It is worth noting that although boosting equalisation transfers is crucial to level differences in local revenue capacity, this solution alone might not be sufficient to level differences in local capacity to implement a sound property tax system. For that purpose, support from the central government can be especially important. This support can be provided in the form of (earmarked) funds, loans or even, in a more extreme situation, a temporary centralisation of the property tax administration. As mentioned before, in case a temporary solution is pursued, having a pre-established date, potentially enforced by law, can help setting expectations and securing that the reform will be implemented fully in the future.

References

Ahmad, E. (2021), “Multilevel financing of sustainable infrastructure in China — policy options for inclusive, resilient and green growth”, *Journal of Infrastructure, Policy and Development*, Vol. 5/1, pp. 1-24, http://dx.doi.org/10.24294/jipd.v5i1.1251. [8]

Ahmad, E. et al. (2019), *Financing inclusive urban development in China*, LSE/CUT Program on Financing Urban Transitions in China and Mexico. [37]

Ahmad, E. and S. Colenbrander (2020), *Financing a sustainable and inclusive urban transition in China*, Coalition for Urban Transitions, London, https://urbantransitions.global/publications. [35]

Almy, R. (2014), “Valuation and Assessment of Immovable Property”, *OECD Working Papers on Fiscal Federalism*, No. 19, OECD Publishing, Paris, https://dx.doi.org/10.1787/5jz5pzvr28hk-en. [12]

Alt, J., I. Preston and L. Sibieta (2010), “The Political Economy of Tax Policy”, *Dimensions of Tax Design*, pp. 1204-1315. [29]

Barvika, S. (2020), *The Property Tax in Latvia: System Structure and Current Challenges*, Lincoln Institute for Land Policy, http://dx.doi.org/WP20SB1. [10]

Belinga, V. et al. (2014), “Tax Buoyancy in OECD Countries”, *IMF Working Papers*, Vol. 14/110. [11]

Blöchliger, H. (2015), “Reforming the Tax on Immovable Property: Taking Care of the Unloved”, *OECD Economics Department Working Papers*, No. 1205, OECD Publishing, Paris, https://dx.doi.org/10.1787/5js30tw0n7kg-en. [4]

Blöchliger, H. et al. (2015), “The stabilisation properties of immovable property taxation: Evidence from OECD countries”, *OECD Economics Department Working Papers*, No. 1237, OECD Publishing, Paris, https://dx.doi.org/10.1787/5js0cqq93djg-en. [21]

Blöchliger, H. and C. Vammalle (2012), *Reforming Fiscal Federalism and Local Government: Beyond the Zero-Sum Game*, OECD Fiscal Federalism Studies, OECD Publishing, Paris, https://dx.doi.org/10.1787/9789264119970-en. [2]

Borge, L. and J. Rattsø (2013), “Capitalization of Property Taxes in Norway”, *Public Finance Review*, Vol. 42/5, pp. 635-661, http://dx.doi.org/10.1177/1091142113489845. [42]

Brys, B. (2011), “Making Fundamental Tax Reform Happen”, *OECD Taxation Working Papers*, No. 3, OECD Publishing, Paris, https://dx.doi.org/10.1787/5kg3h0v54g34-en. [1]

Brys, B. et al. (2013), “Tax Policy and Tax Reform in the People’s Republic of China”, *OECD Taxation Working Papers*, No. 18, OECD Publishing, Paris, https://dx.doi.org/10.1787/5k40l4dlmnzw-en. [28]

CDRF (2020), *Background document on China’s property taxation*, China Development Research Foundation. [24]

Dougherty, S. and K. Forman (2021), “Evaluating fiscal equalisation: Finding the right balance”, *OECD Working Papers on Fiscal Federalism*, No. 36, OECD Publishing, Paris, https://dx.doi.org/10.1787/253da2b8-en. [38]

Färber, G., M. Salm and S. Hengstwerth (2013), *Property Tax Reform in Germany – Eternally Unfinished or an Instrument of a more Equitable Tax System?*, Paper presented at the Fiscal Network Copenhagen Workshop 2013. [36]

Franzsen, R. and W. McCluskey (2012), "Value-Based Approaches to Property Taxation", in *A Primer on Property Tax*, Blackwell Publishing Ltd, Oxford, http://dx.doi.org/10.1002/9781118454343.ch2. [19]

Hagemann, R. (2018), "Tax Policies for Inclusive Growth: Prescription versus Practice", *OECD Economic Policy Papers*, No. 24, OECD Publishing, Paris, https://dx.doi.org/10.1787/09ba747a-en. [41]

Hong, Y. (2012), "Taxing Public Leasehold Land in Transition Countries", in *A Primer on Property Tax: Administration and Policy*, Wiley-Blackwell, http://dx.doi.org/10.1002/9781118454343.ch11. [33]

Joumard, I., M. Pisu and D. Bloch (2012), "Less Income Inequality and More Growth – Are They Compatible? Part 3. Income Redistribution via Taxes and Transfers Across OECD Countries", *OECD Economics Department Working Papers*, No. 926, OECD Publishing, Paris, https://dx.doi.org/10.1787/5k9h296b1zjf-en. [31]

Kim, J. and S. Dougherty (eds.) (2019), *Fiscal Decentralisation and Inclusive Growth in Asia*, OECD Fiscal Federalism Studies, OECD Publishing, Paris/Korea Institute of Public Finance, Seoul, https://dx.doi.org/10.1787/25cf7545-en. [43]

Kim, J. and S. Dougherty (eds.) (2018), *Fiscal Decentralisation and Inclusive Growth*, OECD Fiscal Federalism Studies, OECD Publishing, Paris/Korea Institute of Public Finance, Seoul, https://dx.doi.org/10.1787/9789264302488-en. [40]

Kingdon, J. (2014), *Agendas, alternatives, and public policies*, Pearson Education Limited. [20]

Kitchen, H. (2012), "Property Tax: A Situation Analysis and Overview", in *A Primer on Property Tax*, Blackwell Publishing Ltd, Oxford, http://dx.doi.org/10.1002/9781118454343.ch1. [7]

Liu, Z. (2019), "Land-based finance and property tax in China", *Area Development and Policy*, Vol. 4/4, pp. 367-381, http://dx.doi.org/10.1080/23792949.2019.1610333. [27]

Longobardi, E. (2013), "On the Role of the Property Tax in Financing Local Expenditure: The Case of Italy", *Paper Presented to the Copenhagen Workshop, September 12-13*. [26]

Lutz, B. (2008), "The Connection Between House Price Appreciation and Property Tax Revenues", *National Tax Journal*, Vol. 61/3, http://dx.doi.org/10.17310/ntj.2008.3.13. [15]

Millar-Powell, B. et al. (2022), "Measuring Effective Taxation of Housing: Building the foundations for policy reform", *OECD Taxation Working Papers*, No. 56, OECD Publishing, Paris, https://dx.doi.org/10.1787/0a7e36f2-en. [22]

Neutze, M. (2003), *Leasing of Publicly Owned Land in Canberra, Australia*, Lincoln Institute of Land Policy. [34]

Norregaard, J. (2013), *Taxing Immovable Property Revenue Potential and Implementation Challenges*, https://www.imf.org/external/pubs/ft/wp/2013/wp13129.pdf. [14]

OECD (2020), “COVID-19 and fiscal relations across levels of government”, *OECD Policy Responses to Coronavirus (COVID-19)*, OECD Publishing, Paris, https://dx.doi.org/10.1787/ab438b9f-en. [13]

OECD (2020), “Tax and fiscal policy in response to the Coronavirus crisis: Strengthening confidence and resilience”, *OECD Policy Responses to Coronavirus (COVID-19)*, OECD Publishing, Paris, https://dx.doi.org/10.1787/60f640a8-en. [6]

OECD (2019), *OECD Economic Surveys: China 2019*, OECD Publishing, Paris, https://dx.doi.org/10.1787/eco_surveys-chn-2019-en. [9]

OECD (2018), *Tax Policy Reforms 2018: OECD and Selected Partner Economies*, OECD Publishing, Paris, https://dx.doi.org/10.1787/9789264304468-en. [16]

OECD (2005), *Tax Policy Reforms in Denmark*, OECD Centre for Tax Policy and Administration, https://www.oecd.org/tax/tax-policy/37154664.pdf. [18]

Olofsgård, A. (2003), *The Political Economy of Reform: Institutional Change as a Tool for Political Credibility*, background paper to the World Bank’s 2005 World Development Report. [30]

Rosengard, J. (2012), “The Tax Everyone Loves to Hate: Principles of Property Tax Reform”, in *A Primer on Property Tax*, Blackwell Publishing Ltd, Oxford, http://dx.doi.org/10.1002/9781118454343.ch7. [23]

Rossi, S. (2010), *Aspects of Italian Economic Policy from the 1992-93 Crisis to the Crisis of 2008-09*, Università Roma Tre, Rome. [25]

Simonsen, B. and M. Robbins (2003), “Reasonableness, Satisfaction, and Willingness to Pay Property Taxes”, *Urban Affairs Review*, Vol. 38/6, pp. 831-854, http://dx.doi.org/10.1177/1078087403038006004. [32]

Slack, E. and R. Bird (2014), “The Political Economy of Property Tax Reform”, *OECD Working Papers on Fiscal Federalism*, No. 18, OECD Publishing, Paris, https://dx.doi.org/10.1787/5jz5pzvzv6r7-en. [3]

Smidova, Z. (2016), “Betting the house in Denmark”, *OECD Economics Department Working Papers*, No. 1337, OECD Publishing, Paris, https://dx.doi.org/10.1787/5jln042vd3kk-en. [17]

Swianiewicz, P. and J. Lukomska (2015), “Local Tax Policies in the Limited Autonomy of Revenue Collection System in Poland”, in *Interaction between local expenditure responsibilities and local tax policy*, Copenhagen Workshop, Danish Ministry for Economic Affairs and the Interior and the Korea Institute of Public Finance. [39]

UN Habitat (2013), *Property tax regimes in Europe*, UN Habitat. [5]

Notes

[1] This topic is further discussed in this chapter's transaction section.

[2] For an in-depth discussion on tax reliefs, see Chapter 2.

[3] As mentioned in Chapter 3, this practice is found in Denmark (who aims to produce values that are about 5 percent lower than actual market prices) and in some Canada and US states, which aim to estimate values up to 10% lower than market's (UN Habitat, 2013[5]).

[4] It is worth noting that a country can pursue this practice and, at the same time, raise the desired amount of property tax revenue by adjusting upward the nominal tax rate.

[5] See Slack and Bird (2014[3]).

[6] It is worth noting, though, that it is possible for governments to reduce incentives to under-value properties by penalising this action. For instance, it is possible to establish a system in which when the property owner wants to sell his or her property, the government retains the right of first refusal at the self-assessed price.

[7] Australia offers two interesting and recent examples of phase-outs of transitioning from transaction taxes towards recurrent taxes on immovable property. First, the Australian Capital Territory Government has, since 2012, gradually reduced the tax rates applied to property transactions, while increasing the annual tax on immovable property. This reduction has already led to the end of this charge on transactions of certain types of property such as commercial properties worth AUD 1.5 million or less (for more details, see www.revenue.act.gov.au/tax-reform). Second, the New South Wales Government is considering implementing a similar reform and, to avoid double taxation, is discussing the possibility to give the property buyer a choice as to whether, when purchasing a property, they enter the current regime (transaction taxes plus annual recurrent taxes) or, alternatively, the new regime without transaction taxes but higher recurrent taxes on immovable property. There are also discussions on extending this option to owners of recently purchased properties in a retrospective manner – in this case the transaction tax would be refunded if they elected to switch to the new regime (for details see www.nsw.gov.au/initiative/property-tax-reform).

[8] Due to the fact that recurrent taxes on immovable property are typically managed by local governments, bundling property tax reforms with changes in the inter-governmental framework is especially important and, therefore, deserves a more detailed discussion. The next section digs into this issue in a more detailed manner.

[9] For more see Almy (2014[12]).

[10] See Borge and Rattsø (2013[42]) for evidence.

[11] For more on reforming fiscal federalism see Blöchliger and Vammalle (2012[2]); Kim and Dougherty (2018[40]); as well as Kim and Dougherty (2019[43]). The latter is focused on potential and current fiscal federalism reforms in Asia.

Annex A. Property taxes in China

This annex is based on the OECD Global Revenue Statistics database, accessible at: https://www.oecd.org/tax/tax-policy/global-revenue-statistics-database.htm.

Urban Maintenance and Construction Tax

1. Tax collection body

According to the 1993 Notice on Establishment of Direct Taxation Authorities and Local Taxation Bureaus, the State Taxation Bureaus under central government were collecting Urban Maintenance and Construction Tax (UMCT) from railway companies, as well as headquarters of banks and insurance companies. The Local Taxation Bureaus under local governments were collecting UMCT from other sources (a1; a2).

Since 2018, a reform has been implemented to merge the State Taxation Bureau system and the Local Taxation Bureau system to manage collection for all taxes (b).

2. Setting of tax rate and tax base

China's UMCT is currently governed by the Provisional Regulations of the People's Republic of China on Urban Maintenance and Construction Tax implemented in 1985 (c).

An Urban Maintenance and Construction Tax Law has been drafted by the State Taxation Administration in Beijing and released to the public for comments (d).

Within the Provisional Regulations, details regarding the setting of tax rate and tax base (it is a surtax of VAT, Excise Tax and Business Tax) have been provided. For tax collection, management, exemptions and reductions, UMCT will follow the same regulations as the taxes upon which it is levied. Local governments can decide how to use UMCT revenues as long as they are used for maintenance and construction of public facilities and utility projects. Local governments can draft their own implementation regulations.

In the draft Law, there is no mentioning of local governments' role.

3. Attribution of tax revenues

According to the 1993 State Council Decision, UMCT was a local tax, except for UMCT paid by railway companies, as well as headquarters of banks and insurance companies (e). However, some recent publications treated UMCT as a shared tax due to the allocation of above mentioned exceptions to the central government. Despite this, UMCT revenue was almost entirely received by the local governments. This has not changed based on recent information (f).

4. References

For tax collection

https://www.czj.sh.gov.cn/zys_8908/zcfg_8983/zcfb_8985/sszc_8998/201509/t20150916_158303.shtml (a1: 1993 rule)

http://www.chinatax.gov.cn/chinatax/n810346/n810825/c101434/c15/content.html (a2: 1996 Adjustments)

http://www.gov.cn/guowuyuan/2018-03/17/content_5275116.htm (b: 2018 reform)

For setting of tax rules

http://www.gov.cn/banshi/2005-08/19/content_24817.htm (c: 1985 Provisional Regulations)

http://www.chinatax.gov.cn/chinatax/n810356/n810961/c3816380/content.html (d: draft UMCT Law)

For attribution of tax revenues

http://shanghai.chinatax.gov.cn/zcfw/zcfgk/swzsgl/200210/t284358.html (e: 1993 State Council Decision)

http://www.stats.gov.cn/tjsj/zbjs/201912/t20191202_1713054.html (f: 2019 attribution of budget revenues)

House Property Tax

1. Tax collection body

The Local Taxation Bureaus under local governments were the primary tax authorities collecting House Property Tax in China (a1; a2).

Since 2018, a reform has been implemented to merge the State Taxation Bureau system and the Local Taxation Bureau system to manage collection for all taxes (b).

2. Setting of tax rate and tax base

China's House Property Tax is currently governed by the Provisional Regulations of the People's Republic of China on House Property Tax implemented in 1986 and revised in 2011 (c).

Within the Provisional Regulations, details regarding the setting of tax rate and tax base, tax exemptions, tax calculation methodology, etc. have been provided. When House Property Tax is levied on the original value of a house, local governments can decide a final depreciation ratio (between 10% and 30%) which will be applied to the original value before calculation of tax payments. When taxpayers have difficulty raising money for House Property Tax, local governments can decide whether tax exemptions or reductions are applicable. This is in addition to other tax exemptions specified by the central government. House Property Tax payments are collected annually by instalments and local governments can decide when to collect them. Local governments can also draft their own implementation regulations.

3. Attribution of tax revenues

According to the 1993 State Council Decision, House Property Tax was a local tax (d). This has not changed based on recent information (e).

4. References

For tax collection

https://www.czj.sh.gov.cn/zys_8908/zcfg_8983/zcfb_8985/sszc_8998/201509/t20150916_158303.shtml (a1: 1993 rule)

http://www.chinatax.gov.cn/chinatax/n810346/n810825/c101434/c15/content.html (a2: 1996 Adjustments)

http://www.gov.cn/guowuyuan/2018-03/17/content_5275116.htm (b: 2018 reform)

For setting of tax rules

http://www.chinatax.gov.cn/chinatax/n810346/n810825/c101434/c28479821/content.html (c: 2011 Provisional Regulations)

For attribution of tax revenues

http://shanghai.chinatax.gov.cn/zcfw/zcfgk/swzsgl/200210/t284358.html (d: 1993 State Council Decision)

http://www.stats.gov.cn/tjsj/zbjs/201912/t20191202_1713054.html (e: 2019 attribution of budget revenues)

Stamp Tax

1. Tax collection body

The Local Taxation Bureaus under local governments were the primary tax authorities collecting Stamp Tax in China (a1; a2; b).

Since 2018, a reform has been implemented to merge the State Taxation Bureau system and the Local Taxation Bureau system to manage collection for all taxes (c).

2. Setting of tax rate and tax base

China's Stamp Tax is currently governed by the Provisional Regulations of the People's Republic of China on Stamp Tax implemented in 1988 (d; e).

A Stamp Tax Law has been drafted by the State Taxation Administration in Beijing and released to the public for comments (f).

Within the Provisional Regulations and the draft Law, details regarding the setting of tax rate (provided in a tax rate table) and tax base, tax exemptions, tax calculation methodology, tax collection, etc. have been provided. There is no mentioning of local governments with respect to any tax setting and varying power.

3. Attribution of tax revenues

According to the 1993 State Council Decision, Stamp Tax was a local tax (g). This has not changed based on recent information (h).

4. References

For tax collection

https://www.czj.sh.gov.cn/zys_8908/zcfg_8983/zcfb_8985/sszc_8998/201509/t20150916_158303.shtml (a1: 1993 rule)

http://www.chinatax.gov.cn/chinatax/n810346/n810825/c101434/c15/content.html (a2: 1996 Adjustments) http://www.chinatax.gov.cn/chinatax/n810341/n810765/n812193/n813023/c1204364/content.html (b: 2004 Notice on Enhancing Stamp Tax Collection Management)

http://www.gov.cn/guowuyuan/2018-03/17/content_5275116.htm (c: 2018 reform)

For setting of tax rules

http://www.chinatax.gov.cn/chinatax/n367/c1476/content.html (d: 1988 Provisional Regulations)

http://www.chinatax.gov.cn/chinatax/n367/c1477/content.html (e: Implementation Regulations)

http://www.chinatax.gov.cn/chinatax/n810356/n810961/c3851221/content.html (f: draft Stamp Tax Law)

For attribution of tax revenues

http://shanghai.chinatax.gov.cn/zcfw/zcfgk/swzsgl/200210/t284358.html (g: 1993 State Council Decision)

http://www.stats.gov.cn/tjsj/zbjs/201912/t20191202_1713054.html (h: 2019 attribution of budget revenues)

Stamp Tax on Securities Transactions

1. Tax collection body

The State Taxation Bureaus under the central government were the primary tax authorities collecting Stamp Tax on Securities Transaction (STOST) in China (a1; a2).

Since 2018, a reform has been implemented to merge the State Taxation Bureau system and the Local Taxation Bureau system to manage collection for all taxes (b).

2. Setting of tax rate and tax base

Stamp Tax on Securities Transactions was introduced in 1992 and thus not mentioned in the 1988 Provisional Regulations of the People's Republic of China on Stamp Tax. However, it should still be governed by it as STOST is considered part of general Stamp Tax (c; d).

There are specific sections regarding STOST in the draft Stamp Tax Law (e). Within the draft Law, details regarding the setting of tax rate (one in a thousand of transaction value) and tax base, tax exemptions, tax calculation methodology, tax collection, etc. have been provided. There is no mentioning of local governments with respect to any tax setting and varying power.

3. Attribution of tax revenues

Stamp Tax on Securities Transactions was one of the three shared taxes between central and local governments mentioned in a 1993 State Council Decision (the other two were Resources Tax and VAT). While STOST was solely collected by the central government (see section 1), 50% of STOST revenue would be given to local governments while 50% are retained by central government (f).

In 1996, the State Council decided to change the sharing ratio for STOST from 50:50 to 80% central and 20% local, starting from 1997 (g). However, in 1997, the State Council also adjusted the STOST rate from 3‰ to 5‰ and allocated all the extra revenues to the central government, making the final sharing ratio 88% central and 12% local.

In 2000, the State Council decided to further adjust the sharing ratio from 88% central and 12% local to 97% central and 3% local gradually over the course of 3 years, more specifically, to 91:9 in 2000, 94:6 in 2001 and 97:3 from 2002 (h).

In 2015, the State Council released yet another Notice to adjust STOST sharing. This time STOST revenue will be fully retained by the central government with no sharing with local governments. This change would start from 2016 (i). Thus Stamp Tax on Securities Transactions went from being a shared tax in 1994 to a central tax in 2016.

4. References

For tax collection

https://www.czj.sh.gov.cn/zys_8908/zcfg_8983/zcfb_8985/sszc_8998/201509/t20150916_158303.shtml (a1: 1993 rule)

http://www.chinatax.gov.cn/chinatax/n810346/n810825/c101434/c15/content.html (a2: 1996 Adjustments)

http://www.gov.cn/guowuyuan/2018-03/17/content_5275116.htm (b: 2018 reform)

For setting of tax rules

http://www.chinatax.gov.cn/chinatax/n367/c1476/content.html (c: 1988 Provisional Regulations)

http://www.chinatax.gov.cn/chinatax/n367/c1477/content.html (d: Implementation Regulations)

http://www.chinatax.gov.cn/chinatax/n810356/n810961/c3851221/content.html (e: draft Stamp Tax Law)

For attribution of tax revenues

http://shanghai.chinatax.gov.cn/zcfw/zcfgk/swzsgl/200210/t284358.html (f: 1993 State Council Decision)

http://shanghai.chinatax.gov.cn/zcfw/zcfgk/yhs/200206/t289142.html (g: 1996 State Council Notice)

http://finance.sina.com.cn/2000-09-30/15198.html (h: 2000 State Council Notice news)

http://www.gov.cn/zhengce/content/2015-12/31/content_10543.htm (i: 2015 State Council Notice)

Annex B. Tax rates across OECD countries

Table A B.1. Tax rates across OECD countries

Country - Tax	Tax Rate Description
AUS - Land	Marginal rates of 1.6% land tax are applied above a tax-free threshold of AUD 412 000, and 2% on landholdings that exceed AUD 2 519 000.
AUS - Council	NSW has 152 local governments, each of which applies their own local government rates. It is common practice to apply different rates to residential, business, and farming land. As example, Leichhardt Council (within suburban Sydney) applies ad valorem rates of 0.2021% for residential land and 0.9164% for business land.
AUT	(1) Agricultural land and forest: first EUR 3 633 is taxed at 0.16%; (2) Single family house: first EUR 3 633 is taxed at 0.05% and the next EUR 7 267 is taxed at 0.1%; (3) Rented and mixed use property: first EUR 3 633 is taxed at 0.1% and the next EUR 3 633 at 0.15%; (4) Other property: first EUR 3 633 is taxed at 0.1%. The final rate is calculated by using a Municipal surcharge rate which is decided by the Municipal Parliament but must not be higher than 500%.
CHE-BERNE	The tax is levied only once for land and buildings together and vary from 0 to 1.5%
CHL	The tax rate is 1.0% for agricultural properties, varies between 0.98% to 1.143% for non-agricultural residential properties and is 1.2% for non-agricultural and non-residential properties.
CZE	1 to 6 CZK per square metre, depending on type of property.
DNK	The rate varies between 1.6% and 3.4% but for properties used in agriculture, gardening, nursery, orchards or forestry the land tax rate is reduced by 1.48 percentage points and may not exceed 0.72%.
ESP	For urban property the minimum rate shall be 0.4% and the maximum 1.10%. In the case of rural property rates go from 0.3% to 0.9%. Moreover, the law allows increasing the rate depending on certain circumstances (for instance, when a municipality provides certain services, or it is the capital of a province or region). Considering all possible increases, the tax rate for urban property can reach a maximum of 1.3%. Within these limits, local governments may establish a surcharge of up to 0.5% to the vacant urban properties or different rates depending on the use of the property. On the other hand, another range of rates are established for special kinds of constructions (reservoirs, power plants, etc.)
EST	The tax rate shall be established by the local government council and varies from 0.1% to 2.5%. The rate of land tax for areas under cultivation and for natural grasslands is lower than the regular rate (vary from 0.1 to 2.0%).
FIN	General property taxes (land and commercial buildings) are allowed to vary from 0.93% to 2.00%. Residential building taxes are allowed to range from 0.41% to 1.00%. In addition, separate tax rates can be used for leisure homes, undeveloped residential land and power plants.
HUN	Maximum rates of 3%/3.6% of the adjusted market value or 331/1821 HUF per square metre for lands/buildings. Only the maximum tax rates are defined in the Act, but the local governments define the rate in their jurisdictions (they may as well decide not to levy the tax).
IRL - LPT	For LPT, property values are organised into market value bands: EUR 0 to 100 000 as the first band, followed by 18 bands of increments of EUR 50 000 each and the final band encompassing all properties valued over EUR 1 million. The tax liability is calculated by applying the tax rate to the midpoint of the band. The rate of LPT is 0.18% for properties up to a market value of EUR 1 million. Residential properties valued over EUR 1 million are assessed at 0.18% on the first EUR 1 million in value and 0.25% on the portion of the value above EUR 1 million.
IRL - NPPR	There are different tax rates across local authority areas. Commercial Rates are calculated by applying an Annual Rate of Valuation (ARV) to the Rateable Valuation (RV). The ARV is set by each local authority area and is agreed by each county/city council at its annual budget meeting.

Country - Tax	Tax Rate Description
ITA	Vary from 0.46% to 1.06%
JPN - CPT	Though the limited tax rate set by the central government is 0.3%, the actual tax rates are determined by ordinances of municipalities.
JPN - MPT	Though the standard rate set by the central government is 1.4%, the actual tax rates are determined by ordinances of municipalities.
KOR	Progressive rate from 0.07%/0.1% to 4% for lands/buildings.
LUX	Minimum rate of 3.3%/0.74% for lands/buildings. Buildings have a maximum rate of 4.5%.
LTU	Minimum rate of 0.5%/0.5% and maximum rate of 2%/3% for residential/business properties
MEX	Tax rates vary from 0.13% to 0.33%.
NLD	Tax rates vary: For owner-occupied from 0.0451% to 0.23%; For rented properties from 0.0489% to 0.3836%; For business properties from 0.0623% to 0.4752%
NOR	Tax rates vary from 0.2% to 0.7%.
NZL	There are no tax rate bands.
POL	Tax rates cannot exceed: For land related to an economic activity, PLN 0.89 for 1 m2 of the area; Under lakes, occupied by retention reservoirs or water power stations – PLN 4.56 for 1 ha of the area; For other land, PLN 0.46 for 1 m2 of the area; For residential buildings, PLN 0.74 for 1 m2 of the usable area; For buildings related to economic activity and residential buildings or parts thereof occupied for economic activity, PLN 23.03 for 1 m2 of the usable area; For buildings occupied for economic activity in the field the qualified seed material marketing, PLN 10.75 for 1 m2 of the useable area; For buildings occupied for economic activity in the field of providing health care, PLN 4.68 for 1 m2 of the usable area; For other buildings, PLN 7.73 for 1 m2 of the useable area; For building structures, 2% of the value. Maximum tax rates expressed in PLN are annually indexed according to the inflation rate.
PRT	Tax rates applied to lands are 0.8% while to buildings vary from 0.3% to 0.8%.
SVK	The tax rate on land is recommended to be set at 0.25% but Municipalities may increase or decrease the tax rate up to 5 times the lowest annual tax rate on land set by any Municipality. Tax rate on buildings is recommended to be set at EUR 0.033 per each square metre but Municipalities may increase or decrease the tax rate up to 10 times the lowest annual tax rate on buildings set by any Municipality.
SVN - DPQ	The tax rate depends on the value (progressive) and of the type of property and is set by the State. The tax rate for dwellings varies from 0.1% to 1% of the value. The tax rates on premises used for rest and recreation are in the range 0.2% to 1.5%. The tax rate for business premises varies from 0.15% to 1.25%. For business premises that are not used for attendant activities or are not rented, the tax rate is increased by 50%.
SVN - NUSZ	Charge is set by local communities not through tax rates but as a value of a charge itself. There are no rules about setting the level of the taxation among local communities. Based on comparison of market values with the levels of charge for the use of building ground the effective tax rates is estimated to vary, among local communities, for residential properties from 0.002% to 0.44 % (average: 0.081%) and for business properties from 0.001% to over 3% (average: 0.71%).
SWE	No maximum or minimum tax rates. Instead there are maximum lump-sum values.
TUR	Tax rates vary from 0.1% to 0.3% and are doubled for properties within the borders of metropolitan municipalities and contiguous areas.
USA	Vary by state/local government.

Source: Responses from the OECD Survey on Recurrent Taxes on Immovable Property, updated in 2021.

Annex C. Tax reliefs across OECD countries

Table A C.1. Tax reliefs across OECD countries

Country - Tax	Tax Rate Description
AUS	Pensioners are entitled to local government rates concessions.
AUT(LTA+LTB)	Tax abatements can be granted by most jurisdictions for newly constructed residential buildings for a certain period of time.
BEL - residential property tax	Vary by region. For instance, in the Walloon Region, the rebates of withholding tax on real estate apply to only one dwelling. The rebate for modest dwelling is still expressed as a percentage of the cadastral income. The other reductions are lump-sum reductions, applied to the global withholding tax on real estate (provincial and local surcharges included). These reductions are reduction for modest dwelling, rebate for dependents, rebate for disability and infirmity and rebate for unproductiveness. In addition, in the Brussels-Capital Region, a reduction is granted for the dwelling entirely occupied by the taxpayer himself where the non-indexed cadastral income of all real estate of the taxpayer located in Belgium does not exceed EUR 745. The standard rate of this reduction, which applies to the withholding tax on the main residence, is 25%. In the case of the construction of a new dwelling house or the acquisition of a newly built dwelling house, the reduction amounts to 50% during the first five years in which the withholding tax on that real estate is due. The taxpayer is not granted this reduction if he has received a subsidy for the construction or the acquisition of that dwelling house. The reductions are, in the Brussels-Capital Region: reduction for modest dwelling, rebate for dependents (among which children), rebate for disability and infirmity, rebate for unproductiveness.
BEL - business property tax	BXL: Rebate for unproductiveness, exemption of withholding tax for immovable property used for public services. A tax credit is granted by the Brussels-Capital Region to natural persons or legal entities liable to withholding tax on material and equipment. This tax credit is totally chargeable to the Brussels-Capital Region. This tax incentive for businesses is granted as a tax credit, so as to allow local entities and the urban area of Brussels to keep on collecting additional surtaxes on the withholding tax on real estate.
CHE (Berne)	In Berne, Switzerland, no tax is levied for buildings owned by the Canton, the commune and the churches.
CHL	A tax abatement is granted to old age owners with low incomes, when some requirements are met.
CZE	Land under buildings is exempt.
ESP	Local authorities are allowed to establish tax deductions for installed systems to use thermal or electrical energy from the sun.
EST	Local governments may exempt recipients of pensions paid on the basis of the State Pension Insurance Act and for repressed persons and persons treated as repressed persons as defined in the persons Repressed by Occupying powers Act. Owners of the land where they live will be freed of land tax liability up to 0.15 hectares in town and up to 2 hectares elsewhere.
FIN	The properties owned by non-profit organisations may be exempt from property taxes, these decisions are made at the municipal level.
GBR - residential property tax	There are a number of discounts and exemptions based on occupation/occupiers.
GBR - business property tax	The central government rating system has many various national exemptions and reliefs including exemptions for agricultural uses, certain property used for the disabled, religious worship, relief for small properties in sole ownership, relief for certain properties in small rural settlements up to a threshold, relief for empty properties in some specified circumstances and a flat relief for most types of retail properties up to a threshold. Additionally, local government has the power to grant any relief they wish.
HUN	The local government can supplement the range of exemptions, benefits and allowances specified in the Act, but only in case of the non-business properties.
IRL - LPT	Certain properties are exempt from LPT such as charities, properties situated in unfinished housing estates, nursing homes, properties vacated by their owners due to illness, diplomatic properties and property purchased, built or adapted to make it suitable for occupation by a permanently and totally incapacitated individual . A system of deferral arrangements is available where there is an inability to pay off liable owners and certain specified conditions are met.
IRL - NPPR	State Owned Properties and also Agricultural Land are not subject to Commercial Rates.

Country - Tax	Tax Rate Description
LTU	1) owned by natural persons and used for: - social welfare, agricultural activities, education endeavours; individual creative activities, located in the territory of a cemetery; - non-commercial purposes (including dwellings, garages, farms, real estate used for leisure and etc.) not exceeding EUR 150 000 (for taxpayers with 3 or more children or disabled children the non-taxable rate of real estate value is EUR 200 000). 2) owned by legal persons immovable property of: - diplomatic missions and consular posts of foreign states; state or municipalities; undertakings of free economic zones; bankrupt undertaking; the Bank of Lithuania; - traditional religious communities; charity and sponsorship funds; property located in the territory of a cemetery; enterprises of the disabled persons; associations; trade unions; - science and study institutions; educational establishments; establishments providing social services; used for the provision of health care services; Artists organisations; - entities, co-operatives more than 50% of their income are earned from agricultural activities; property, used for environmental protection and fire prevention; multi-occupancy dwelling owners associations, home building societies, garages maintenance and gardeners' societies, used solely for non-commercial activities; In addition, Municipal councils have the right to reduce the tax or completely exempt from payment at the expense of their budgets.
ITA	Abatements for low income properties may be applied by local governments.
JPN - CPT	Tax abatements are granted for certain types of spending on property, for example, residential lands. Tax abatements to low-income property owners are left to municipalities' judgements.
NLD	Only properties in development areas under specific ruling are subjected to tax reliefs.
NOR	Tax abatement allowed for new dwellings for 20 years. Discretional tax abatement/reduction may be granted for low-income earners.
NZL	The central government provides a subsidy (rates rebate) for low income homeowners who may have difficulty paying their rates liabilities (rates rebate scheme).
PRT	Basic exemption for one property: main residence, for a limited property, for households with income below EUR 153 300, for properties with value below EUR 125 000; tax abatements granted to low income property owners with low value properties (main residence); business exemptions for real estate funds, pension funds and retirement savings funds.
SVK	Tax administrators (municipality) have the possibility to reduce tax rate for pensioners, disabled persons and for people in material need.
SVN - DPQ	Exemptions to the property tax include buildings used for agricultural purposes; business premises used by the owner or user for business activity; cultural or historical monuments. In addition, there is a temporary exemption for ten years to taxpayers who own a newly constructed building or repaired or renovated residential property, if the value of the property has increased as a result of renovation by more than 50%. For a taxpayer with more than three family members, who live in the owner's house, the tax decreases by 10% for the fourth and every additional family member. There is also a reduction of the tax base that could be treated as a tax exemption. The tax base for the residential property, if permanently occupied by the owner or close relative, shall be reduced by an amount corresponding to the value of 160 square meter living area.
SVN - NUSZ	Exemptions are set for land and buildings, used by the army, churches, embassies and international organisations. A temporary exemption for five years is set for new or renovated residential properties. Partial or full exemption can be set for people with low incomes. Full exemption is set for building land planned for public infrastructure (health, social security, schools, culture, science, sports and public and public administration, etc.) and developed building land under public infrastructure.
TUR	If a property owner fulfils certain criteria, the property tax rate is 0% for one residence. Some tax exemptions are granted based on the type, position and owner of the property. Buildings and lands that belong to the special budget administrations, special provincial administrations, municipalities, village legal entities, universities established by law and state-owned buildings/land are exempted from tax permanently. The other permanent or temporary exemptions have generally social, economic and ecological purposes.

Source: Responses from the OECD Survey on Recurrent Taxes on Immovable Property, updated in January 2021.

Printed by Libri Plureos GmbH in Hamburg,
Germany